A Spontaneous Order:

The Capitalist Case For A Stateless Society

CHASE RACHELS

DEDICATION

This work is dedicated to my son, Micha Rachels. May he grow up with a free spirit, critical mind, and warm heart.

ACKNOWLEDGEMENTS

I would like to first and foremost thank my wife, Michelle Ferris, for standing by my side as an active participant in the fight against tyranny. Her loving encouragement and support enabled me to see this project to its end. Stephan Kinsella's mentorship was likewise invaluable in its relation to the precision and rigor of this book. My editor, Mattheus von Guttenberg, also deserves recognition for his professional assistance in editing this work and verifying the accuracy of its content. I would like to express my gratitude for Will Porter, who was gracious enough to contribute one of his brilliant essays (Chapter 0: Epistemology and Praxeology). I would also like to give thanks to the following people who provided their support in a variety of ways, though bear in mind this list is by no means exhaustive or in any particular order: Luis F. Duran-Aparicio, Blake Williams, Jason Bassler, Justin Stout, Chris Calton, Gary Simon, Mike Martelli, Joel Richardson, Walter Block, Jeff Berwick, and many more!

CONTENTS

Foreword

MODERN LIBERTARIAN THEORY is only about five decades old. The ideas that have influenced our greatest thinkers can be traced back centuries, of course,[1] to luminaries such as Hugo Grotius, John Locke, Thomas Paine, Herbert Spencer, David Hume, and John Stuart Mill, and to more recent and largely even more radical thinkers such as Gustave de Molinari, Benjamin Tucker, Lysander Spooner, Bertrand de Jouvenel, Franz Oppenheimer, and Albert Jay Nock.[2]

The beginnings of the modern movement can be detected in the works of the "three furies of libertarianism," as Brian Doherty calls them: Rose Wilder Lane, Ayn Rand, and Isabel Patterson, whose respective books *The Discovery of Freedom*, *The Fountainhead*, and *The God of the Machine* were all published, rather remarkably, in the same year: 1943.[3] But in its more modern form, libertarianism originated in the 1960s and 1970s from thinkers based primarily in the United States, notably Ayn Rand and Murray Rothbard. Other significant influences on the nascent libertarian movement include Ludwig von Mises, author of *Liberalism* (1927) and *Human Action* (1949, with a predecessor version published in German in 1940); Nobel laureate F.A. von Hayek, author of *The Road to Serfdom* (1944); Leonard Read, head of the Foundation for Economic Education (founded 1946); and Nobel laureate Milton Friedman, author of the influential *Capitalism and Freedom* (1962).

The most prominent and influential of modern libertarian figures, however, were the aforementioned novelist-philosopher Ayn Rand, the founder of "Objectivism" and a "radical for capitalism," and Murray Rothbard, the Mises-influenced libertarian anarcho-capitalist economist and political theorist. Rothbard's seminal role is widely recognized, even by non-Rothbardians. Objectivist John McCaskey, for example, has observed, that out of the debates in the mid-1900s about what rights citizens ought to have,

---

[1]   For more on this, see Brian Doherty, *Radicals for Capitalism: A Freewheeling History of the Modern American Libertarian Movement* (New York: Public Affairs, 2007) and David Boaz, *The Libertarian Reader: Classic and Contemporary Readings from Lao-tzu to Milton Friedman* (New York: Free Press, 1997).
[2]   See Boaz, *The Libertarian Reader*.
[3]   See Doherty, *Radicals for Capitalism*.

6

grew the main sort of libertarianism of the
last fifty years. It was based on a principle
articulated by Murray Rothbard in the
1970s this way: No one may initiate the use
or threat of physical violence against the
person or property of anyone else. The
idea had roots in John Locke, America's
founders, and more immediately Ayn
Rand, but it was Rothbard's formulation
that became standard. It became known as
the *non-aggression principle* or—since
Rothbard took it as the starting point of
political theory and not the conclusion of
philosophical justification—the *non-
aggression axiom*. In the late twentieth
century, anyone who accepted this
principle could call himself, or could find
himself called, a libertarian, even if he
disagreed with Rothbard's own insistence
that rights are best protected when there is
no government at all.[4]

We can date the dawn of today's libertarianism to the works of
Rand and Rothbard: to Rand's *Atlas Shrugged* (1957); and, especially, to
Rothbard's *Man, Economy, and State* (1962), *Power and Market* (1970), and *For
A New Liberty* (1973), plus his journal *The Libertarian Forum* (1969–1984). *For
A New Liberty* stands today as a brilliant, and early, bold statement of the
radical libertarian vision. By the mid-60s, the modern libertarian movement
was coalescing, primarily behind the non-initiation of force principle and
the "radical capitalism" of Ayn Rand, and Rothbard's systematic libertarian
corpus based upon the non-aggression principle or axiom. It is no surprise
that the Libertarian Party was founded in 1971, as these ideas, and the
liberty movement, were gaining steam.

In the ensuing decades many other influential works appeared
expounding on the libertarian idea, such as Linda and Morris Tannehill, *The
Market for Liberty* (1970), John Hospers, *Libertarianism: A Political Philosophy
for Tomorrow* (1971), David Friedman, *The Machinery of Freedom* (1973), Robert
Nozick, *Anarchy, State, and Utopia* (1974), Henri Lepage, *Tomorrow, Capitalism*
(1978), Samuel Edward Konkin III, *New Libertarian Manifesto* (1980), Jan

---

[4]   John P. McCaskey, "New Libertarians: New Promoters of a Welfare State"
     (published as a blog post on johnmccaskey.com, April 14, 2014).
     http://www.johnmccaskey.com/joomla/index.php/blog/71-new-libertarians. See
     also, Wendy McElroy, "Murray N. Rothbard: Mr. Libertarian," (published on
     LewRockwell.com, July 6, 2000).

Narveson, *The Libertarian Idea* (1988), Anthony de Jasay, *Choice, Contract, Consent: A Restatement of Liberalism* (1991), Richard Epstein, *Simple Rules for a Complex World* (1995), Charles Murray, *What It Means to Be a Libertarian: A Personal Interpretation* (1996), David Boaz, *Libertarianism: A Primer* (1998), Randy E. Barnett, *The Structure of Liberty* (1998), and, more recently, Jeffrey A. Miron's *Libertarianism, From A to Z* (2010), Jacob Huebert's *Libertarianism Today* (2010), Gary Chartier's *The Conscience of an Anarchist* (2011), and Gerard Casey's *Libertarian Anarchism* (2012).

These and other works expounding on the ideas of liberty have their own strengths and merits, and many of them have their own deficiencies and idiosyncrasies as well. Some, for example, are statements only of the author's personal vision and do not purport to describe libertarian thought in general; some are minarchist, at best, and do not even recognize anarcho-libertarianism as a type of libertarianism (Miron, for example, says "libertarianism accepts a role for government in a few, limited areas: small government, not anarchy");[5] and some do not sufficiently appreciate Austrian economics and its crucial role in informing political theory. And many of the earlier works are simply dated at this point—how could they not be, being written before the rise of the Internet (1995) or even before the fall of communism (1989–91)?

As libertarian thought develops and matures, there is a continual need to restate our basic principles, to search for new ways of understanding and conveying our views about the nature of human society, the state, conflict, cooperation, and liberty. The way forward, if we wish to spread and develop the intellectual edifice of libertarian thought, is to extend and advance the most consistent, scientific, and rigorous foundation for libertarianism. This is, in my view, the basic vision laid out by Rothbard, which relies heavily on free market economic theory, chiefly that of Rothbard's mentor Mises, and as supplemented by the work of Rothbard's colleague and protégé Hans-Hermann Hoppe, author of *A Theory of Socialism and Capitalism* (1989), *inter alia*. This type of libertarianism is distinct from others in many ways. It is principled and rights-based, not utilitarian (not to say that it is impractical; as Rand pointed out, the practical *is* the moral);[6] it is radical, anarchist, and anti-state, not minarchist; it is anti-war; it is systematic and rigorous, not a collection of *ad hoc* policy points; it is realistic, sober and sophisticated about the nature of the state; and it is heavily influenced by insights of free market and Austrian economics, especially those of Mises and his "praxeological" understanding of human

---

5   Jeffrey A. Miron, *Libertarianism, from A to Z.* (New York: Basic Books, 2010).

6   See Randy E. Barnett, *The Structure of Liberty: Justice and the Rule of Law* (Oxford: Clarendon, 1998), arguing for a distinction between consequentialism and utilitarianism; also *idem*, "Foreword: of Chickens and Eggs—The Compatibility of Moral Rights and Consequentialist Analysis," 3 *Harv. J. L. Publc. Pol'y* 611 (1989), available at www.randybarnett.com.

action.

Thus, Rothbard, influenced by and building on the insights of earlier and contemporary thinkers, such such as Mises and Rand, first presented a systematic vision of modern, radical libertarianism: anti-state, pro-market, Austrian. This enabled Rothbard to adumbrate a broad framework for liberty, from property to contract to punishment theory. Rothbard's analysis extends also to, or draws on, other disciplines as necessary, such as epistemology, history, the nature of the sciences, and the like.[7]

Additional advances to the essentially Rothbardian perspective on social theory have been made over the years. Hoppe, for example, a diligent student of both Mises and Rothbard, has emphasized the essential role of *scarcity* in the need for interpersonal property norms, leading to a more rigorous and streamlined restatement of the basic Lockean approach which underlies Rothbard's own radical libertarian system. Hoppe has also extended Rothbardian analysis in the realm of political ethics with his "argumentation ethics" defense of libertarian rights. Modern Hoppean-Rothbardians are not only pro-market and anti-state: they are pro-technology, anti-democracy and anti-intellectual property as well. They promote the use of the Internet, smart phones and video cameras, blogging, podcasting, Youtube, social media and phyles, encryption, anonymity, VPNs, open source software and culture, torrents, wikileaking, crowdsourcing and crowdfunding, MOOCs, 3D printing and Bitcoin to network, communicate, learn, profit and spread ideas—and to counter, monitor, fight, and circumvent the state. To increasingly render the state irrelevant and to reveal it as retrograde, crude, and antiquated, not to mention inefficient, cold, and evil.

Thus, while there is reason to welcome all new works, thinkers and approaches that advance liberty and libertarian ideas, there remains a need for treatments of the ideas of liberty that are explicitly anchored in anti-state, Austrian-Misesian, and systematic Rothbardian ideas. We need sound analyses and ideas, whether broad or narrow, personal or general, current or timeless, academic or aimed at the general reader. Chase Rachels's *A Spontaneous Order* is one such work. This is a fresh approach which has all the right ingredients: it is anchored in and aware of the anarcho-capitalist and Austrian economic literature and insights, rather than trying to reinvent the wheel; it is accessible and aimed at a wide audience; it is up to date; it is lively and the author's passion for liberty is clearly evident throughout. Importantly, Rachels recognizes the fundamental role that economic scarcity plays in the formation of social and property norms, as Professor

---

[7]   For a superb overview of the significance and scope of Rothbard's work, and for an incisive comparison of the systematic Rothbardian approach to the dilettantish "razzle-dazzle" of Nozick, see Hans-Hermann Hoppe, "Introduction," in Murray N. Rothbard, *The Ethics of Liberty* (2nd ed., 1998)

Hoppe has repeatedly emphasized. And while *A Spontaneous Order* is not some dense, thousand page musty tome, it is wide-ranging in scope, covering the major issues of concern to advocates of liberty: from the basics, such as epistemology, justifications for libertarian norms, and foundational issues like property and the theory of contract, which is informed by Rothbard's underappreciated and revolutionary title-transfer theory of contract. This focus on essentials and on clarity of expression enables Rachels to tackle several important applications, many of which receive short shrift in other works—such as corporate limited liability, intellectual property law, money and banking, monopolies and cartels, and a host of other practical issues and applications such as health care, defense, roads, environmentalism, education, and others. The book concludes, appropriately, with a stirring and inspirational final chapter, "Getting There," which is full of practical and principled insights about what is to be done to achieve a freer society. To "Get there," we will need the ideas of liberty to be explicated and spread, to be learned, practiced, and taught. *A Spontaneous Order* admirably contributes to this mission.

Stephan Kinsella
Houston, Texas
SEPTEMBER 2014

Introduction

SCARCITY IS AN immutable characteristic of the physical realm. As humans, we require the consumption of various scarce (aka economic) goods for our sustenance and pleasure. Fortunately, the digital age has produced a superabundance of non-scarce goods for our pleasure. However, as marvelous as this advent is, it cannot wean us entirely from our dependence on economic goods. The enjoyment of many non-scarce goods may only be enabled by the use of those goods which are scarce, i.e., by servers, microchips, monitors, phones, cell phone towers, satellites, and at the very least the standing room for this equipment, infrastructure, and personnel, etc.

The problem of social order, then, stems from mutually exclusive desires for how to employ such scarce goods. Being scarce, there are a limited number of these goods, and the desire for them exceeds their availability. Thus, over time, there have been innumerable attempts to solve this dilemma through the formulation of various property norms and the erection of various States to create, interpret, and enforce them. Property norms themselves simply refer to the criteria used to determine who has the rightful authority to employ a given scarce good. When conflicts inevitably rise regarding the use of scarce goods, it is such property norms that serve as the philosophical and legal basis for arbitrating between the conflicting parties. Thus, the efficacy of a norm is measured by the degree to which, if followed, it is able to mitigate or eliminate interpersonal conflict.

The thesis put forth regards the Private Property norm as the one best suited for such conflict avoidance and, hence, the optimal production of wealth. This norm will be extended to its fullest to show how it may also be applied towards those functions traditionally assumed by the State. Simultaneously, it will be revealed how the State owes its very existence to the continued violation of the Private Property norm, and must therefore be dissolved for both practical and ethical reasons.

What is the Private Property Norm?

The Private Property norm first and foremost states that every person is the exclusive owner of his/her own body. This is referred to as the principle of self-ownership. This entails respecting another's agency by not initiating the uninvited use of physical force against him. The principle of self-ownership allows for any action that respects the autonomy and liberty of others. For example, only Joe has the exclusive *right* to employ his body as he sees fit, so long as such employment does not involve uninvited physical interference with the bodies or external property of others. The Private Property norm permits one to acquire ownership over external economic goods through original appropriation or voluntary exchange. To acquire property via original appropriation, one simply need be the *first* to mix his labor with an unowned good. This is commonly referred to as the first-user or homesteading rule. A careful examination of this rule should reveal that it is necessarily conflict-free, as being the first user and claimant implies there can be no valid competing claims over said good at the time of its acquisition. Voluntary exchange is the second and only other means by which one may acquire rightful ownership over a good, according to the Private Property norm. This includes any voluntary transfer of title over a given good to someone else. This may take the form of a monetary sale, barter exchange, gift, inheritance, etc. Once again, because such exchange is voluntary, it too is free of conflict and is therefore in accordance with the purpose of norms: conflict avoidance. An important derivative of the Private Property norm is the non-aggression principle (aka the NAP) which states that no one may rightfully commit aggression against the persons or property of others. To clarify, aggression in this context and for the remainder of the book will entail the *initiation* of uninvited physical interference with the persons or property of others, or threats made thereof.

Finally, what the Free Market refers to is simply the social arrangements that develop in the absence of coerced exchanges, which implies the widespread adoption of the Private Property norm. That is to say, it refers to that environment which is comprised of a myriad of voluntary exchanges and acts of original appropriation. In such an environment, one is only able to increase his wealth through the production of desired goods and services, which are valued more than the sum of their individual separate components. Thus, the self interests of the individual are beautifully harmonized with the interests of greater society. The Free Market, then, is a system which only takes for granted that humans are self interested and that they seek to use means to achieve various ends. Hoppe expounds on the nature of the Private Property norm:

INTRODUCTION

Contrary to the frequently heard claim that the institution of private property is only a *convention*, it must be categorically stated: a convention serves a *purpose, and* it is something to which an *alternative* exists. The Latin alphabet, for instance, serves the purpose of written communication and there exists an alternative to it, the Cyrillic alphabet. That is why it is referred to as a convention.

What, however, is the purpose of action norms? If no interpersonal conflict existed — that is: if, due to a prestabilized harmony of all interests, no situation ever arose in which two or more people want to use one and the same good in incompatible ways — then no norms would be needed. It is the purpose of norms to help avoid otherwise unavoidable conflict. A norm that generates conflict rather than helping to avoid it is *contrary to the very purpose of norms*. It is a dysfunctional norm or a perversion... With regard to the purpose of conflict avoidance, however, the institution of private property is definitely *not* just a convention, because no alternative to it exists. Only private (exclusive) property makes it possible that all otherwise unavoidable conflicts can be avoided. And only the principle of property acquisition through acts of original appropriation, performed by specific individuals at a specific time and location, makes it possible to avoid conflict *from the beginning of mankind* onward, because only the *first* appropriation of some previously unappropriated good can be conflict-free — simply, because — *per definitionem* — no one else had any previous dealings with the good.[8]

What is the State?

       Throughout this book, there will be innumerable references to the "State." This should not be confused with, say, California or North Carolina. Rather, it is interchangeable with what is more commonly referred to as the "government." However, using the term "government" in place of the "State" can be misleading as it insinuates that a Private Property or Free Market Anarchist society is absent a governing presence in a more general sense. In a Free Market Anarchist society (aka Anarcho-Capitalist or Voluntaryist society), the market *is* the governing presence and enforceable rules and norms still exist, e.g. the NAP. In the Free Market, *no one* may rightfully or legally commit aggression against the persons or property of others. In distinct contrast, however, the State is that institution which has the exclusive legal right to commit aggression against others in a geographical area. More specifically, the State is that institution which confers upon itself the status of ultimate arbiter in all conflicts, as well as the *exclusive privilege* to create, interpret, and enforce law. In addition to these privileges, it also retains the unique power to lay taxes on its citizens, i.e., to make them pay for its "services" or else face fines, imprisonment, or even death if arrest is resisted. Hoppe summarizes the defining characteristics of the State:

> First, the state is an agency that exercises a territorial monopoly of ultimate decision making. That is, the state is the ultimate arbiter in every case of conflict, including conflicts involving itself. It allows no appeal above and beyond itself. Second, the state is an agency that exercises a territorial monopoly of taxation. That is, it is an agency that unilaterally fixes the price that private citizens must pay for the state's service as ultimate judge and enforcer of law and order.[9]

---

[8]   Hans-Hermann Hoppe, "State or Private Law Society?" (lecture presented at Mises Brasil, São Paulo, Brasil, April 9, 2011).

[9]   Hoppe, ibid.

INTRODUCTION

The illegitimacy of the State rests on the fact that it exercises control over resources that its agents never acquired through original appropriation or voluntary exchange, and it does so without the consent of the rightful owners of said resources. This is what separates the so called "social contract" of the State from a restaurant owner who expects a customer to pay after he has enjoyed a meal. In the first place, the restaurant owner offers the good *upon the customer's specific request*, and only *then* asks for payment. In distinct contrast, the State first expropriates or steals wealth from its citizenry in the form of taxes, and we are told this is payment for its services. In the second place, the restaurant owner would have acquired his establishment and the food that he serves through original appropriation or voluntary exchange, and would thus have the legitimate authority to dictate how it is to be run and to expect payment from his customers for services rendered. The State, on the other hand, cannot claim to own the land of an entire country, as it never homesteaded or purchased it from prior owners (at least not with funds generated through original appropriation or voluntary exchange).

Logical and Economic Errors of the State

As normally understood, the primary role the State is charged with is to serve as the authoritative institution in the creation, interpretation, and enforcement of law and to protect the property of its citizens. However, as noted earlier, before it can embark on any task it must first confiscate a portion of its citizens' property without their genuine consent so that it may have the means to perform the aforementioned services. Thus, the means the State uses to achieve the ends of conflict mitigation and property protection themselves generate conflict and violate the property rights of its citizens from the outset. This "logical error" associated with State operations explains the inherently destructive economic consequences of this arrangement. Hoppe explains:

> First of all, among economists and philosophers two near-universally accepted propositions exist:
>
> Every "monopoly" is "bad" from the viewpoint of consumers. Monopoly is here understood in its classic meaning as an exclusive *privilege* granted to a single producer of a commodity or service, or as the absence of "free entry" into a

particular line of production. Only one agency, A, may produce a given good or service, X. Such a monopoly is "bad" for consumers, because, shielded from potential new entrants into a given area of production, the price of the product will be higher and its quality lower than otherwise, under free competition.

The production of law and order, i.e., of security, is the primary function of the state (as just defined). Security is here understood in the wide sense adopted in the American Declaration of Independence: as the protection of life, property, and the pursuit of happiness from domestic violence (crime) as well as external (foreign) aggression (war).

Both propositions are apparently incompatible with each other. This has rarely caused concern among philosophers and economists, however, and in so far as it has, the typical reaction has been one of taking exception to the first proposition rather than the second. Yet there exist fundamental theoretical reasons (and mountains of empirical evidence) that it is indeed the second proposition that is in error.[10]

In addition to the State's monopolistic complacency, the fact that it receives payment through aggressive confiscation and not voluntary sale severely hinders its ability to ascertain which activities are "worth" pursuing. In the market, this would be determined by comparing one's costs with his revenue. Profits occur when revenue exceeds costs, and losses when costs exceed revenue. One's productivity in the Free Market is reflected by his degree of profits or losses. Profits and losses are only able to measure productivity because they reflect the purchasing preferences of consumers. If one is profitable, this means he is generally satisfying consumer preferences; if he is, on the other hand, making losses, this means he is

---

[10]   Hoppe, ibid.

transforming the goods at his disposal in such a way that their resulting configuration is worth less to the consumer than the sum value of the individual goods used in the process. Thus, profits equate to a *production* of wealth, and losses equate to a *destruction* of wealth. Fortunately, in a Free Market those who destroy wealth or generate losses tend to lose command over ever more resources, freeing them up for more productive use in the market place by more capable market participants. However, no such regulating mechanism exists for the State. Because the revenue the State generates comes from violent confiscation, its resulting profits or losses do not necessarily correspond with the creation or destruction of wealth. Thus, it has no rational means by which to make economic decisions such as where a good should be produced, what materials to produce it with, who should produce it, where it should be allocated, nor how it should be produced. Even if agents of the State could miraculously determine the "correct" answers to these questions at a given point in time, the very next second the answers would become obsolete because consumer preferences continually fluctuate along with the available technology and supplies to satisfy them.

Navigating A Spontaneous Order

Some of the more common criticisms of the Free Market are that it fails to address externalities, the collective-action problem, a lack of uniformity in safety and other quality standards, the free rider problem, and of course that it provides insufficient protection for the common man against the predations of the greedy business man. All of these allegations and many more will be addressed throughout this book.

The book starts off with Chapter 0 covering the epistemological limitations of empiricism in the realm of economics. It is due to such limitations that much of the discussion throughout this book will be based in theory, logical proofs, and analogies as opposed to seeking credibility through the lens of empirical data. Of course, some empirical examples will be utilized, but this should not be misconstrued as an attempt to prove the propositions made throughout this book. They are instead used to help illustrate some of the concepts which will be discussed.

The next few chapters will then be geared towards providing a conceptual foundation for the remainder of the book by providing a rational proof for the Private Property norm, defining the scope and nature of property, examining the characteristics of enforceable contracts, and establishing the economic boundaries and role of insurance in a Free Market.

The remaining chapters will speculate on how various services and social problems may be addressed in a Free Market in contrast with the State. The topics covered will range from: health care, monopolies and cartels, money and banking, road production, law and order, security production, environmentalism, poverty, education, and the corporation. The book will then culminate with a discussion on some effective means one may employ to diminish the power of the State and help usher in a free and voluntary society in its stead.

The Utopian Allegation

The purpose of this work is not to suggest that a society based on free market principles will necessarily be a Utopian one, nor does it require a change in "human nature" in order for such a society to arise and be sustained. Rather, it is to argue that a free market society is both ethically and economically superior to a State managed one, regardless of what form the State may take. For this proposal to be true, it does *not* require people to become better than they are or to adopt a greater social awareness. It must only assume that they are and forever will be self-interested creatures. This is not to say that all members of such a society will be misers or misanthropes. There will still be crime, and there will still be charity. These too are motivated by self-interest. However, the incentive structure that is created by the Free Market most closely aligns the self-interest of the individual with the interests of the members of greater society, and therefore crime and other anti-social behavior are most effectively dealt with in this environment. When reading through the pages of this book, I encourage you to be skeptical, challenging each proposal that is made, and to be relentless in your pursuit of truth. I would also encourage you to employ this same level of critique to the State itself, and to allow your objectivity to take precedence over the comfort of the familiar.

End the State. Free the Market. Liberate your Mind.

Chapter Zero

EPISTEMOLOGY AND PRAXEOLOGY

-Will Porter, 2014

Introduction: Science & Knowledge

THE PRIMARY TASK of epistemology is to construct a theory that describes knowledge and how it is attained. Epistemology grapples with the nature and nuances of knowledge: its function, its operation, and its boundaries. The systematic pursuit of knowledge and understanding may be deemed *science*, or, in its more antiquated usage, *philosophy*. This pursuit must be rooted in an epistemological theory – an understanding of knowledge and the various ways it is acquired.

There are virtually endless fields of scientific inquiry, from meteorology to anatomy, but all of them may be categorized as one of two types. Economics, the primary concern of the present work, is a "social" science, along with fields such as history and sociology. In contrast to the "natural" sciences, like physics and chemistry, social science deals with people's behavior, interactions, and choices. While both seek to understand and explain certain aspects of reality, social and natural science are categorically distinct from one another. It is only with a coherent epistemological foundation that one can distinguish between the two main types of science, and begin one's pursuit of systematic knowledge about the world, people, and their interactions.

Ludwig von Mises & Praxeology

During his long career, Ludwig von Mises – the 20th century social scientist and founder of the modern Austrian School of economics – made scholarly breakthroughs which have implications reaching beyond the narrow study of economics. Underlying the Misesian project is a core theory of knowledge and an understanding of choice-making in human behavior. Because this body of thought approaches social science in a unique and novel way, Mises employed the term *"praxeology"* to describe and distinguish it. Praxeology studies the logical implications of *human action*, but it also provides more general insights into the nature of science itself. The role that knowledge plays in human action is vital for the Misesian understanding of epistemology and, more particularly, economics. Mises' theory of knowledge deeply influenced his approach to science – establishing ever-more distinct boundaries between the two branches of scientific inquiry. The epistemological theory offered in the present work will utilize the concepts and terms of praxeology, analyze important distinctions regarding knowledge, and arrive atop a sound edifice from which one can proceed into the sciences. As we will see, the work of Ludwig von Mises has paved the way for much of this analysis.

A Priori vs. A Posteriori

The first task in building a foundation is to determine the difference between *"a priori"* and *"a posteriori"* knowledge.[11] *A priori* and *a posteriori* represent two avenues by which one can attain, or verify, knowledge: by logical deduction and by empirical observation. Attaining *a posteriori* knowledge requires specific experiences or observational data of some kind, while *a priori* deductions may occur in the absence of such data. For example, take the claim that no object can be both black all over and white all over at the same time. This can be verified *a priori*, by deduction alone, because "white all over" and "black all over" are mutually exclusive properties. Due to mutual exclusivity, one may reason that no object can exhibit both properties at once. This is an example of the law of contradiction, which states that no object or entity can exhibit two contradictory properties simultaneously. It is an instance of truth, or knowledge, which can be verified *prior* to any particular experience – it requires only that one reason through the necessary implications of the concepts in question. On the other hand, knowledge derived through experience, observation, and testing is deemed *a posteriori*. The fact that water runs downhill, or that oranges contain vitamin C, can only be affirmed by some particular experience. Without the data attained during observation, there is no way to verify or refute an *a posteriori* truth-claim. In order to find the answers to *a posteriori* types of questions, it is necessary to conduct tests and make observations, to investigate and gather data.

A priori knowledge, once established, holds true at all times and in

---

11 The approximate literal translations of the Latin terms *a priori* and *a posteriori* are "Before the fact," and "After the fact," respectively. Also, to avoid confusion, note that in the course of this essay the terms "knowledge," "claim," "proposition," and "truth" will be used to refer to the same concept.

all places, like the propositions of logic and arithmetic. *A posteriori* truths are, instead, hypothetical and tentative, meaning future observations can come along and refute them. In light of stronger evidence, new data, or innovations in measuring capabilities, empirical knowledge can potentially always be overturned with a better explanation. Knowledge acquired from observational data is, in other words, always theoretically *falsifiable*, or potentially disprovable by new findings.

To avoid confusion, it should be noted that while *a priori* knowledge can be verified as true through deduction alone, the "building blocks" of our concepts and language are initially attained through the senses, empirically. Once such concepts are learned, however, the possibility arises that they may be employed to discover and establish new propositions that are true *a priori*. *A priori*, then, does not refer to knowledge attained before all or any experience whatsoever, but merely to what can be verified as true, logically, in the absence of any *particular* empirical data. To recognize an *a priori* truth, it clearly requires prior life experience of *some* sort, but once grasped it is immediately apparent that such knowledge is true by virtue of logic alone. To illustrate, one must already understand the meaning of the words "black" and "white" before he can determine that it is impossible for an object or entity to exhibit both properties exclusively.

Thus, the avenues to knowledge may be split into two distinct realms: *a priori* and *a posteriori*. This important distinction will serve as the basis for a *dualist* epistemology, or one that demonstrates the fundamentally "dual" nature of knowledge, acquired and verified by two different modes of cognition.

Necessary Truths & Regularity in the Natural Sciences

A priori knowledge is attained by reasoning and reflecting on what is necessarily true. A necessary truth is one that couldn't possibly be otherwise, like the law of contradiction. To dispute a necessary truth, one must do so on the grounds of logical validity, rather than with data gleaned from empirical observation. This is clearly applicable to basic mathematics. One would only demonstrate their own confusion if they attempted to refute "2+2=4" with some new, cutting-edge data. Austrian economist and rationalist philosopher Hans-Hermann Hoppe provides another example of a necessary, *a priori* truth:

> Whenever two people A and B engage in
> a voluntary exchange, they must both
> expect to profit from it. And they must
> have reverse preference orders for the

goods and services' exchanged so that A
values what he receives from B more
highly than what he gives to him, and B
must evaluate the same things the other
way around.[12]

A posteriori knowledge, in contrast, involves the material world, whose governing laws must be discovered by empirical means. The natural sciences are largely comprised of this type of knowledge. In the study of physics, for example, hypotheses are only affirmed or falsified by data gathered from empirical observation. Scientists study this data and attempt to learn about certain constantly-operating relations of cause and effect: the laws which regulate and "guide" all natural events. Observational science cannot avoid assuming that there are *constants* in nature, and that due to this regularity, natural phenomena can be understood using data gathered during past observations. In this sense, *a posteriori* causal laws may be described as "mechanical," as they are predictable and remain stable over time.

Natural scientists conduct experiments by exposing their object of study to a controlled stimulus, observing, and measuring the resulting response. After repeating a series of tests, the observer hopes to extract from his data some general regularity between causes and effects, allowing him to formulate the trend into an empirical law. Because *a posteriori* knowledge is dependent upon specific observations and experiences, it is always possible for newly-gathered data to falsify current empirical laws. A theory in the natural sciences holds up only so long as the current data fails to falsify it.

Causal chains may also vary in their degree of constancy. In physics, laws adhere to a strict regularity with virtually no possibility for deviation, whereas a study like biology may only find *frequent* regularities. Nonetheless, the method of the natural sciences is *induction* – otherwise known as "causal inference" – where general laws are inferred from a series of tests and observations of the phenomenon in question.[13] The laws of physics are especially significant here because every natural phenomenon is subject to them. While the laws of biology or chemistry have their own

---

[12]   Hans-Hermann Hoppe, "Praxeology and Economic Science" in *Economic Science and the Austrian Method* (Auburn: Ludwig Von Mises Institute, 1995). — This quote illustrates the concept of mutually-beneficial exchange, an important idea in the study of economics. It is necessarily true that when two parties trade, each expects to gain from the exchange. If this weren't the case for both parties, the transaction wouldn't take place. The very meaning of both parties' willingness to trade is wrapped up in the fact that each sees more value in what they will receive, as compared to what they're asked to give up in exchange.

[13]   Induction is commonly known as the "scientific method": create a hypothesis, test and observe, affirm or falsify the hypothesis, revise if necessary, re-test and repeat.

narrower purview, the laws of physics apply to every natural event. It is this background of regularity that allows the inductive sciences – and everyday experience – to successfully understand the causal relations between various phenomena, and to make accurate predictions concerning the future of such phenomena. The method of induction, then, is fundamentally different in nature from that of logical deduction; they are distinct, separate modes of cognition.

Analytic vs. Synthetic & the Synthetic A Priori

With the *a priori*/ *a posteriori* division in mind, another important distinction is commonly made in regard to "analytic" and "synthetic" propositions. An analytic claim is one that refers purely to definitions, such as the claim "All bachelors are unmarried." Even though this statement *is* true logically, it is entirely a matter of linguistic convention. A claim whose truth depends on nothing more than a definition is also known as a "tautology". In contrast, a synthetic truth is one that reveals something beyond what may be inferred from the individual definitions of the words used in a claim. For instance, the claim that "Children prefer candy to vegetables" is established as true or false by neither the definitions of "children," "prefer," "candy," *etc.* It is instead reliant upon additional facts, beyond what can be found in a dictionary.

If a claim is analytic, it doesn't yield any new information, and refers only to the definitions of the words used in the claim. Since analytic propositions refer only to linguistic conventions, they cannot give new ground on truth or information external to the terms themselves. If a claim is synthetic, on the other hand, it tells us something new, relevant to properties, entities, or concepts *beyond* the words employed in the claim.

Most, if not all, *a posteriori* claims are also synthetic, since they always make reference to information external to the terms employed. These are called synthetic *a posteriori* propositions and again refer to the same kind of empirically-contingent, observational knowledge discussed above. Analytic claims, in distinction, are always provable by *a priori* means – such as the "bachelors" example – because no additional information is required to verify a tautology.[14] Once one learns the meaning of the word "bachelor," it is unnecessary for him to go around surveying unmarried men to verify that they are bachelors. Other than the definition itself, no additional information is needed, and so long as the word continues to be used with the same meaning, the analytic claim will remain true, making it

---

14 As shown earlier, one must already know the meaning of certain words before he can conclude the validity of any claim. Making *any* proposition will always require *some* understanding of the terms employed.

verifiable *a priori*, but no more useful for discovery of new truth.

While these distinctions may appear negligible, the fundamental difference between the two sets of terms – *a priori/a posteriori* and analytic/synthetic – is that the former deals with whether or not particular experiences are required to verify a claim, while the latter set distinguishes between claims concerning *only* definitional conventions from those that refer to additional concepts, entities, or properties.

Finally, and most importantly, knowledge can be synthetic (non-tautologous), *and*, at the same time, *a priori* (verifiable prior to any particular experience). In the following discussion regarding epistemology and social science, the synthetic *a priori* will carry great significance. As opposed to empty definitional claims (analytic), or facts attained by empirical observation (*a posteriori*), the synthetic *a priori* is an altogether unique, special class of knowledge.

Some of you may be thinking: this is impossible, it must involve a contradiction. How might one attain new, synthetic insights by way of logical deduction alone? Does this imply some sort of infallibility – a capacity to discover new facts about the world solely by power of reason? Initially, it might seem strange, but to fully understand how this type of truth is possible, why it is so important for epistemology, and how it applies to science, exploration into the different types of *phenomena* is necessary.[15]

Human Action, Teleology, & "Natural" Phenomena

The two main branches of science investigate two different types of events, or phenomena. Natural science seeks to explain a wide multitude of observable events, from the climate, to chemical reactions, to the biological processes of living beings. Purposeful behavior, or "action," however, is a unique exception.[16] The holistic study of action is instead within the purview of the social sciences.

---

[15] The "analytic *a posteriori*" type of claim is a subject of controversy, and therefore has been left out of the main discussion. Nonetheless, various thinkers have tried to construct examples of such a truth. An analytic *a posteriori* truth would have to be attained through experience, yet its meaning would be, at the same time, tautologous. This might relate to how language is learned. That "azule" means "blue" in Spanish is known only *a posteriori*, yet the claim that "azule is blue" *itself* is analytic; effectively saying "blue is blue."

[16] While humans are currently the only life form we *know* to live up to the status of "actor," one should not reject outright the possibility that there exist actors on other planets, or that certain other complex Earth species are also actors. This, however, is the task of zoology, not praxeology. The scope of the present work is to define action and elaborate its implications, not to determine which particular beings happen to be actors.

Action may be described as "teleological" in nature. Action simply refers to that behavior which is conducted in light of one's conceptual understanding of causal relationships and how they affect the achievement of his ends. Hence, any change in observable reality can be described as either a "natural" phenomenon, or as a teleological one, brought about by an actor who deliberately interferes in the natural course of the world's events.[17]

The domain of natural science is primarily made up of synthetic *a posteriori* knowledge. Physical laws, like gravity, operate on a constant basis of cause and effect, and so are said to be *causally-structured*. Knowledge about such causal regularities is gained through particular experiences, using the scientific method of induction. Future observations may, again, falsify or disprove conclusions derived from past observations, as induction establishes only hypothetical truths. Though one may repeatedly affirm a hypothesis, he cannot reach *ultimate* or *absolute* knowledge through the inductive method of causal inference.

Despite induction's inability to reach absolute certainty regarding particular causal relationships, the principle of causality itself must nonetheless be considered to govern all events that take place in the external, material world. In this context, Mises writes:

> ... It is impossible for the human mind to
> think of uncaused change. Man cannot
> help assuming that every change is caused
> by a preceding change and causes further
> change.[18]

In contrast, the realm of synthetic *a priori* knowledge is concerned with action. Action can only be understood when a conceptual being (*i.e.* an actor) reflects on what is logically necessary to his own nature. Here it is especially useful to distinguish action as teleological, or *purposeful*.[19]

---

[17] Here I refer to the term "nature" only to mean "that which occurs in the absence of any purposeful changes created by an actor." I do not mean to exclude human beings from the "natural" environment which produced them, and which they are a part of, but only to firmly distinguish the phenomenon of action from all other natural events.

[18] Ludwig Von Mises, *Theory and History* (New Haven: Yale University Press, 1957). – It is important to note that it very well may be the case that "action" ultimately operates on the same basis of causality as the rest of the natural world. However, regardless of whether actions are freely taken or causally determined, it retains unique traits which distinguish it from all natural events. No other phenomenon involves the use of conceptual knowledge (particularly the understanding of causal relations) like action does.

[19] The term "purposeful behavior" is commonly used as synonymous with "rational behavior". "Rational" in this sense simply means choice-making behavior. In

Teleology is the branch of philosophy which deals with purpose, which is intrinsic to the concept and process of *choice-making*. When a being makes a conscious choice regarding his behavior, he demonstrates that he *values* a particular state of affairs over his available alternatives. Choice, then, implies purpose, and since action always involves a choice, it is deemed a purposeful phenomenon. Thus, social science, because it seeks to understand the teleological type of event, must study the acts of purposeful beings – it must study the behavior of *actors*.[20]

The spheres of natural and teleological phenomena are distinct, but are also inextricably linked to one another. In the first place, nothing could be said or understood about the natural world without a concept-using, teleological entity there to experience it. At the same time, the existence of action presupposes some external reality in which it can take place. While abstract conceptual thought has no tangible, concrete existence, it *is* the product of a scarce, material body, subject to nature's causal laws. Indeed, actors rely on the regularity of such causal laws to successfully reach their goals.

When actors make choices, utilizing their knowledge and preferences, they deliberately implement causes in the world for the sake of creating particular effects. If an actor's environment did *not* operate on reliable, causal laws, action would be impossible. An actor could never hope to predict the effects of his behavior based on past experiences, and therefore the achievement of his ends would have to take place without any expectation that one particular cause leads to a particular effect. Without a causally-stable external reality, every behavior would produce new, unique effects, about which no systematic prediction could ever be made. Actors would exist in a perpetual state of random flux, wherein any type of planning or prediction would be impossible. In sum, the world in which action takes place *is* and must be governed on the basis of cause and effect.

Whether or not action is itself ultimately governed by causal laws is beyond the scope of the present work; however the answer to that question has no effect on the logical truths offered by praxeology. Regardless of what empirical data tells us about action's ultimate source, actors

---

common usage, "rational" refers to someone who makes relatively *good* choices, whereas in the study praxeology it simply means that a being makes conscious choices (utilizing concepts) at all. Either one of the above terms may be used interchangeably with the term "action".

[20] To clarify, any life form that is unable to comprehend the notion of purpose – perhaps by virtue of complete instinct-dominance – is a non-actor. Such organisms are incapable of formulating preferences and conceptual knowledge into plans on which they can act. In contrast to actors, the behavior of this type of being is considered non-teleological, that is, a part of the natural realm of events. Similarly, phenomena like bodily functions or reflexes – even of actors – are not considered actions. An actor has little to no control over certain bodily operations, leaving them outside the realm of teleological, or purposeful, phenomena.

themselves cannot escape the logical and argumentative necessities imposed on them by their own conceptual nature.

Equipped with vital epistemic distinctions between the various types of knowledge, as well as an understanding of how the sciences must apply those types of knowledge to distinct realms of phenomena, we may now explicitly delve into the content of praxeology – a series of inter-connected synthetic *a priori* axioms.

Praxeology, The Action Axiom, & The Categories of Action

The statement "Man acts" must reside in the realm of synthetic *a priori* knowledge: it is true by logical necessity, yet it also offers something beyond mere definitions. If one attempts to deny this claim – known as the "action axiom" – he must inevitably affirm it in the course of his denial, because a denial is itself a kind of action. This is known as a performative contradiction. When one demonstrates the validity of a claim in the very *act* of denying it, the claim becomes axiomatic.[21] One cannot deny an axiom without thereby engaging in self-refutation. Originally formulated by the late economist Ludwig von Mises, the action axiom serves as a synthetic *a priori* starting point for the entire study of praxeology. In addition to being argumentatively indisputable, axioms can also serve as a foundation from which additional insights may be derived.

Due to the inherent undeniably of this concept, any coherent theory of knowledge is compelled to consider action as its inalienable starting point – any and all discussion of epistemology necessarily takes place within the context of specific actions. Thus, beginning with the action axiom, we may extrapolate the fact that action must involve the use of "means" that are intended to achieve particular "ends". An actor's desires or goals are described as his ends, whereas his means consist of the knowledge (particularly knowledge concerning causes and effects), skills, and scarce resources which he uses to reach his ends. For example, if one's goal is to go to the library, he might decide to use a vehicle, various roads, and his knowledge/ability to drive, all as means to help him get there.

Means and ends are inextricably linked to action, and they directly

---

21   The notion of the "axiom" itself – as defined in the present work – is fundamentally a praxeological insight. The very meaning of a proposition which one cannot argumentatively deny is tied to the idea that there are *presupposed* truths which lie behind the concept of "action" (and/or argumentation – see below "Knowledge, Truth, & Argumentation"). It is this which gives axioms their significance. An axiom is considered undeniable only because one must affirm it in his very *act* of denial. Thus, the only truths which could ever be shown to be axiomatic are ones with some ultimate relation to the concept of action.

follow from the action axiom. Every conceivable action can be described or expressed in terms of the end an actor aims at, and the means he employs to accomplish that end. In Kantian fashion, Mises terms the concepts of means and ends as "categories of action," that is, logically implicit components in the concept of action itself. Because no purposeful conduct could occur without the use of means to achieve ends, they are considered categories of action. The categories are, in other words, "essential elements" of action. Thus, not only is the action axiom itself a synthetic *a priori* truth, but so are each of the categories derived from it. They are equally indisputable, as their denial, too, must entail self-contradiction. The concepts of value, choice, preference, cost, profit, and loss are also categories of action, each implicit in purposeful behavior and its means-ends framework. Hoppe elaborates further on how these synthetic *a priori* categories are axiomatic and inherently contained in the action axiom:

> For any attempt to disprove the validity of what Mises has reconstructed as implied in the very concept of action [the categories] would have to be aimed at a **goal**, requiring **means**, excluding other courses of action, incurring **costs**, subjecting the actor to the possibility of achieving or not achieving the desired goal and so leading to a **profit** or a **loss**. Thus, it is manifestly impossible to ever dispute or falsify the validity of Mises' insights. In fact, a situation in which the categories of action would cease to have a real existence could itself never be observed or spoken of, since to make an observation and to speak are themselves actions.[22] [*Emphasis mine*]

And also:

> All of these categories which we know to be the very heart of economics – values, ends, means, choice, preferences, cost, profit and loss – are implied in the axiom of action.[23]

---

[22]   Hoppe, "On Praxeology and on the Praxeological Foundation of Epistemology," *Economic Science*.

[23]   Hoppe, ibid.

Elsewhere, Hoppe maintains that the action axiom and its categories are not "self-evident," or tautologous, and that their elucidation provides us with new, synthetic knowledge, affirmed as true out of logical necessity. This strikes to the very core of what it means for a truth to be both synthetic and *a priori*. While they may not be, and often are not, *explicitly* understood immediately, once one is confronted with these insights, he cannot coherently deny them.

Prediction, Observation, & Reflection

The teleological concepts of purpose and choice are not observable to the five senses. Hence, in studying the phenomenon of human action one cannot go forward on empirical data alone. Empirical science studies causal regularities, and this allows for predictions to be made based on past observations. Social science, due to the unique conceptual traits of its object of study, cannot proceed in such a manner. For example, in the natural science of chemistry, predictions can be made about chemical reactions based on observations and tests conducted with certain chemicals in the past. If one tried to apply the same method to the phenomenon of action, he would soon learn that no two individuals respond to external events in precisely the same way. A stimulus – or cause – which provokes a particular response – or effect – from one actor may radically differ for another, due to their unique preferences, values, and knowledge-sets. The same holds true even for a single actor at different instants, as his values and knowledge-sets constantly fluctuate over time. The *only* conceivable way one *could* determine the future actions of another would be *if* action is truly dictated solely by observable causal forces, *and* if he could take into account all the observable factors affecting this other person. This would include a given actor's genetic disposition, the configuration of his brain and how it is affected by all types of stimuli, the physical capabilities of his body, his surrounding environment, etc. The observer would *then* have to understand how this immense set of factors affects each other, and *only* at this point may he hope to extrapolate a prediction of another's actions with certainty. This is, of course, currently outside of mankind's technical abilities. However, whether or not this sort of prediction is even theoretically possible will have no impact on the insights derived from praxeology nor will it in any way affect the epistemic boundaries established by it. A good analogy would be to think of praxeology as providing the formula and empiricism as providing the variables. One requires insights from praxeology in order to meaningfully and coherently interpret empirical economic data, and only through praxeology may incontrovertible economic laws or principles be formulated.

In praxeology, action is not understood using empirical data, but only through *a priori* reasoning, or "reflection," on necessary, axiomatic truths (*i.e.* the axiom of action and its categories). To verify the truths of praxeology, one need not go further than the conclusions generated by his own thoughts, rendering empirical data utterly extraneous. Due to the vantage-point of an actor, he is in a unique position to observe, or reflect on, the concept of action – a position he can never be in while observing any external, natural phenomena. (The existence and specific traits of natural phenomena can only be known through the inductive scientific method.)

Since all of man's observations are necessarily those of a choice-making actor, one could not attempt any empirical observation *of* action without already presupposing its existence and the validity of all its categories. Any attempt to observe action is *itself* an action, guided by value and purpose, using scarce means and aimed at a desired end, taken in place of other alternative actions, and thereby incurring the cost of lost opportunities. One could, therefore, never hope to step outside his status as an actor to observe action in any way at variance with the insights of praxeology. These insights take logical precedence to any observational data, as man's observations themselves logically must conform to the structure and existence of action in general.

If one *does* attempt to observe an instance of human action, he will only see an entity moving around in some particular way. Nothing about choice, value, cost, profit, means, or ends will ever be made apparent to the senses of an outside observer. While purpose can be conceptually *inferred* from observations of an actor's bodily movement, purpose is itself never actually seen or understood as a result of a mere observation. It is only by reflecting on the logical, conceptual nature of action that one can truly understand it. Thus, no entity *but* an actor could have access to such information.

A clear example of this sort of reflection can be found in the recognition that every conceivable action is comprised of means intended to achieve ends. This is not apparent to empirical observation, but only deduced from reflecting on the nature of action. It is unnecessary, and indeed impossible, to take measurements and conduct tests in order to prove that actions always make use of means and are aimed at ends. To verify that claim, one needs only to reflect on what it means to act toward a goal (something all actors are necessarily capable of doing).[24] This should

---

[24]   To clarify, it is not the specific content of an actor's values and ends that can be known *a priori*, but only the general fact that actors desire the achievement of ends at all. One could not deny this without implicitly affirming its truth, as again, any denial would involve the use of means intended to achieve an end, and would thereby constitute an action itself.

illustrate the fundamental difference between facts learned through empirical observation, and axiomatic truths attained and verified via reflective reasoning.

Thus, it is confirmed that action is conceptually distinct from all other phenomena. Unlike any other type of event, one can derive logical insights concerning action prior to any specific experiences, while still revealing new, non-tautologous information. This is the fundamental distinction upon which the entire edifice of praxeology is built, and it has serious implications for scientific inquiry in general, and for social science in particular.

The notion of a synthetic *a priori* truth – once seemingly contradictory – now becomes wholly viable and indeed inescapable when one begins to examine the nature of purposeful behavior. One could not undo the truth of these claims, since actors implicitly demonstrate their validity in any attempt to deny them, as well as in any attempt to observe a situation that did not comport with them.

Knowledge, Truth, & Argumentation

With the idea of purposeful behavior elucidated, the next task is to explore the vital role that knowledge itself plays in action, as well as the roles that language, proposition-making, and truth-validity play in knowledge.

Knowledge is the product of a conceptual mind sorting out sensory data and merging it into an integrated experience, allowing an actor to navigate and understand his environment. Deliberately utilizing means in order to reach goals, or ends, requires the use of knowledge and technical know-how, without which, purposeful behavior would be impossible. Before one engages in action, he must first identify his current situation, determine a more preferable state of affairs, and finally discover how he might reach that condition through his behavior. An actor must figure out the proper changes he is to inflict into the world in order to bring about the desired effects, *i.e.*, in order to reach his end. This process involves "filtering" sensory data through one's mind to extract the relevant information, with the additional ability to *conceptualize*, allowing an actor to structure his knowledge in an explicit and concrete way suitable for the realization of his purposes.

Errors, of course, are always possible, and knowledge regarding certain causal chains or facts about the world may not, in reality, hold true. Nevertheless, knowledge – correct or not – is more than just sensory data, but sensory data interpreted and conceptualized by a purposeful, choice-making agent.

The only way to formulate and express conceptual knowledge is by means of language, either verbal or symbolic. Indeed, it is difficult to even imagine conceptual thought totally detached from language, as language gives expressible form to concepts by assigning their meaning to shapes, symbols, and sounds. A language-using entity essentially cannot escape the use of language in formulating his ideas; language is his primary faculty of expression for any knowledge, information, or concept at all. Besides spoken and written language there are also forms of gestural and pictorial communication, but only insofar as such gestures and images can play the same role as words in carrying the meaning of concepts can a truth-claim be expressed in this way.

A truth-claim, or argument, is an affirmation or negation of some facet of reality or some causal relationship. When two language-users reach a disagreement regarding a claim to truth, they are able to engage in *argumentative exchange* in an attempt to resolve it. Both sides give their own account and each weighs the other's claims against some standard of validity to reach a conclusion. Argumentation is the necessary result of an actor's ability to categorize entities and properties into a conceptual framework. Without the ability to organize concepts, not only argumentation, but action itself would become altogether impossible.

It is the expression of one's concepts using sounds and symbols that other language-users can understand as meaningful. If one tried to deny that language had meaning, he would find himself in a performative contradiction. An objection to *any* given proposition implies the objector considers his words meaningful, thereby directly contradicting the content of the objection: "language has no meaning". Since the existence of argumentation is itself argumentatively indisputable, we may also deem it axiomatic. In other words, one cannot reasonably argue that one cannot argue.

It therefore becomes equally impossible for one to deny that he knows the meaning of truth-validity, since in his very act of denial he demonstrates his possession of such knowledge. To dispute any claim whatever, the speaker must appeal to some standard of truth – otherwise, on what grounds could he possibly dispute *anything*? To support any position, or to undercut the position of an opponent, one must make use of truth-claims in the course of an argument. Hence, that language, argumentation, and truth-validity are genuinely meaningful concepts must already be presupposed if one is to make a case for, or against, anything at all.

The propositions made during an argument, further, are verified or refuted primarily on the basis of *logic*. In claiming the validity of any proposition, an actor presupposes some objectively-ascertainable standard of truth. If, on the contrary, each person could have his "own truth," it would be meaningless to argue over the validity of any proposition.

Arguments are only meaningful at all when the participants realize that claims to knowledge must be consistent with some basic standard of verifiability, not merely based in their own subjective whims.

Thus, implied in the meaning of truth-validity are, at least, the logical laws of *existence* ("Something exists"), *identity* ("Things have distinguishing properties that separate them from all other existing things"), and *contradiction* ("Because things have particular identities, they cannot exhibit mutually exclusive properties simultaneously" or, more simply, "A cannot be both A and not A at the same time").

When one says something is true, he means most fundamentally that it is in accord with these basic logical laws. Additional empirical data may be required to verify a particular proposition, but if a claim is directly at variance with a logical law, it can be immediately rejected as false. Logical laws, then, are implied – wrapped up – in the very concept of argumentation.

To illustrate: during argumentation one cannot conceivably avoid assuming that *something* exists; that is to say, the existence of entities, objects, and matter is indisputable. An argument has to be made by *some* entity in order to be expressed at all. Also implied in argumentation is the fact that existence is made up of more than just one homogeneous thing; it implies a diversity of entities and properties. Language, and therefore argument, would lose all meaning if there were zero distinctions to be made about anything in reality. To negate or affirm anything using language in the course of an argument, one implicitly assumes a diverse range in the identities of things, to which different concepts and words refer. Finally, related to the presupposition of identity is the fact that objects and entities cannot, at once, exhibit 100% of one property, and 100% of another mutually exclusive property. In other words, contradictions cannot occur in reality, because each extant entity has its own unique set of properties which distinguish it from all other things. No matter how hard one tried, any argument imaginable would implicitly assume the validity of these three logical laws – they underpin the very meaning of truth itself. Again, even if one is ultimately in error regarding a particular truth-claim, to express that claim at all the same presuppositions must still apply.

Similar to the broader concept of action, a necessary component of argumentation is knowledge. The determination of truth-validity and the subsequent use of that knowledge is an essential element to choice-making, regardless of whether or not a particular actor's conclusions turn out to be actually true. The same holds true for argumentation.

Without at least the *faculty* to distinguish between truth and falsehood, one could not formulate arguments, nor could he engage in any choice-making behavior at all. As with means and ends, knowledge is a category of action because no specific action could be conceived of that did not contain knowledge as a necessary ingredient. It might be deemed a special type of the "means" category, but knowledge is nonetheless essential to the concept of action.

Furthermore, because knowledge is subject to validity-verification, it serves an active or "positive" function in choice-making. Means and ends are neutral categories, in that all that can be done with them is to simply fill them with the particular content of a given action. Knowledge, on the other hand, is true or false, right or wrong, correct or incorrect. Determining the validity of specific claims is an essential part of how an actor guides his behavior.

Knowledge is only useful insofar as it can provide actors with causally-effective means to achieve their ends. When one acts on incorrect knowledge about the effectiveness of a means, the likelihood that he will actually achieve his end is severely diminished. An actor's means, ends, and preferences are all determined based on what he *knows* about his own values, and the current environment in which he is situated. Each actor's surrounding circumstances will also, in turn, influence his knowledge, preferences and decisions, as different situations offer unique experiences and obstacles to overcome. We may conclude here that the ultimate role of knowledge is to enable actors to succeed in achieving their ends.

***

The task of epistemology has traditionally been to explore the nature of knowledge. The true function of knowledge, as we have seen, lies with man's ultimate nature as a choice-maker. Actors use knowledge to navigate between truth and falsehood for the sake of enabling effective action. One may also formulate knowledge into a truth-claim, expressed by language, and such a claim is verified or refuted primarily on the grounds of presupposed logical axioms, and if necessary, empirical data as well.

Epistemology also asks whether there is more than one type of knowledge and, if so, it distinguishes where one ends and the other begins. We have discovered how "action" is the only area of study that can yield synthetic discoveries in an *a priori* manner. This further illustrates the dualist character of our epistemology – there are only two routes to attain *new* knowledge: deductive reflection and empirical observation.

Kant, Dualism, & the Empiricists

With praxeological insights at hand, an age-old empiricist objection – that dualism leads to a form of metaphysical idealism – can now be successfully addressed.[25]

EPISTEMOLOGY AND PRAXEOLOGY

Depending on one's interpretation, the work of traditional rationalists, like Gottfried Leibniz and Immanuel Kant, seems to imply that external reality must conform to the mind, rather than the other way around. This would clearly entail some sort of idealism, where thought either creates or distorts reality.

In contrast to the empiricist model of the mirror-like mind – inspired by thinkers such as David Hume and John Locke – where *all* knowledge is derived purely from sensory data, the traditional rationalist model is one of an active mind which meets reality with its own structure of *a priori* knowledge. This mental structure, Kant believed, was comprised of various "categories of thought". For example, Kant considered the principle of causality as such a category. He correctly thought that the general existence of cause and effect was not to be observed through the senses, but rather that it was necessarily understood prior to any specific observation. Indeed, as Mises suggests, the human mind cannot even fathom the notion of an observable change in reality that was not the effect of some prior cause. The rationalist accounts for causality by deeming it part of the logical structure of the human mind, rather than something to be seen, heard, or felt. For Kant *and* Mises, then, the principle of causality is an *a priori* presupposition, not a falsifiable empirical fact.

In the same way that praxeology uses the term "category" to mean a logically essential element or component, the traditional rationalist notion of categories also consists of truths that are necessary, presupposed ingredients of experience. The principle of causality, while not observable, cannot be detached from any human experience; its existence is presupposed and indisputable. Along with causality, Kant deemed "time" and "space" as categories of thought as well, on the premise that one cannot experience or observe anything without implicitly assuming a general existence of time and space. One could never experience a situation completely devoid of space, nor could any experience take place outside the unrelenting flow of time.

Because raw observational data is nothing more than light photons, sound waves, touch-textures, *etc.*, no part of it is inherently logical or conceptually-structured in any way. Kant's categories of thought are concepts which help the mind to organize such sense data into something rationally understandable. In other words, a conceptual being does not merely utilize sensory data alone; it is organized by, and integrated with, *a priori* presuppositions (in Kant's terms, the categories of thought). This insight strikes at the very meaning of human rationality, a faculty of conceptual understanding which goes *beyond* mere sensuous stimulation.

The essential rationalist claim is that the human mind must meet

---

25   "Idealism" in this context simply means that the objects of physical existence are somehow reliant upon, or created by, the mind.

observational reality with its own toolbox, so to speak. Kant referred to this as the "manifold of apperception," where the human mind processes raw sensory input through the categories of thought, resulting in a unified conceptual understanding. In order to coherently grasp the plethora of data with which man is always bombarded, Kant thought that man's mind must, from the outset, order conscious experience causally, temporally, and spatially.

To this claim, the empiricist might retort that if such an *a priori* structure of thought was really in place, prior to, or independent of, all experience, in what way could this structure have anything to do with actual, observable existence? If the rationalists were correct, the empiricists charged, this would mean either that the human mind would have to create our reality according to that logical structure, or that the mind distorts reality into something different than what it truly is. In other words, the empiricists argued that the only way for the rationalist to proceed was to adopt some flavor of idealism, where the structure of the human mind distorts reality in order to render it understandable.

However, in light of praxeological theory, we can further elaborate on the notion of an active mind as one that is constrained by the categories of *action*. With this idea, we can now answer the empiricist's objection.

Unlike any other phenomena, action is unique in that it simultaneously has a foot in both the teleological realm of thought and the natural realm of existence. One might say that action is the intermediary between the two – where conceptual thought meets observable reality. Indeed, action is the *external* implementation of *internal* knowledge and preferences – transforming some aspect of the natural world with the intention of bringing about a more preferable state of affairs.

The categories of action – means, ends, value, choice, knowledge, (the principle of) causality, *etc.* – are unavoidably valid once the meaning of action is formulated, expressed, and its implications unpacked. Hence, rather than being free-floating figments of the mind with no foundation in reality, as were Kant's categories of thought, the categories of action are rooted to the very real – and indisputable – concept of purposeful behavior.

We can now see that Kant's idealistic mental categories become the praxeological categories of action. The difference here is that the praxeological account puts vital emphasis on the notion of action, which has immediate relevance to external reality. The traditional rationalists focused more exclusively on the nature of reason and experience, whereas praxeology seats conceptual thought within its function in action, thereby linking abstract thought to the *concrete reality* in which action must navigate. On this, Mises comments:

> The main deficiency of traditional
> epistemological attempts is to be seen in

> their neglect of the praxeological aspects.
> The epistemologists dealt with thinking
> as if it were a separate field cut off from
> other manifestations of human
> endeavor. They dealt with the problems
> of logic and mathematics, but they failed
> to see the practical aspects of thinking.[26]

Kant's free-floating categories of time, space, and causality are, instead, directly contained in the action-categories of means and ends. Thus, an end is accomplished only *after* some means is employed; time necessarily elapses between the two. Furthermore, all action must take place in some physical environment, unavoidably understood by any actor as spatially-structured. Even if reaching one's end did not involve much bodily movement, all action must take place *somewhere* in space. At the very least, all action involves the utilization of standing room and the time consumed by the action itself. Causality, finally, is also integral to action, as ends are only reached as the *effect* of some means; actors deliberately inflict causes into the world in order to reap their effects.

A Realistic Epistemology & Re-Formulating the Categories of Action

Because actions take place in a concrete reality, the action-categories must fundamentally reflect that reality in some way as well. In understanding the role that action plays in our theory, we can bridge from abstract conceptual thought into concrete reality, yielding a very *realistic* epistemology. As opposed to an untenable idealism that cannot account for the connection between thought and reality, our theory offers precisely that connection. Thus, the traditional rationalists are correct in claiming that certain synthetic truths can be known *a priori*, but it is only the concept of action that can ground these truths to observable reality and escape all forms of idealism. Since action is guided by thought, yet also affects change into the external world, the categories of action are not only laws of thought, but laws of reality as well.[27]

---

[26] Ludwig von Mises, "Some Preliminary Observations Concerning Praxeology," in *The Ultimate Foundation of Economic Science* (New York: Van Nostrand LTD., 1962), 2.

[27] This serves to reconcile the small quarrel between Ludwig von Mises and Murray N. Rothbard, two giants in the field of praxeology. The latter maintained that praxeology furnished existential laws, whereas Mises held that they are epistemological laws. We can now see that they are both. This reconciliation opens the possibility for an action-based theory of metaphysics, but that will have to be the

Now that we understand how the action-categories are legitimately synthetic *a priori*, their function in purposeful behavior, and their uniqueness among all other knowledge, we can further derive a complete list of them. We have already explored the categories of **means, ends, knowledge, existence, identity, contradiction, causality, space, and time**, but we only briefly touched upon the categories of **preference, choice, cost/price, profit/loss, and value**. All of these concepts are directly deduced from the action axiom: the seemingly basic claim that man acts.

Let us now explicitly demonstrate each category's inextricable role in action, by way of a hypothetical objection – an attempted denial of the action axiom and each of its categories. In the very act of objection (and, indeed, in any act whatsoever), one must pursue an **end** to which he attaches **value**. One aims to accomplish this end by employing some number of **means; knowledge** necessarily being one of them. Further implied in the concepts of means and ends are the categories of **space, time**, and **causality**. In his objection, the speaker must additionally make a **choice**, setting another course of action aside, thereby incurring the **cost** of a foregone opportunity. From the costs assumed by choosing one thing in favor of another, the **price** of each opportunity emerges in respect to the person's set of **preferences**. If the speaker accomplishes his end and satisfies his preference (something we know to be impossible, assuming the speaker's end is to meaningfully refute the concept of action), he can be said to have attained a **profit**.[28] If the end reached by the actor does not satisfy his expectations, to the extent that his costs exceed his benefits, he takes a **loss**. Finally, all of this must imply an **existence** in which to take place, comprised of various objects, things, and entities. Each thing exhibits its own unique **identity**, which rules out the possibility of **contradictions**.

It is possible that there are additional action-categories, and so while the list may not be exhaustive, it constitutes what can be known about reality *a priori*. It provides various existential facts that can be deduced, logically, each fact having a direct logical relation to human action.

Due to the way praxeology applies to all actors, the conclusions it yields are universal. They are not unique to social, ethnic, national, psychological, or any other distinction; instead, they apply to each and every acting agent. With an overarching theory that encompasses all purposeful behavior and the knowledge which guides it, we may proceed into the social sciences carrying some vital epistemological assumptions. In the study of economics, we utilize praxeological insights to derive economic laws, which are used to properly interpret the data that reflects purposeful behavior. When analyzing the complex, interwoven patchwork of actions on the scale

---

subject of another essay.

[28]   Note that "profit" does not necessarily mean monetary profit, as the term is commonly understood. An actor may profit only mentally, or psychologically, but in the context of praxeology, it is profit nonetheless.

of an entire society, this methodology becomes indispensable.

Empiricism in the Social Sciences

There are schools of thought that actively seek to refute the existence of such synthetic *a priori* truths as the action axiom. Two camps emerged in 20th century German academia who opposed the notion of the synthetic *a priori:* empiricists and, their more radical variant, the Logical Positivists. The empiricists and their more exciting positivist cousins – while supporting the relatively tame epistemology that knowledge is primarily gained through the senses – were very skeptical that anyone could deduce a corpus of epistemological philosophy through *a priori* axioms.

Such a philosophical foundation would establish the potential legitimacy of *science* conducted on the basis of *a priori* truth, rather than by induction alone. It was, in fact, Ludwig von Mises who discovered that social science – and more particularly, economics – could *only* deal with the logical implications of human action. Working from the typical understanding of his predecessors, Mises revised economic method to fit into the framework of praxeology. Contrary to the popular intellectual fashion of his time, Mises concluded that economics was necessarily a study of action, and could not be based in the traditional Baconian scientific method. In economics, observations can only be *interpreted* with the aid of an *a priori* theoretical structure, which is precisely what praxeology provides. If one tried to forego praxeology in an attempt to derive a theory from only observational data, he would run into problems immediately. The conclusions of praxeology are, indeed, inescapable.

The positivist objects to this; he maintains that the only two possible kinds of truth are analytic definitions (tautologies) and tentative empirical hypotheses. This perspective essentially states that *certainty* cannot be claimed about *anything* unless it is definitional, which can only involve linguistic conventions. Positivism attempts to introduce a skepticism regarding the human capacity for attaining genuinely absolute knowledge. These academics claimed that the realm of *a priori* knowledge is exclusively comprised of mere linguistic conventions, representing only arbitrary transformation rules of various symbols (language and/or mathematics) without any scientifically relevant relation to observational reality.

Although the positivists accepted that there *is* indeed a dichotomy between the realms of *a priori* and *a posteriori* knowledge, they postulated that nothing from the former realm could give us any new or meaningful information. To them, *a priori* truths were virtually free of content in regard to the reality of the world as it exists. Concerning this claim itself, however, one must ask: what kind of truth is *that?* According to positivist epistemology, the claim that "*A priori* knowledge can only be tautologous" is either a tautological definition that tells us nothing new, or only a hypothesis, in which case, such a claim may well be falsified in an experiment. Before verifying such a theory, scientists would have to go around "testing" every conceivable proposition to make sure it was in accordance with their epistemological account (that all knowledge is either empty and tautologous or hypothetical and tentative).

If we apply the positivist logic to its own epistemological claim, it is self-refuting. Because the positivists do not regard their own epistemology as tentative and hypothetical – but rather necessarily binding for all knowledge-claims – they must, on pain of contradiction, reject their own methodology. Recall how the positivists want to assert that only two types of knowledge exist: logical relations of the type "All bachelors are unmarried men," and empirical facts, which can potentially always be falsified by future experiments. When this distinction is applied to the positivist epistemic claim, there can be no solution. According to their own criteria, it must be either logical-tautologous (as in the bachelor example), or empirical; but in either case, they are doomed. For positivists clearly *do* regard their methodology as helpful and able to offer new information, yet at the same time believe their methodology to be true without requiring any corroborating empirical data to prove it. Contrary to their own position, the positivists must consider their epistemological claim to be *non-empirical* (because no experiment could falsify it) and also *useful* because it claims to offer more than a mere definition. The central claim of positivism, then, cannot survive its own distinction. The only way they could ever hope to salvage it would be to concede that it indeed *is* a synthetic *a priori* claim, at which point they would have conceded the entire argument, as that is precisely what they were trying to dispute in the first place.

But that is not all – there is a second critique which must be addressed in regard to this school of thought. Sociologists and economists employing a purely empirical method are essentially mimicking the natural sciences, like chemistry or physics. A tentative hypothesis is posited and empirical observation and experimentation are used to affirm or invalidate the proposed theory. Ignoring the obvious objection that there is no sociological or economic laboratory where variables can be steadily controlled, there is an even more fundamental error associated with the attempt to apply the empirical method to any study concerning human action. This error is best illustrated when we analyze the basic assumptions implicit to the empirical method. In absence of such assumptions, empirical science would be either impossible or meaningless. But by incorporating them into our explicit understanding, it soon becomes apparent that no *strictly* empirical method – free of all *a priori* assumptions – could ever yield fruitful discovery in the study of action, further demonstrating the vital importance that praxeology has to the field of social science.

EPISTEMOLOGY AND PRAXEOLOGY

If one were to conduct consecutive experiments with the goal of refuting or confirming a proposed theory, it seems one could not consistently commit to the empiricist idea that *all* non-tautologous knowledge must be empirically-attained. Causes and effects, as Hume famously noted, are themselves nowhere to be seen in observation. But while Hume thought this meant that causality did not itself exist, the truth is that causality is only known through *non*-empirical, or *a priori*, means.

If reality were not causally-structured, it would not make sense to say that a past observation could be either confirmed or falsified by any future observation. For example, ask yourself: if observing Experiment A at time T1 is to have any relevance whatsoever to observations made during Experiment B at time T2, what must be true for this relationship to exist? What is to bind these observations to one another, so to speak, and allow a scientist to apply information gathered about *past* events when making predictions about *future* events? In other words, why is it not simply that at T1 we see one thing happen and at T2 we see another? Why should there ever be a problem? Why is it true that T2's results could "falsify" or "confirm" the results from T1? Without the use of any *a priori* knowledge regarding causality, this question could not be coherently answered. Any given set of observations would have to be seen as simply logically incommensurable with any other set; no hypothesis could ever be tested, confirmed, or refuted. When a scientist derives a theory from his past observations, the only possible way for him to test that theory is with the assumption that future instances of the same phenomena will operate on the basis of the same causal relations. Without this *a priori* assumption of the principle of causality, the empirical scientist has no coherent or systematic way in which he can test his theories; every new set of observations is completely independent from and irrelevant to the last set.

But it would seem quite ridiculous to deny the acute success of the observational sciences. The astonishing advances in technology and scientific understanding over the 20th century *alone* clearly demonstrate the practical validity of assuming the existence of a causally-structured reality. The *a priori* assumption made by empiricists – that physical reality operates on constant and stable relations over time – is *not* justified under the positivist-empiricist theory of knowledge. Due to the principle of causality, however, scientists are able to make successful and accurate predictions about empirical events based in what they have learned from past observations.

Contrary to empiricist doctrine, then, the principle of causality must be taken to be a meaningful synthetic *a priori* statement. In fact, *no* empirical science could be undertaken without this basic, non-observable, non-falsifiable, understanding that causes create effects in constant and predictable ways.[29]

It is important not to mistake any of the above as an attempt to render the scientific method illegitimate or invalid, quite the contrary. Rather, the question concerns the *scope of applicability* for the inductive scientific method. The traditional scientific method may still have some limited uses in social science, but the implications of praxeology must be taken as our primary methodological tool. Data in the social sciences can only be *interpreted* on the basis of a theory, and so theoretical insights are required for a systematic understanding of any kind. In the social sciences, data never speaks for itself, but requires the application of a sound (*a priori*) theory in order to extract any meaningful conclusions. Praxeology furnishes this theoretical structure.

In regards to predictions, one *can* say that specific types are inherently *untenable*. Any prediction that is at variance with the *a priori* truths derived from the action axiom can be immediately rejected as systematically flawed. For example, one could not reasonably predict that an actor will *not* employ the first unit of a given set of homogeneous goods toward its currently most-valued end (and the second to its second-most valued end, and so on). The fact that actors employ resources to their most valued ends is part of the economic law of "diminishing marginal utility," which is derived, *a priori*, from the action axiom. This all-important axiom, then, serves to confine the logical scope of prediction in the fields of social science.

With the above in mind, it becomes quite clear why a *strictly* inductive method has no place in a discipline like economics. The mainstream economic orthodoxy constantly makes a variety of impossible predictions using statistics, linear regression techniques, and econometrics. One who takes data about the past and lumps it into a statistical aggregate can only yield a historical account of past economic relations. One can never use such aggregates alone to *scientifically* forecast future economic phenomena.[30] Attempting to do so is akin to Ptolemaic astronomers trying

---

[29] To quickly address the possible objection that certain aspects of quantum physics somehow disprove the idea of a stably-structured reality, one can only answer: as far as praxeology is concerned, quantum states and infinitesimally small measurements of time and space are not relevant for actors. Action is always concerned with the *marginal* – not the quantum – level. Man is not able to act on the basis of such inconceivably small distinctions, but only those which he can actually detect. Quantum physics may well upset or shake up conventional notions of causality, but so long as the discussion is focused on human action, we have no reason to assume that the principle of causality is invalid. On the contrary, action *per se* implies that actors recognize their actions as demonstrably affecting their natural surroundings on the basis of cause and effect. Quantum physics could not refute the fact that there is a significant degree of stability in the world in which man acts, and that, in acting, he implements and observes definite causes to reap (and, in the case of science, study) their effects.

[30] It is important to distinguish systematic *scientific* prediction from the type of

to force math and science to fit their incorrect notion of a geocentric universe. Such an exercise can only result in overly-complicated falsehoods that serve to muddy the waters for future scientific inquiry.

Conclusion

Human action, and the sciences which study it, must be examined with the tools which are attained through reflective contemplation of our own nature as choice-makers. Only the logical ramifications of action can provide tools wholly useful for social science. While the action-categories prohibit one from attaining predictively-helpful *causal* relations from empirical data, the application of the action-categories *does* still allow for fruitful analysis, scientific insight, and the use of economic law.

Epistemological dualism allows one to distinguish between the two, categorically distinct, areas of knowledge. The two branches of science which closely correspond with that distinction are also elucidated by this dualism. Economics, history, sociology and the like all involve human action as their primary subject matter, and thus require an entirely different method than that of the physical sciences. The fundamental distinctions made by rationalist philosophy have carved the way for an action-based epistemology; one that recognizes the fundamental difference between *a priori*-deductive and *a posteriori*-inductive knowledge. This understanding provides a rock-solid edifice from which an entire science of market exchange can be derived – known as economics, or, as Mises terms it, "catallactics."

In closing, praxeology offers more than just epistemological truth, but truth regarding the nature of the social sciences and economic methodology. No longer is economics a discipline which aims to ape the methods of the physicist, but one that has its own toolbox to deal with its own unique set of problems and questions. With the conceptual framework of action established, one may move into the realm of economic science well-equipped. It is the concept of purposeful behavior which ultimately grounds our theory of knowledge, and, proceeding into science, it is this action-based epistemological framework which grounds economic theory.

The age-old quarrel between the rationalist and the empiricist frameworks of knowledge can now finally be laid to rest. Whether for physical or social science, one cannot avoid the necessity of employing

---

forecasting that entrepreneurs commonly employ in the market. Entrepreneurs discover or follow trends in an attempt to anticipate the desires of other actors; however they are useless, by themselves, in formulating a scientific "law." Such trends can yield no information regarding causal relationships, but merely illustrate facts about historical trends and events.

synthetic *a priori* knowledge. Rationalism – as espoused by the likes of Immanuel Kant, Ludwig von Mises, and Hans-Hermann Hoppe – has truly validated the human faculty of *reason*, and man's capacity to grasp genuine existential truths: truths regarding the marvels of the rational mind, and the universe which it relentlessly endeavors to master.

Chapter One

LIBERTARIANISM

The Purpose of Property Norms

BECAUSE THE DESIRE for many resources exceeds their availability, there exists potential for interpersonal conflict to emerge over how they are to be employed. To address this issue, property norms are established to provide an objective basis for reconciliation. Without such norms, the alternative would be destructive interpersonal conflict where presumably "might makes right" would reign as a social paradigm. Although there exist many variations of property norms, the purpose of this chapter is to demonstrate why any *valid* norm must be logically compatible with private property and its libertarian implications. Hoppe expounds upon the function of property norms in general:

> To develop the concept of property, it is necessary for [economic] goods to be scarce, so that conflicts over the use of these goods can possibly arise. It is the function of property rights to avoid such possible clashes over the use of scarce resources by assigning rights of exclusive ownership. Property is thus a normative concept: a concept designed to make a conflict-free interaction possible by stipulating mutually binding rules of conduct (norms) regarding scarce resources.[31]

---

[31]   Hans-Hermann Hoppe, "Property, Contract, Aggression, Capitalism, Socialism" in *A Theory of Socialism and Capitalism: Economics, Politics, and Ethics* (Boston: Kluwer Academic, 1989), 18.

The Nature of the Libertarian/Private Property Ethic

The Libertarian Ethic (aka the Private Property Ethic) holds that all legitimate rights are derived from property rights. The most fundamental of which concerns one's relationship to his own physical body i.e., that he and he alone has an exclusive claim to it. This is commonly referred to as "the principle of self-ownership."

To own something, especially one's body, means to have final say over the employment or use of whatever is "owned", provided that such employment does not entail the initiation of uninvited physical interference with another person's body or their justly-acquired property. Simply put, only the owner(s) of something have the exclusive right to use it; they are likewise justified in resisting demands made on their property by others.

From the concept of property rights, one may derive the Non-Aggression Principle (NAP), which states that no one may justifiably initiate uninvited physical force against another person's body or property, or make threats thereof. Thus, when "aggression" is referenced in this work it will be referring to the uninvited initiation of physical interference with one's person or property.

The only two legitimate methods of acquiring property, according to the Libertarian Ethic, are original appropriation and voluntary exchange. Original appropriation simply entails that the first claimant *and* user of a previously unowned good found in nature is the rightful owner of the good. Put differently, if one mixes his labor with an unowned good and claims it as his own, then he would become this good's rightful owner.

It is critical that this "mixing of labor" criterion is met. Asserting that a mere verbal declaration would suffice in obtaining property rights over any good would yield a host of logical and practical problems. More specifically, such "mixing of labor" for the sake of "original appropriation" may include the transformation, possession, and/or embordering of a scarce good.

The second just means of acquiring property is through voluntary exchange. Voluntary exchange is a derivative of "original appropriation" in that economic (aka scarce) goods must be captured and appropriated before they can be traded or given away. Hoppe provides a cogent summary for the Libertarian Ethic:

> Unlike bodies, which are never 'unowned'
> but always have a natural owner, all other
> scarce resources can indeed be unowned.
> This is the case as long as they remain in
> their natural state, unused by anyone. They
> only become someone's property once

they are treated as scarce means, that is, as soon as they are occupied in some objective borders and put to some specific use by someone. This act of acquiring previously unowned resources is called 'original appropriation.' Once unowned resources are appropriated it becomes an aggression to uninvitedly change their physical characteristics or to restrict the owner's range of uses to which he can put these resources, as long as a particular use does not affect the physical characteristics of anyone else's property—just as in the case of bodies. Only in the course of a contractual relationship, i.e., when the natural owner of a scarce means explicitly agrees, is it possible for someone else to utilize and change previously acquired things. And only if the original or previous owner deliberately transfers his property title to someone else, either in exchange for something or as a free gift, can this other person himself become the owner of such things. Unlike bodies, though, which for the same "natural" reason can never be unowned and also can never be parted with by the natural owner completely but only be 'lent out' as long as the owners' agreement lasts, naturally all other scarce resources can be 'alienated' and a property title for them can be relinquished once and for all.[32]

Generous use of the term "rights" has been made in this chapter. Prior to moving forward, it would behoove us to examine what exactly rights are and what they entail. For this task, I will take advantage of the insight provided by Murray Rothbard:

When we say that one has the right to do certain things we mean this and only this, that it would be immoral for another, alone or in combination, to stop him from

---

[32] Hoppe, ibid, 11.

> doing this by the use of physical force or
> the threat thereof. We do not mean that
> any use a man makes of his property
> within the limits set forth is necessarily a
> moral use. [33]

It is important to expand upon the above definition in a few important ways. Rights provide a framework for the justification of force. To say one has a right against being coerced unjustly or being murdered implies that the right is defensible by one's own use of force. In other words, if one's rights are violated, then the use of physical force, or the threat thereof, may be justifiably employed against the perpetrator. Such measures may be used for either defending those rights or for seeking retribution/restitution for their violation. To be clear, this is not to say that physical force, or the threat thereof, *must* be used; it is simply saying that such force would be justified. This force would be *reactionary*, not *initiatory*, and hence satisfies the non-aggression principle. In the future chapters of this book, there will be discussion regarding some non-violent means by which criminal behavior may be effectively combated, but for now the scope of this discussion will be limited to identifying what the Libertarian Ethic is, how it may be rationally justified, and what rights it entails.

 Finally, the above definition of rights should not be misconstrued so as to think that any breach of "morality" warrants the use of physical force. For instance, if a man promises his girlfriend that he will take her to the movies on Saturday night, and then reneges on this promise in order to go out with her best friend, this act may be immoral. However, if in response his girlfriend slashes his tires, then she would be guilty of violating his property rights despite his recent unsavory act. It is important to note the greater specificity of a discussion on "rights" as compared to "morals." All too often the topics are confused and this confusion has been used to justify assaulting others for a great many "victimless crimes."

 So to be clear, from this point forward, I will be speaking in terms of "rights" and not the greater scope of "morals." The actions of others may offend our moral code, however we must determine which of these actions warrant physical force and which of them are just aesthetically displeasing.

The Criteria for Moral Agency

How do we determine to whom/what the Libertarian Ethic

---

[33] Rothbard, "Natural Laws and Natural Rights," in *The Ethics of Liberty*, 24.

applies? More specifically, what makes someone or something a "moral agent?" Perhaps the ability to engage in discourse is the right criterion? Hoppe suggests:

> ...[O]nly if both parties to a conflict are capable of engaging in argumentation with one another can one speak of a moral problem and is the question of whether or not there exists a solution meaningful. Only if Friday, regardless of his physical appearance (i.e., whether he looks like a man or like a gorilla), is capable of argumentation (even if he has shown himself to be so capable only once), can he be deemed rational and does the question whether or not a correct solution to the problem of social order exists make sense... Only if this other entity can in principle pause in his activity, whatever it might be, step back so to speak, and say 'yes' or 'no' to something one has said, do we owe this entity an answer and, accordingly, can we possibly claim that our answer is the correct one for both parties involved in a conflict.[34]

In other words, the Libertarian Ethic applies to beings capable of argumentation or of propositional exchange (discourse). However, Hoppe reasons that if a being is not capable of argumentation, then whether or not said being is capable of recognizing the rights of others cannot be known with certainty. (It is important to clarify that such capacity to communicate a proposal or to argue is not limited to verbal communication. Any form of communication would suffice and may theoretically range from physical gestures, to telepathy, to drawings...etc.) For rights to exist between two or more beings, there needs to exist a certain degree of reciprocity. This must entail the ability to both recognize and *deliberately* respect the other's right to his own body and property. Such ability is the minimum criterion for one to be considered a moral-agent.

To say that a moral agent (e.g. a mentally healthy adult human) must not aggress against a non-moral agent (e.g. a wasp) would be to put the non-moral agent in a position of moral superiority over the moral agent.

---

[34] Hans-Hermann Hoppe. "The Problem of Social Order" in *Economics and Ethics of Private Property: Studies in Political Economy and Philosophy* (Boston: Kluwer Academic, 1993), 5.

For instance, the moral agent is capable of consciously respecting the NAP in regards to this non-moral agent. In contrast, the non-moral agent is incapable of deliberately respecting the NAP, and will be able to act outside its confines without being said to have violated the moral agent's rights, or to have committed an unethical act. The reason this non-moral agent could not be held ethically accountable for such actions is that, being such, it would have no capacity to conceptualize the NAP let alone deliberately abide by it.

This has great implications in regards to so called "animal rights." Really, it would be more appropriate to recognize that rights are only applicable to those beings which satisfy the minimum criterion for moral agency listed above. Which animals, if any, are "moral agents" as defined above, I will leave to the zoologist.

In conclusion, the Libertarian Ethic is not necessarily limited to humans, but applies to all moral agents be they human, extra-terrestrial, or otherwise.

Philosophical Groundwork

Some additional groundwork is needed before diving into the justifications of the Libertarian Ethic. Let us first examine what it means for an ethic or right to be "justified." First, it must be "universalizable" or consistent. That is to say, for something to be a valid or justified ethic, it must apply to all moral agents at all times and in all places.

A rule stipulating that stealing is wrong is a universalizable ethic. A rule stipulating that stealing is permitted by people over 6 feet tall is not. This introduces arbitrary distinctions between types of moral agents and therefore fails the universalization test. This concept is commonly referred to as the "Golden Rule of Ethics" or the "Kantian Categorical Imperative."

A second and more obvious criterion for an ethic or right to be justified is that it must be practically achievable. If one cannot physically act in accordance with an ethic, then the ethic is null and void. For instance, the proposition that occupying a physical space with one's body is unjustified is absurd because one cannot but take up standing room.

Third and finally, for an ethic to be justified, it cannot come into conflict with other norms which must be presupposed in the act of discourse or argumentation. For if a proposed norm did come into conflict with the necessary norms of argumentation, then the person proposing the ethic would fall into what is known as a "performative contradiction." That is to say – the person's actions would come into conflict with the proposal he was making. *To justify anything means to justify it in argumentation.* As the act of argumentation presupposes certain norms, any proposed norm that was in conflict with these must be rejected as logically unsound. It is important to remember argumentation is a conflict-free exchange of ideas; it may be as simple as a truth claim proposed by one individual to another.

The next layer of groundwork requires examining the nature of axioms. According to Ayn Rand, "an axiom is a proposition that defeats its opponents by the fact that they have to accept it and use it in the process of any attempt to deny it." This definition will be pertinent when discussing Hans Hermann Hoppe's argumentation ethics later in this chapter.

The particular axiom upon which the whole of Austrian Economics is based is that of "Human Action." Ludwig Von Mises defines this axiom:

> Human action is purposeful behavior. Or
> we may say: Action is will put into
> operation and transformed into an agency,
> is aiming at ends and goals, is the ego's
> meaningful response to stimuli and to the
> conditions of its environment, is a person's
> conscious adjustment to the state of the
> universe that determines his life.[35]

Simply put, the axiom of action tells one that action is purposive; that people deliberately employ means for the sake of achieving particular ends. Furthermore, for anyone to act he must be doing so with the intention of "profiting" in some manner. That is to say, if he is acting, he necessarily must view such actions as bringing him closer to a more preferable state of affairs. This is not to say his actions *will* accomplish this, but rather that he believes they will. This is true necessarily, for if he felt a given action would take him further from his preferred state of affairs, then he would either refrain from acting or act differently.

This does not mean that people do not sometimes act to help others at a cost to themselves, but rather that they view such an act to yield more to them (in this case a feeling of personal psychic pleasure) than what is being given up. Such psychic pleasure may also be referred to as "psychic profit."

An additional insight made by Austrian economists is that all value is necessarily *subjective*. The mere fact that voluntary trades occur is indicative of this truth. For example, if I buy a candy bar from you for a dollar then this demonstrates that I value the candy bar more than a dollar whereas you value it less than a dollar, otherwise we would have never bothered expending the time and energy required to make said trade in the

---

35   Ludwig von Mises, "Acting Man," in *Human Action: A Treatise on Economics* (New Haven: Yale University Press, 1949), 11.

first place. From this insight one may deduce that all voluntary trades must be seen as mutually beneficial ex ante to both parties involved, otherwise they would not have occurred.

The "*a priori* of communication/argumentation/discourse" will serve as the final piece of groundwork (from here on in I shall refer to this concept as the "*a priori* of argumentation," though "communication" and "discourse" are also appropriate). Hans Herman Hoppe defines the "*a priori* of argumentation:"

> The argument shows us that any truth claim, the claim connected with any proposition that it is true, objective or valid (all terms used synonymously here), is and must be raised and settled in the course of an argumentation. Since it cannot be disputed that this is so (one cannot communicate and argue that one cannot communicate and argue), and since it must be assumed that everyone knows what it means to claim something to be true (one cannot deny this statement without claiming its negation to be true), this very fact has been aptly called 'the a priori of communication and argumentation.'[36]

This fact is logically incontestable. There is no way anyone can assert something to be true without making an argument – for the very act of asserting something to be true is itself an argument. Furthermore, one cannot coherently claim *not* to know what truth is, for in so doing he is claiming that it is true that he does not know what it means for something to be true. Thus, our actor finds himself in a performative contradiction. It may be concluded, then, that for one to make any argument, it must first be presupposed that he understands the concepts of truth and validity and that a given proposition may only be shown as such in the course of an argument.

Justifying The Libertarian Ethic

---

[36] Hoppe, "From the Economics of Laissez Faire to the Ethics of Libertarianism" in *Private Property*, 314.

Now that the necessary groundwork has been laid, we may proceed in justifying the Libertarian Ethic by means of Hoppe's "Argumentation Ethics." Hoppe describes the nature of this approach:

> It [Argumentation Ethics] only makes explicit what is already implied in the concept of argumentation itself, and in analyzing any actual norm proposal its task is merely confined to analyzing whether or not it is logically consistent with the very ethics which the proponent must presuppose as valid insofar as he is able to make his proposal at all.[37]

Put differently, if one proposes an ethic which contradicts the necessarily presupposed ethics of discourse, then this proposed ethic must necessarily be rendered invalid by his own action (the fact that he engaged in argumentation). Thus, the ethical norms presupposed in the making of any proposal must themselves be the logical benchmark by which all future ethical proposals are evaluated. If a given ethic runs counter to the presupposed ethical norms of proposal making, then it *cannot* be valid.[38]

Argumentation ethics are a logical extension of the *a priori* of argumentation. The purpose of any argument is to establish a proposition as being true and/or justified, or conversely to show a given proposition to be false/unjustified. Argumentation, then, is by its very nature persuasive and non-coercive. If one were to attempt to use physical coercion in the course of an argument, this would undermine the intent of discovering truth or falsehood, thereby precluding such an act from being compatible with argumentation. As such, for someone to engage in argumentation with another would require an implicit acceptance that the other party has the right to exclusive control over his own body.

To demonstrate this, let us assume that one does not recognize the other's exclusive control over his own body, and proceeds to slap him in the face when confronted with a point he is unable to counter. This coercive act would immediately end the argument and begin violent conflict. To reinforce this fact, let us assume that one of our interlocutors does not hit the other, but rather threatens to assault him if he does not concede. Again, this act of coercion falls outside the realm of argumentation as it undermines the goal of discovering a truth or a

---

[37] Hoppe, ibid, 315.

[38] To clarify, when the term "ethic" is brought up in this book, it will more specifically be referring to interpersonal ethics, which are intimately related with "rights." For instance, if I have a "right" to do something, it would be considered unethical for you to attempt to stop me from doing it via aggressive means.

falsehood by substituting conflict for resolution.

By establishing as a precondition of argumentation the mutual recognition and acceptance of each party's agency, the principle of self-ownership has been justified *a priori*. Thus, it may be concluded that any proposition(s) which conflict(s) with the principle of self-ownership cannot be coherently justified. For the sake of thoroughness, I will proceed to run the principle of self-ownership through a Justification Schema.

1. Is it universalizable? Yes. The principle of self-ownership states that every moral agent, without exception, is the sole and legitimate owner of his body.
2. Is it practically achievable? Yes. Every moral agent has the capacity to own his body.
3. Is it compatible with the necessary presuppositions of argumentation? Yes. In fact, the principle of self-ownership *is* a necessary presupposition of argumentation.

Next, I will provide a justification for the private ownership of external economic goods. Hoppe explains lucidly:

> I first demonstrate that argumentation, and argumentative justification of anything, presupposes not only the right to exclusively control one's body but the right to control other scarce goods as well, for if no one had the right to control anything except his own body, then we would all cease to exist and the problem of justifying norms – as well as all other human problems – simply would not exist. We do not live on air alone; hence, simply by virtue of the fact of being alive, property rights to other things must be presupposed to be valid, too. No-one who is alive could argue otherwise.[39]

A practical precondition for argumentation is that the actors involved are alive. To be alive, and to even argue, requires the right to exclusively control and consume external resources. Naturally, one must also have the right to occupy a given amount of physical space with his body before he may be able to argue at all. Rothbard supplements this argument:

---

[39] Hoppe, ibid, 321

> Now, *any* person participating in any sort
> of discussion including one on values, is,
> by virtue of so participating, alive and
> affirming life. For if he were *really* opposed
> to life, he would have no business
> continuing to be alive. Hence, the *supposed*
> opponent of life is really affirming it in the
> very process of discussion, and hence the
> preservation and furtherance of one's life
> takes on the stature of an incontestable
> axiom.[40]

This argument should not be misconstrued as saying that people are *entitled* to having a particular set of scarce resources, but rather that it is within their right to own them provided that they are acquired via just means. The distinction here may seem trivial but the implications are vastly different. For instance, if one is entitled to a particular resource, this would mean that he would have a right to it and that if this right is not fulfilled, then physical force or the threat thereof would be justified in either fulfilling it or seeking retribution for its violation.

This is what is known as a positive right. For a positive right to be fulfilled, someone is required to take an action in order to fulfill it. For example, if I had a *right* to healthcare, this would oblige someone else to provide this service to me or to at least provide me with the funds necessary to purchase it. Thus, "positive rights" necessarily conflict with private property rights, as they limit to some degree a person's right to exclusive control over his own body or external property.

In contrast, having the right to own something simply entails that others may not commit aggression against this owned good or make threats thereof. For that to be fulfilled requires no action taken on the part of anyone else. These types of rights are known as "negative rights." In contrast to positive rights, negative rights simply *preclude* others from taking certain actions, whereas positive rights oblige others *to* act. Finally, the validity of the private ownership over external economic goods will be verified by running it through the justification schema:

1. Is it universalizable? Yes. The right to own external economic goods is shared by all moral agents and can thus claim to satisfy the test of universalization.
2. Is it practically achievable? Yes, everyone has the capacity to own external economic goods or scarce resources at all times.
3. Is it compatible with the necessary presuppositions of

---

[40] Rothbard, "A Crusoe Social Philosophy," ibid, 32-33.

argumentation? Yes. In fact, the right to own external scarce resources is a necessary precondition of argumentation.

In light of the above proofs for the principle of self-ownership and the right to own external property, one may deduce that the Non-Aggression Principle (NAP) must also be valid. To further demonstrate the validity of the NAP we will run it through the justification schema:

1. Is it universalizable? Yes, the NAP condemns uninvited initiations of physical force against all moral agents and their property.
2. Is it practically achievable? Yes, everyone has the capacity to refrain from committing aggression against others or their property at all times.
3. Is it compatible with the necessary presuppositions of argumentation? Yes, in fact the NAP *is* a necessary presupposition of argumentation.

Original appropriation (aka homesteading) and voluntary exchange are the only two legitimate means of acquiring property. Hoppe has this to say:

> If a person did not acquire the right of exclusive control over other, nature-given goods by his own work, that is, if other people, who had not previously used such goods, had the right to dispute the homesteader's ownership claim, then this would only be possible if one would acquire property titles not through labor, i.e., by establishing some objective link between a particular person and a particular scarce resource, but simply by means of verbal declaration. This solution – part from the obvious fact that it would not even qualify as a solution in a purely technical sense in that it would not provide a basis for deciding between rivaling declarative claims – is incompatible with the already justified ownership of a person over his body. For if one could indeed appropriate property by decree, this would imply that it would also be possible for one to simply declare another person's body to be one's own. However, as we have seen,

to say that property is acquired not
through homesteading action but through
declaration involves a practical
contradiction: nobody can say and declare
anything, unless his right to use his body is
already assumed to be valid simply because
of the very fact that regardless of what he
says, it is he, and nobody else, who has
homestead it as his instrument of saying
anything.[41]

The argument Hoppe uses here is known as an *argumentum a contrario*. This is an argument type that entertains the possible alternatives to a given proposal to demonstrate how they are either invalid or less suitable for a particular end. In this case, Hoppe demonstrates how the alternatives to original appropriation/homesteading must be in conflict with the principle of self-ownership, and by extension the necessary presuppositions of argumentation. The alternatives fail the third step of the justification schema. Moreover, unlike the "first user" homesteading rule, such a declarative alternative creates the possibility for multiple people to lay claim to a given scarce resource at the same time. With homesteading, however, the laws of physics do not permit two bodies (human) to occupy the same space at the same time so only one person has the capacity to mix his labor with a given resource *first*. It is this mutually exclusive characteristic of space occupation that permits the homesteading theory to avoid any possible violent conflict where two or more claimants have equally valid claims to a given good or area of land. Again, if verbal declarations were in themselves considered sufficient to acquiring title over property, then anyone could simply make a competing claim against a given piece of property and propose that his evidence of ownership over said property is equally legitimate to the currently recognized owner. Thus, any future rulings over competing claims of property would ultimately have to be offered on the basis of arbitrary criteria. Alternatively, if a judge decided not to rule in favor of one party over another (because as we said the declaration in itself was sufficient in acquiring rights over property), then the number of parties having title to specific economic goods would increase drastically, thereby increasing the likelihood that multiple parties will attempt to use the good(s) in question in mutually exclusive ways. Because there would be no way to arbitrate between mutually exclusive plans for the same good, such a situation would only serve to generate conflict thereby defeating the very purpose of establishing a property norm – i.e., to serve as a conflict avoidance/dispute resolution mechanism.

---

[41] Hoppe, ibid, 336.

Perhaps one may then object: "Why does the first appropriator/homesteader get the stuff? Why not some late-comer?" If economic goods were able to be owned by some unknown person who may arrive in the future to claim them, then no one could act without infringing on the property rights of these future-comers. We would all be paralyzed, lest we violate the property rights of said future-comers. Thus, to reject the first-user ethic would be to put the nail in our own coffins. No economic goods could be consumed in the present for doing so would deny said good to future-comers. Because this particular proposal would render its followers dead, it must be considered invalid. Moreover, the practical requirement for an effective property norm is that it enables objective arbitration between competing claims to a given scarce resource. Such arbitration is intended to confer rightful ownership to that party which may demonstrate a "superior objective link" between himself and the good in question. If someone is a first user of a scarce resource, then by definition he is the only one who could have any objective link to it at all. Thus, being the only one with such a link, it is necessarily superior to all others. With this being the case, any future-comer may only establish such a link with the disputed resource by violating the first user's previously established property right to the good.

The very purpose of ethics and norms is to help avoid otherwise unavoidable conflict. To say a latecomer or a "possible-future-comer" is the rightful owner of a given good would only serve to *generate* conflict between the first and late comer(s), and would therefore be completely contrary to the very purpose of a norm. Thus, the only ethic or norm which would serve to avoid conflict would be to grant a given scarce good to its first user. This would be inherently conflict-free, because by definition there would be no valid competing claims. Hoppe elaborates on this first-user necessity:

> What is wrong with this idea of dropping the prior-later distinction as morally irrelevant? First, if the late-comers, i.e., those who did not in fact do something with some scarce goods, had indeed as much of a right to them as the first-comers, i.e., those who did do something with the scarce goods, then literally no one would be allowed to do anything with anything, as one would have to have all of the late-comers' consent prior to doing whatever one wanted to do. Indeed, as posterity would include one's children's children—people, that is, who come so

late that one could never possibly ask them—advocating a legal system that does not make use of the prior-later distinction as part of its underlying property theory is simply absurd in that it implies advocating death but must presuppose life to advocate any thing. Neither we, our forefathers, nor our progeny could, do, or will survive and say or argue anything if one were to follow this rule. In order for any person—past, present, or future—to argue anything it must be possible to survive now. Nobody can wait and suspend acting until everyone of an indeterminate class of late-comers happens to appear and agree to what one wants to do. Rather, insofar as a person finds himself alone, he must be able to act, to use, produce, consume goods straightaway, prior to any agreement with people who are simply not around yet (and perhaps never will be). And insofar as a person finds himself in the company of others and there is conflict over how to use a given scarce resource, he must be able to resolve the problem at a definite point in time with a definite number of people instead of having to wait unspecified periods of time for unspecified numbers of people. Simply in order to survive, then, which is a prerequisite to arguing in favor of or against anything, property rights cannot be conceived of as being timeless and nonspecific regarding the number of people concerned. Rather, they must necessarily be thought of as originating through acting at definite points in time for definite acting individuals.[42]

An alternative argument put forth by Hoppe:

---

[42] Hoppe, "The Socio-Psychological Foundations of Socialism or the Theory of the State" in *Socialism and Capitalism*, 170.

If a person A were not the owner of his physical body and all goods originally appropriated, produced or voluntarily acquired by him, there would only exist two alternatives. Either another person, B, must then be regarded as the owner of A, or both parties, A and B, must be regarded as equal co-owners of both bodies and goods.

In the first case, A would be B's slave and subject to exploitation. B would own A and the goods originally appropriated, produced, or acquired by A, but A would not own B and the goods homesteaded, produced, or acquired by B. With this rule, two distinct classes of people would be created-exploiters (B) and exploited (A)-to whom different "law" would apply. Hence, this rule fails the "universalization test" and is from the outset disqualified as even a potential human ethic, for in order to be able to claim a rule to be a "law" (just), it is necessary that such a rule be universally-equally-valid for everyone.

In the second case of universal co-ownership, the requirement of equal rights for everyone is obviously fulfilled. Yet this alternative suffers from another fatal flaw, for each activity of a person requires the employment of scarce goods (at least his body and its standing room). Yet if all goods were the collective property of everyone, then no one, at any time and in any place, could ever do anything with anything unless he had every other co-owner's prior permission to do what he wanted to do. And how can one give such a permission if one is not even the sole owner of one's very own body (and vocal chords)? If one were to follow the rule of total collective ownership, mankind would die out instantly. Whatever this is, it is not a human ethic either.[43]

The first ethic clearly fails the universalization test and therefore we need not go any further. However, it is important to note that this ethic is also incompatible with the third criterion of the justification schema, which states that any valid ethic must be consistent with the presupposed ethical norms required for engaging in argumentation. In this case, it would conflict with the principle of self-ownership.

Next is the scenario where "everyone owns an equal share of everything, to include the bodies of one another."

1. Is this universalizable? Yes. This ethic proposal does indeed pass the universalization test as "everyone owns everything" does not entail distinctions among moral agents.

2. Is this practically achievable? No. Acting according to this norm would be impossible. Not only would acquiring the prior approval of all seven billion people on earth be virtually impossible in itself, but no one person could even give permission in the first place, as giving permission is itself an action requiring the use of scarce resources. As each person needs everyone else's approval in order to utilize communal resources, each of them would need everyone else's approval simply in order to give approval. Thus, this norm falls victim to the logical quagmire of infinite regression, thereby prohibiting all actors from acting at all! Any attempt to follow this norm would lead to a speedy death.

3. Is this compatible with the necessary presuppositions of argumentation? No, as it conflicts with the principle of self-ownership which asserts that everyone is the exclusive owner of his or her own body. If everyone owned an equal share of everyone else's body, then no one would have right to *exclusive* control over his own body. It also conflicts with the right to exclusively own external property, which is a necessary precondition of life, and life a necessary precondition to being able to put forth any argument.

Now that the alternatives have been shown to fail the justification schema, let us see if the acts of acquiring property via original appropriation and voluntary exchange suffer the same or a different fate:

1. Are they universalizable? Yes, the requirement for one to use either original appropriation or voluntary exchange to justly acquire property applies to all moral agents.

---

43 Hans-Hermann Hoppe, introduction to *The Ethics of Liberty* by Murray N. Rothbard (New York: New York University Press, 1998), xvi-vii.

2. Are they practically achievable? Yes, everyone has the capacity to acquire property over scarce goods through original appropriation or voluntary exchange.
3. Are they compatible with the necessary presuppositions of argumentation? Yes, in fact they are corollaries of such presuppositions.

Common Objections to Argumentation Ethics

At this point, critics may object on the basis of Hume's fact-value dichotomy (otherwise known as the "is-ought problem"). Formulated by David Hume, this perspective states that one cannot derive an *ought* from an *is*. Normative claims – that is, claims regarding how things *should be* – cannot be derived from explanations from how the world *is* – otherwise known as descriptive claims. Critics of Hoppe's perspective will often attribute normative positions to his libertarian argument; they understand his argumentation ethics as saying that nobody *should* commit aggression. However, raising this objection indicates a misunderstanding of Hoppe's proposal, as he does not claim to derive an "ought" from any "is." Argumentation ethics merely identifies which ethical propositions are logically sound or justifiable, and which ones are not. Hoppe defends himself from these assertions:

> It [Hoppe's style of argumentation ethics] remains entirely in the realm of is-statements and never tries to derive an 'ought' from an 'is.' The structure of the argument is this: (a) justification is propositional justification-a priori true *is-statement*; (b) argumentation presupposes property in one's body and the homesteading principle-a priori true *is-statement*; and (c) then, no deviation from this ethic can be argumentatively justified-a priori *is statement*.[44]

The truth of Hoppe's argument is unaltered by one's willingness or unwillingness to abide by it. Whether or not man accepts the Libertarian Ethic as valid or justified has no bearing on whether or not it *is* valid and

---

[44] Hoppe, "On the Ultimate Justification of the Ethics of Private Property" in *Private Property*, 345.

justified. He summarizes the point thusly:

> 'So what? Why should an a priori proof of the libertarian property theory make any difference? Why not engage in aggression anyway?' Why indeed?! But then, why should the proof that $1+1=2$ make any difference? One certainly can still act on the belief that $1+1=3$. The obvious answer is "because a propositional justification exists for doing one thing, but not for doing another." But why should we be reasonable, is the next comeback. Again, the answer is obvious. For one, because it would be impossible to argue against it; and further, because the proponent raising this question would already affirm the use of reason in his act of questioning it. This still might not suffice and everyone knows that it would not, for even if the libertarian ethic and argumentative reasoning must be regarded as ultimately justified, this still does not preclude that people will act on the basis of unjustified beliefs either because they don't know, they don't care, or they prefer not to know. I fail to see why this would be surprising or make the proof somehow defective. More than this cannot be done by propositional argument.[45]

The Implications of the Libertarian Ethic

One of the shocking implications of the Libertarian/Private Property ethic is that it is not logically compatible with the State. The State is defined as:

> ... That organization in society which attempts to maintain a monopoly of the use of force and violence in a given

---

[45]   Hoppe, ibid, 407-408.

> territorial area; in particular, it is the only
> organization in society that obtains its
> revenue not by voluntary contribution or
> payment for services rendered but by
> coercion. While other individuals or
> institutions obtain their income by the
> production of goods and services and by
> the peaceful and voluntary sale of these
> goods and services to others, the State
> obtains its revenue by the use of
> compulsion; that is, by the use and the
> threat of the jailhouse and the bayonet.[46]

The first characteristic of the State is that it *exercises a territorial monopoly* of ultimate decision-making. The State, as final arbiter of disputes, does not allow the verdict of competing arbitration agencies to supersede its own. By definition, any uninvited initiation of physical force or the threat thereof against the persons or property of others is condemned by the NAP. Thus, the State's status as "ultimate arbiter," and the means by which it is enforced, are illegitimate and unjustified.

The State's supposed legal "right" to lay taxes is also incompatible with the NAP. Taxes require people to surrender their earnings to the State despite an individual's lack of genuine consent. Thus, because taxation amounts to taking one's property against his will via aggressive means, it must be considered theft. To illustrate, one's refusal to pay taxes ultimately leads to arrest and imprisonment. If one decides to resist such an arrest, the agents of the State will not hesitate to assault or murder this person.[47] To

---

[46] Murray N. Rothbard, "Anatomy of the State" in *Egalitarianism as a Revolt against Nature, and Other Essays,* 57. Washington, D.C.: Libertarian Review, 1974. See, where Schumpeter says in *Capitalism, Socialism, and Democracy*: "The friction or antagonism between the private and the public sphere was intensified from the first by the fact that. . . the State has been living on a revenue which was being produced in the private sphere for private purposes and had to be deflected from these purposes by political force. The theory which construes taxes on the analogy of club dues or of the purchase of the service of, say, a doctor only proves how far removed this part of the social sciences is from scientific habits of mind." See also, Murray N. Rothbard, "The Fallacy of the 'Public Sector,'" New Individualist Review (Summer, 1961): 3ff.

[47] Lysander Spooner explains the practice of taxation in *No Treason: The Constitution of No Authority,* 1867, Ch. III: "Go to A_____ B_____, and say to him that "the government" has need of money to meet the expenses of protecting him and his property. If he presumes to say that he has never contracted with us to protect him, and that he wants none of our protection, say to him that that is our business, and not his; that we choose to protect him, whether he desires us to do so or not; and that we demand pay, too, for protecting him. If he dares to inquire who the individuals are, who have thus taken upon themselves the title of "the government," and who assume

add insult to injury, most people do not directly enjoy the benefits of all the so called "services" they are forced to fund via taxes. (e.g. one who has no children having to pay taxes which go towards public elementary schools...etc.)

Finally, the State exercises jurisdiction over a given territory despite the fact that its agents have not acquired property rights over it through legitimate means, i.e., via original appropriation or voluntary exchange. This clearly indicates that the State's claim of authority over this geographical area is unfounded. Only the legitimate owners of a given piece of property may exercise jurisdiction over it and may determine the rules under which its residents may live. Simply put, if one does not homestead a thing/space or acquire it through voluntary exchange, then he has no just authority over the people who occupy or have themselves homesteaded said thing/space.

---

to protect him, and demand payment of him, without his having ever made any contract with them, say to him that that, too, is our business, and not his; that we do not choose to make ourselves individually known to him; that we have secretly (by secret ballot) appointed you our agent to give him notice of our demands, and, if he complies with them, to give him, in our name, a receipt that will protect him against any similar demand for the present year. If he refuses to comply, seize and sell enough of his property to pay not only our demands, but all your own expenses and trouble beside. If he resists the seizure of his property, call upon the bystanders to help you (doubtless some of them will prove to be members of our band.) If, in defending his property, he should kill any of our band who are assisting you, capture him at all hazards; charge him (in one of our courts) with murder; convict him, and hang him. If he should call upon his neighbors, or any others who, like him, may be disposed to resist our demands, and they should come in large numbers to his assistance, cry out that they are all rebels and traitors; that "our country" is in danger; call upon the commander of our hired murderers; tell him to quell the rebellion and "save the country," cost what it may. Tell him to kill all who resist, though they should be hundreds of thousands; and thus strike terror into all others similarly disposed. See that the work of murder is thoroughly done; that we may have no further trouble of this kind hereafter. When these traitors shall have thus been taught our strength and our determination, they will be good loyal citizens for many years, and pay their taxes without a why or a wherefore... It is under such compulsion as this that taxes, so called, are paid."

Chapter Two

PROPERTY

AT THE CORE of every political theory is a methodology for the assignment of property rights. In fact, this must be so; for in order to determine the aggressor and victim in any violent interpersonal conflict, one requires some theoretical basis for determining who owns the good in contention (this good in contention may include one's very own body). If the source of conflict does not concern a dispute regarding the control of a scarce resource, then said conflict would fall outside the scope of property norms. The distinguishing factor between conflicts which involve a dispute over the rightful control of scarce resources and those which do not is that the employment of violence *may* be a just means to reconcile the former type of conflict, however such violence would *never* be warranted when addressing the latter.

For instance, if I take a mango from you, whether or not this is an act of aggression (as defined by the NAP) is entirely dependent upon who actually owns the mango. If you picked this mango from my yard without my consent, then my seizing it would be just. However, if you bought this mango at the store, or picked it from your own mango tree, then my seizing it would be unjust and would constitute an act of aggression against your property. Thus, a theory of property is integral to any objective system of interpersonal ethics. Without such a theory, all attempts to resolve such disputes would ultimately be arbitrary, and in all likelihood unjust.

Of course, the characterization made above is contingent upon accepting the libertarian theory of property. If one used a more collectivist theory of property, then it may very well be the case that the role of victim and aggressor would be the reverse.

To use another example, the libertarian principle of "self-ownership" would condemn rape as being an unjust act, not because of the aesthetics of rape (or the lack thereof), but rather because the rapist has infringed upon the victim's property right over his/her body. However, if our theory of property permitted someone to own another person, as is the case with chattel slavery, then this same act would be considered a justified exercise of one's property right over his slave.

It is important to keep in mind the distinction between "ethics" and "aesthetics." We must be careful not to conflate the two as is so often done. The practical significance behind such a distinction is the ability to determine in which context violent recourse is justified, and in which context it is not. In other words, violence used as a response to that which is merely distasteful but not aggressive, is, and must always be, unjustified.

Naturally, the question you may be asking yourself is "how do we distinguish between ethics and aesthetics?" The answer is by formulating a rational theory of property. However, before we expound upon such a theory, let us first reflect upon the function and purpose of having a theory of property in general. Hoppe explains his meta-ethical position:

> Only because scarcity exists is there even
> a problem of formulating moral laws;
> insofar as goods are superabundant
> ("free" goods), no conflict over the use of
> goods is possible and no action-
> coordination is needed. Hence, it follows
> that any ethic, correctly conceived, must
> be formulated as a theory of property, i.e.,
> a theory of the assignment of rights of
> exclusive control over scarce means.
> Because only then does it become
> possible to avoid otherwise inescapable
> and unresolvable conflict.[48]

In other words, the function of a theory of property is to provide a means to determine the just acquisition and transfer of property. That is to say, to determine who gets what.

In essence, the core of many conflicts between individuals is a dispute over the use and control of some scarce (economic) good. This could be a bowling ball, money, land, a factory, etc. It is because we live in an environment where the desire for many resources exceeds their availability that we must apply some arrangement of property laws if we wish to mitigate and resolve violent conflict amongst individuals. As only those goods which are scarce can be the objects of violent conflict, non-rivalrous goods are not subject to ownership claims. Therefore, we may conclude that the concept of "property" may only be applicable to that which is scarce and rivalrous. Tucker and Kinsella dispel some common misconceptions of what it means for something to be scarce:

> But let's be clear what we do *not* mean by
> the term scarce in the sense that it applies
> to this discussion. Something can have
> zero price and still be scarce: a mud pie,

---

[48] Hoppe, *Socialism and Capitalism*, 158.

soup with a fly in it, a computer that won't boot. So long as no one wants these things, they are not economic goods. And yet, in their physical nature, they are scarce because if someone did want them, and they thus became goods, there could be contests over their possession and use. They would have to be allocated by either violence or market exchange based on property rights.

Nor does scarcity necessarily refer to whether a good is in shortage or surplus, nor to whether there are only a few or whether there are many. There can be a single "owner" of a non-scarce good (a poem I just thought of, which I can share with you without your taking it away from me) or a billion owners of scarce goods (paper clips, which, despite their ubiquity, are still an economic good).

Nor does scarcity necessarily refer to tangibility only, to the ability to physically manipulate the thing, or to the ability to perceive something with the senses; airspace and radio airwaves are intangible scarce goods and therefore potentially held as property and therefore priced, while fire is an example of a tangible good of potentially unlimited supply.[49]

What indicates the rivalrous or non-rivalrous nature of something is whether use of it inhibits future use or another's simultaneous use. That is to say, if my use of something X precludes any other use of that same something X, then X is rivalrous. Conversely, if my use of something X does *not* preclude *any* other use of X, *and* if my use of X does not subtract from any future use of X, then X is *not* rivalrous, and could therefore never achieve the status of "property." Moreover, because property is only applicable to goods or things which have the capacity for mutually exclusive usage, then those things which are super abundant cannot be considered

---

[49] Kinsella, Stephan, and Jeffrey Tucker, "Goods, Scarce and Nonscarce" (editorial published at Ludwig Von Mises Institute, Auburn, Alabama, August 25, 2010). mises.org/daily/4630.

property, as no conflict over them may possibly arise. Thus, only *scarce* (economic) goods may warrant the application of property norms to govern their usage. Jeffrey Tucker and Stephan Kinsella expound further upon rivalry and scarcity as being the essential elements of property:

> Instead, the term scarcity here refers to the possible existence of conflict over the possession of a finite thing. It means that a condition of contestable control exists for anything that cannot be simultaneously owned: my ownership and control excludes your control... An example of a necessarily non-scarce good is a thing in demand that can be replicated without limit, so that I can have one, you can have one, and we can all have one. This is a condition under which there can be no contest over ownership. As Hoppe says, under these conditions, there would be no need for (property) norms governing their ownership and use... This non-scarce status might apply to many things but it always applies to non-finite things, that is, goods that can be copied without limit, with no additional copy having displaced the previous copy and with no degradation in the quality of the copied good from the original good... So it is with all things: if there is a zero-sum contest over its possession, it is scarce; if there need not be rivalry over its ownership, and its capacity for copying and sharing is infinite, it is non-scarce...[50]

Property, necessarily being comprised of scarce, rivalrous goods, requires acquisition. The concept of property is only coherent or relevant with the acquisition and use of scarce resources. According to libertarian theory, there are exactly two just means of acquiring property:

- Original Appropriation (i.e., homesteading/first user)
- Voluntary Exchange (i.e., giving, trading, buying, selling, etc.)

---

[50]   Kinsella and Tucker, "Goods, Scarce and Nonscarce."

A common objection to the practicality of the "original appropriation" means of acquiring property is that hardly any person is able to trace the ownership of land to the time when it was originally appropriated. As such, whether or not the chain of title to a good is legitimate can be impossibly difficult to ascertain. Rothbard trenchantly answers this concern:

> It might be charged that our theory of justice in property titles is deficient because in the real world most landed (and even other) property has a past history so tangled that it becomes *impossible* to identify who or what has committed coercion and therefore who the current just owner may be. But the point of the "homestead principle" is that if we *don't know* what crimes have been committed in acquiring the property in the past, or if we don't know the victims or their heirs, then the current owner becomes the legitimate and just owner on homestead grounds. In short, if Jones owns a piece of land at the present time, and we don't know what crimes were committed to arrive at the current title, then Jones, as the current owner, becomes as fully legitimate a property owner of this land as he does over his own person. Overthrow of existing property title only becomes legitimate if the victims or their heirs can present an authenticated, demonstrable, and specific claim to the property. Failing such conditions, existing landowners possess a fully moral right to their property.[51]

Finally, to own something means to have the exclusive right to employ this good in any way one sees fit, so long as such employment does not entail aggression against the property of another. As a practical matter, property must have objectively verifiable borders if one wishes to demonstrate the validity of his title.

---

[51] Murray N. Rothbard, "Justice and Property Rights," in *Property in a Humane Economy*, Edit. Samuel L. Blumenfeld (Lasalle: Open Court, 1974), 121.

PROPERTY

Intellectual Property

Intellectual property (IP) is a classification given to the class of legally-protected rights to non-scarce goods – such as ideas, music, and the expression of patterns. The three most common categories of intellectual property are copyrights, patents, and trademarks. In his monograph "Against Intellectual Property," Stephan Kinsella provides a cogent definition of each of the categories of intellectual property:

> Copyright
> Copyright is a right given to authors of 'original works,' such as books, articles, movies, and computer programs. Copyright gives the exclusive right to reproduce the work, prepare derivative works, or to perform or present the work publicly. Copyrights protect only the form or expression of ideas, not the underlying ideas themselves.[52]

> Patent
> A patent is a property right in inventions, that is, in devices or processes that perform a 'useful' function. A new or improved mousetrap is an example of a type of device which may be patented. A patent effectively grants the inventor a limited monopoly on the manufacture, use, or sale of the invention. However, a patent actually only grants to the patentee the right to exclude (i.e., to prevent others from practicing the patented invention); it does not actually grant to the patentee the right to use the patented invention.[53]

---

[52] Stephan Kinsella, "Property Rights: Tangible and Intangible," in *Against Intellectual Property*. (Auburn: Ludwig Von Mises Institute, 2008), 10.

[53] Kinsella, *Against Intellectual Property*, 10.

Trademark

A trademark is a word, phrase, symbol, or design used to identify the source of goods or services sold, and to distinguish them from the goods or services of others. For example, the Coca-Cola® mark and the design that appears on their soft drink cans identifies them as products of that company, distinguishing them from competitors such as Pepsi ®. Trademark law primarily prevents competitors from "in-fringing" upon the trademark, i.e., using "confusingly similar" marks to identify their own goods and services. Unlike copyrights and patents, trademark rights can last indefinitely if the owner continues to use the mark.[54]

Intellectual property (IP) is a concept that entails granting the "creator" exclusive rights over particular patterns of information, be they a process, design, picture, painting, song, book, or logo. It must be understood that these so called "IP rights" do not grant to a given creator the permission to reproduce original works; rather, they grant them the legal authority to prevent others from replicating these original works with their own property.

For instance, under a system of intellectual property, if one were to patent a go-kart design, and the next day he discovered that you were building a go-kart to the very same specifications that he had just patented, then he would be able to legally threaten to have force initiated against you as a means to halt your go-kart production. The fact that you would have been building this go-kart with your own supplies would be immaterial.

Herein lies the logical issue with upholding IP: that the enforcement of such rights necessarily results in the delimiting of someone's rights over his legitimate (scarce) property. Rights believed to exist by IP proponents come into conflict with rights to legitimate property. Thus, we know on the outset that the coexistence or compatibility of "IP rights" with legitimate property rights may not be coherently defended.

Moreover, the goods to which intellectual property rights are asserted fail to meet the criteria for property because a structure of IP rights attempts to grant ownership over patterns of information which are

---

[54] Kinsella, ibid, 12.

themselves neither rivalrous nor scarce. Once discovered or created, their production is inexhaustible; they are "free goods" for which neither ownership nor economization is needed.

Though the coexistence of intellectual property with legitimate property is conceptually incoherent, it would nonetheless behoove us to go over some of the common assertions made in favor of IP:

I own my labor and that which I create, including intellectual products, therefore IP is valid!

This is a point that is brought up quite often, and has proven to be very misleading. In the first place, one does not "own" his labor, for labor is just something you *do* and not a thing to be *owned*. It is true you do own your body, and you can use your body for labor if you wish, but it is the body that is owned, not the labor. Thus, what grants one the right to sell his services is the ownership he has over his body not his labor.

In the second place, creation itself is not sufficient in establishing property rights. For example, if I go to your house and use your ingredients to create a cake, I do not thereby own the resulting cake with the attendant ability to repel those who invade upon it! If I make a cake with my own ingredients, I do not own the resulting cake because I "made it," but rather because I owned the materials used for its creation. Again, we only own that which we originally appropriate or receive through voluntary exchange.

Further, the term "creation" itself is a bit misleading, for we never actually *create* anything. Rather, we transform matter that is already in existence into a form that we find to be more suitable to our ends. The right to own "created goods" must finally rely on them being scarce; there must be a possibility to use these goods in incompatible ways if they are to be ownable.

But wouldn't using someone else's creation without his permission be theft?

This is a very common misconception, even within the libertarian movement. This idea pervades our culture with common phrases like "you stole my idea!" or "you pirated my music!" Whether or not something may be stolen is contingent upon whether or not it can be owned, as stealing is the unjustified taking of someone's owned goods. It has already been established that patterns of information are not "ownable" since they are neither rivalrous nor scarce. What cannot be owned cannot be stolen.

Beyond this, stealing requires the legitimate owner to no longer have access to that which has been stolen. If I take your car, you no longer have access to your car. However, if I copy your recipe, your access to your recipe has in no way been impeded by my copying. You still possess this recipe. It just so happens that now I, too, have the recipe. No theft has taken place. It would be absurd for me to accuse you of stealing my car if it were sitting in my driveway and you just happened to build one yourself with the same design. Similarly, it would be equally preposterous to assert that copying is stealing, when the supposed "victim's" access to that which he claims has been stolen has in no way been diminished.

If someone profits from my idea without my permission, then the money he made is essentially money he has stolen from me!

Often times a musical artist or an inventor will claim that the unpermitted reproduction of his music or invention will dig into his profits, because such reproduction would yield a larger supply of the good in question relative to his monopoly production. This addition to supply thus renders him unable to sell his music or invention for as much as he would have otherwise been able. His belief that this unauthorized reproduction and sale is tantamount to theft would suggest that he owns the buyers' money before they hand it over to him. This is, of course, fallacious reasoning.

We only have legitimate claim to that which we originally appropriate or receive through voluntary exchange. We do not own someone's money before he gives it to us. The fact that a customer may have given his money to the original artist had he not purchased a product from a copycat does not change this fact. Furthermore, one is not entitled to and does not own the value of something. For example, if my neighbor refuses to mow his lawn, the value of my property may be reduced in the eyes of most people, but this in no way means that my neighbor has infringed on my property rights. Again, no one has legitimate claim over the value of anything, because value is simply a subjective determination and we certainly do not own the subjective determinations or evaluations of others.

If there is no IP system, people won't be as incentivized to create and innovate!

While the claim has a plausible ring to it, it is dubious at best. The IP system actually serves to *suppress* ingenuity! But how is this? Well, because as a creator of any sort, one would immediately experience limitations upon what information he would be permitted to use in pursuit of his invention, song, or whatever else he is attempting to create. In other words, the suppression of innovation would take the form of all the information whose use and access would be safeguarded under the auspices of copyright, patents, trademarks, etc. One would not be able to avail himself of the body of many others' work as it would be "protected" by IP and thus become inaccessible or costly to attain.

Moreover, IP is approximate; it does not simply preclude the reproduction of exact replicas, but rather the reproduction of that which is *too* similar to the original. So let's say I take your go-kart design and make some small improvements to it. I could still be sued under IP law for patent infringement. *So, the limitations, whether they are the threshold for similarity or the longevity of the IP in question, must always be arbitrary.*

Above and beyond this are the time, resources, and energy spent on the training and employment of the overseers of an IP system, as well as the time and money used to apply for a copyright or patent. These are all factors which, had it not been for the IP system, could have gone into products or services actually demanded by the consumer.

The threat and practice of litigation associated with the enforcement of IP laws create further costs. Such lawsuits have cost many millions to conduct and many millions more are used to keep legal teams on staff for larger businesses. Again, this represents huge amounts of resources and time that could have been spent in more productive ways, but are instead wrapped up in the legal system.

A less obvious cost of the IP system is the chilling effect it has on small businesses. There are thousands upon thousands, if not millions, of patents and other IP certifications of which one may never be apprised and yet will still be subject to a forfeiture of his liberties if he is found to be in violation of any one of them. Powerful corporations have the advantage of being able to afford a legal team to keep on staff to secure many hundreds of IP certifications, be they patent or copyright, and to use them as leverage against other large businesses to deter them from suing on the grounds of IP infringement. This tactic is tantamount to a "mutually assured destruction" defense, where one company will refrain from suing the other on the grounds of IP infringement for fear that this other company may sue them in return and on similar grounds.

Smaller businesses, however, do not have the capital to build up such a defense or gain such leverage, so they are at an artificial disadvantage in the battle for IP weapons as compared to their larger counterparts. Worse yet, many may decide to abandon their plans for entrepreneurship, as IP liabilities would constitute one more cost that they are simply unwilling to bear.

Last, but certainly not least, are the guaranteed sacrifices of liberty associated with the IP system. To enforce IP is to limit, at least to some degree, an innocent person's peaceful use of his property. Those who advocate for IP on purely utilitarian grounds would do well to recognize these costs and rethink their position. The burden of proof that IP increases innovation falls upon the advocates for such a system. Some of the costs are concrete, and ironically include factors which hinder innovation itself.

Finally, even if it were proven to enhance innovation and prosperity, would it be our place to impose such a system, given that it necessarily abridges one's rights to his property? The truth of the matter is: the only things that must be done to maximize wealth are to refrain from committing aggression and to pursue our own self-interests. Coercion may still exist, but an institution which has the sole right and obligation to commit aggression as the primary means to solve complex social problems should never exist. Time and time again it has been shown that appealing to the State to solve social problems only serves to exacerbate such problems and in so doing generate more unforeseen consequences.

The market, on the other hand, serves to regulate, allocate, and equilibrate much more efficiently and effectively than any mixed or controlled economy can, precisely because it does not rely upon central planning to effect such adjustments. In freed markets, everyone has to play by the same rules, and every voluntary interaction is mutually beneficial. However, under a Statist paradigm, a select group of people are able to ignore the limitations set upon the rest of the citizenry, and benefit themselves at the expense of others. In essence, free markets promote win-win outcomes, whereas the State can only produce win-lose or zero-sum games.

What if someone puts their name on my work and publishes it as his own?!

Let's say I publish a book and claim to be the author when in reality I am not. My patrons would be buying what they believed to be a book written by me, but in actuality, and contrary to my advertisements, it is not. Once discovered, I may be tried on grounds of fraud, rendering the use of IP as a legal remedy in this scenario superfluous. In other words, doing this would be held as a violation of property rights (theft), as I would be accepting the property of others without fulfilling my condition of the contract, which is to provide an original work.

Could I make a contract telling the buyer not to reproduce my thing?

Yes, however there are two detrimental effects associated with this choice. First, this may deter the consumer from purchasing your product as he may not be comfortable with assuming such liability. Second, it would not be binding to third parties. Let's say that you bought a movie and I came over to your place and watched it, then proceeded to make a movie of my own with a very similar plot. Even though I am in essence copying this movie, I could still not be held legally liable as I am not a signature on the "no copy" contract. As a practical matter, such a method to reduce free riders may prove to be ineffective.

PROPERTY

<u>Am I just supposed to let everyone copy my work now?</u>

Not necessarily. The only actions prohibited to you as a means to protect your work from being copied without your permission would be using or threatening physical force against others or their property. Drive-thru movie theaters, for instance, used to attract loiterers attempting to enjoy the show without paying. In response, theaters began installing individual car speakers to prevent free riders from hearing the movie, thus incentivizing them to purchase a ticket. Information held on CDs is protected by the use of elaborate encryption methods and registration requirements to effectively mitigate free riders. Book authors or musical artists still have the advantage of being first to market and can rely upon tours, book signings or readings, and other live performances or merchandising as a way to reap profits. The truth is there are countless numbers of ways in which one can protect himself from free riders without resorting to aggression.

Chapter Three

CONTRACT

ANY THEORY OF contract will be a divisive one, as few people today, even in libertarian circles, see eye to eye on the precise philosophical criteria needed to ground specific ownership claims. This is due, in part, to an ignorance of the foundations of interpersonal ethics. Perhaps the most notable misconception due to such ignorance is the notion that *all* voluntary agreements, no matter what their content, are justifiably enforceable.

As we learned before, in order for something to be eligible for the status of "property," it must be scarce. This is because the function of property is to provide a mechanism by which one may determine who has the right to control what resource, and, of course, no such determination would be necessary for any non-scarce good. Thus, the ultimate goal of the concept of property is to assist in the avoidance of conflict between two or more individuals over the employment and use of scarce (aka economic) goods. Though property, and more specifically private property, is in fact a norm, this fact does not render the concept itself meaningless or without significant purpose.

It is commonly accepted that we live in a world where the desires for various resources exceed their availability. Unavoidable conflict would ensue were everyone to engage in a perpetual free-for-all for these scarce goods. This is not to say the adoption of property norms would immediately eradicate all conflict. Rather, it would serve as the logically justified foundation from which to arbitrate inevitable disputes over the control of scarce goods. Therefore, it is important to formulate a theory of property, such that if followed, all violent interpersonal conflict would be avoided from the beginning of its adoption onward and, at the same time, allows for justified action prior to any agreement. Man must have justifiable actions to take – which imply the use of scarce goods – prior to any contact or arrangement with anyone else.

The libertarian theory of property, otherwise known as the "private-property ethic," accomplishes this task. This theory also demonstrates that any other theory of property which comes into conflict with it, such as the Marxian principle "from each according to his ability, to each according to his need," only serves to generate conflict, not diminish it. Thus, such competing theories fail the very purpose of a norm.

The original appropriation of goods is necessarily conflict free, as the first user and claimant of a good has no competing legitimate claimants with whom he must contend (such is the nature of being first). Voluntary exchange is also, by definition, free of conflict, as both parties are free to abstain from the exchange.

Finally, to own something means to have the exclusive *right* to control or employ it without uninvited physical interference, so long as such employment does not entail an uninvited physical interference with someone else's person or property. Libertarians believe that all individuals are self-owners, in so far as they have exclusive rights to control over their own physical bodies. From the principle of self-ownership, and the subsequent ability to acquire exclusive claims to external economic goods, the Non-Aggression Principle (NAP) is established. The NAP merely restates what is implicit in the concept of ownership, i.e., that no one may justifiably *initiate* uninvited physical force against another person's body or justly acquired property.

It is important to note that the above is not meant to be an authoritative proof of private property or the NAP; rather it is simply intended to identify the fundamental concepts of property and ownership as the ground work for expounding upon a theory of contract. Stephan Kinsella defines "Contract" as being "a relation between two or more parties which includes legally enforceable obligations between them."[55] The term "enforceable," in this context, means that the use of physical force or the threat thereof would be a *justifiable* response to any breach of a contract.

There exist two general categories of contract: "to do" and "to give." The former being an agreement to perform a given task or service, and the latter an agreement to exchange some specified good(s). Regarding the breach of "to do" contracts, otherwise known as "performance contracts," judges generally prefer to award monetary damages, as such damages are easier to oversee and administer than a compulsion to perform a given task.

For example, if you contract with a singer to perform at your wedding and he fails to do so, it would be quite difficult to measure whether or not any successive performances ordered by a given judge would be of the same quality as that which you originally contracted. That is to say, the singer may feel upset about having to be compelled to perform, and thus deliberately sabotage his own performance. Moreover, to determine whether or not this was the case would be very difficult as performance levels or qualities are completely subjective, whereas a transfer of a given amount of money in damages can easily be objectively verified. Finally, it should be added, that though judges may not be willing or practically able to compel performance, the threat of monetary/property

---

[55] Stephan Kinsella, "A Libertarian Theory of Contract," in *Journal of Libertarian Studies 17.II* (2003): 12.

damages and reputation loss provide sufficient incentive to render the process of contracting for such services useful.

It is important to understand what distinguishes a legitimately enforceable arrangement (contract) from a non-enforceable arrangement. Recall the non-aggression principle (NAP), which states that no one may justifiably *initiate* uninvited physical force against another person's body or justly acquired property; from this principle one may conclude that the only force which is justified is *responsive* force. That is, physical force, or the threat thereof, in *response* to aggression perpetrated by someone else. Thus, the only arrangements which are legitimately enforceable (i.e., are considered "contracts") are those which, if breached, would entail an NAP violation.

Let us apply this concept to a mere promise that involves no transfer of title to scarce goods: Suppose Bob promises his sister Sue that he will attend her wedding, but fails to show up. Would it be justified to initiate force against Bob? Of course not! This is because Bob's failure to show up did *not* constitute an uninvited physical invasion of anyone's person or property. Though there may be moral implications associated with lying or neglecting to perform, they are completely irrelevant to the point of whether or not such an arrangement may be considered a "contract."

Now, let us examine a separate scenario, where Jill decides to trade Charlie three dollars for his hat. This arrangement is known as a "conditional transfer of title." This means that Jill would be offering Charlie title to her three dollars on the condition that Charlie offered the title over his hat to Jill in exchange. Thus, if Charlie agreed and accepted Jill's three dollars yet refused to give Jill his hat, or if he gave Jill something other than his hat, then he would be guilty of stealing Jill's property (the three dollars), and hence be in violation of the NAP. As such, Jill would be justified in using force, or the threat thereof, to retrieve her stolen property, and perhaps some damages.

From this insight, one may discover that the only arrangements which may be enforceable are those which involve the transfer of title to property. This is what is known as the "Title Transfer Theory of Contract." However, before we apply our theory to some real world examples, take note of one final implication of any contractual arrangement: the title to any good in a contract must be in the possession of the obliged party (promisor) at the time of specified completion, if it is to be enforceable.

For example, imagine person A (the promisee) lends person B (the promisor) his stereo, on the condition that, in one week's time, person B transfers title to his yoyo to person A. Suppose person B's yoyo is destroyed before the week's end and he comes up empty handed. Would person A be justified in using force or making threats thereof against person B to receive remuneration? No, he would not, because at this point person B would not be causing uninvited physical interference with person A's property as it no longer exists.

Instead of the exchange being immediate and simultaneous between person A's and person B's economic goods, Person A is providing Person B with temporary title to the stereo *now* on the condition that Person B provides Person A with title to his yoyo in the *future*. Thus, when Person B utilizes Person A's stereo in the interim he is not violating the NAP or the arrangement, as use of the stereo in the interim had already been accepted by Person A. Contrary to the previous contract example, Jill only consented to giving Charlie title to her three dollars on the condition that Charlie provides the hat *now* as well. Since he failed to do so, Charlie was therefore in breach of contract when he accepted her three dollars; *any* use of Jill's three dollars on Charlie's part would be a breach of contract so long as he failed to provide Jill with his hat. Stephan Kinsella elaborates on this seemingly counter-intuitive point:

> The simplest title transfers are contemporaneous and manual. For example, I hand a beanie baby to my niece as a gift. However, most transfers are not so simple, and are conditional. Any future-oriented title transfer in particular is necessarily conditional, as are exchanges of title. For example, before dinner, I tell my niece that she gets the beanie baby after dinner *if* she behaves during dinner. The transfer of title is future-oriented, and conditional upon certain events taking place. *If* my niece behaves, *then* she acquires title to the beanie baby. Future transfers of title are usually expressly conditioned upon the occurrence of some future event or condition.

> In addition, because the future is uncertain, future-oriented title transfers are necessarily conditioned upon the item to be transferred *existing* at the designated time of transfer. Title to something that does not exist cannot be transferred. Consider the situation where I own no hamster but tell my niece, "Here, I give this hamster to you." In this case, "this hamster" has no referent so no title is

transferred. Likewise, the future beanie baby transfer is conditional not only on the expressly stated condition—the niece performing the specified action (behaving) —but also on the unstated condition that the beanie baby *exists* at the designated future transfer time. During dinner, the cat might destroy it, or it might be lost, or consumed in fire. Even if the niece behaves, there is no beanie baby left for her to acquire. In effect, when agreeing to a future title transfer, the transfer is inescapably accompanied by a condition: "I transfer a thing to you at a certain time in the future—if, of course, the thing exists."[56]

In such future-oriented conditional transfer of title arrangements, it is the buyer of future goods that implicitly bears the risk of default. The buyer of present goods suffers from no default risk – he receives his half of the transaction instantly as soon as the contract is made. In this type of exchange, the promisee agrees to transfer something in the *present* which is certain. Thus, if he is unable to produce the item at present, then the arrangement ends before it ever begins. However, if the promisee – acting as a buyer of future goods – provides his goods and enters into a *future* oriented conditional transfer of title arrangement, he is inevitably accepting the risk, because the future is uncertain, that whatever he is expecting to receive in return in the future actually exists upon the completion of his end of the arrangement.

In contrast, if person B did indeed possess title to the yoyo in question, and was simply refusing to give it up, then this would constitute a violation of person A's property right to the yoyo, and would entail a situation in which person A may justifiably use force against person B in response to said violation. There are, of course, ways in which the effects of such a default may be mitigated or remunerated through other contractual mechanisms, which will be discussed shortly. Finally, such title transfers do not have to be written on a piece of paper. They may simply be formed by "manifesting one's intent to transfer ownership or title to another."[57]

Let us now apply this theory to a monetary loan contract. A loan is simply one more example of a future oriented, conditional transfer of title, whereby the creditor (the promisee) grants title to the debtor (the promisor)

---

[56] Kinsella, "A Libertarian Theory of Contract," 12.
[57] Kinsella, ibid, 21.

over a specified amount of money now (the loan), on the condition that the debtor pays back the principal of this loan, plus interest, at some specified time in the future.

Remembering the condition that the promisor must have title over this loan, plus interest, at the time specified in order for the creditor to expect full repayment, the creditor may decide to proactively add certain clauses to this contract to mitigate financial losses in the case of default. These clauses may say something to the effect of: "on the condition the debtor (promisor) is unable to pay back the loan, plus interest, at the agreed time, we will garnish 30% of his wages from that point forward until the loan has been fully paid."

This, of course, is just one of many non-aggressive solutions to the problem of default risk. Introducing default terms in the contract stipulates what is to follow should a promisor be *unable* to fulfill his agreed to conditions due to a lack of title to the amount of money owed in full at the time of the contract's completion. Requiring collateral be placed as a precondition to entering into a loan contract is another solution. Such a contract may read as "I hereby transfer to you title to my car on the condition I do not fulfill the loan obligation at the specified time." This is a way of creating incentive for the debtor to make good on the loan. Perhaps title to the car would be held in escrow until the loan has been paid in full. Details of the collateral transfer can take as many forms as the parties wish.

Another, and perhaps more obvious, proactive measure a creditor may take to reduce the risk of default is to run a credit check on the prospective debtor prior to providing him/her with a loan. Such a credit history would help the creditor determine the likelihood that the prospective debtor will make good on the loan. With this information in mind the creditor may very well decide not to offer this prospective debtor with a loan at all.

At no point would it be justified to place debtors into a "debtor's prison" if they fail to pay their loans in full, *due to their lacking title to the full amount owed*. Recall earlier that the implicit assumption of future oriented, conditional transfer of title contracts (for instance, a loan contract) is that whatever is being contracted for *exists* at the time of the contract's completion. Thus, if the debtor simply does not have enough money to cover the loan in full, then he cannot be justifiably punished via violent means or threats thereof. Put differently, the debtor is not causing a rights violation as the creditor voluntarily exchanged titled property for a promise of future goods. If the future goods fail to manifest, there can be no title issued nor transferred for them. Hence, the debtor is in no way violating the NAP, and therefore any force used against him would be considered *aggression* and therefore unjustified.

With regards to employment arrangements, they are generally not binding on the part of the employee, as they are typically set up in the following manner: "I hereby transfer title to X amount of money to you on the condition you perform task Y." Thus, if the employee decides not to perform task Y, then he/she simply is not compensated with pay X. However, if the employer wanted some assurances that the employee would not refuse to show up to work, he may provide an employment contract that reads something to the effect of: "I hereby transfer title to X amount of money to you on the condition that you perform task Y; on the condition you fail to perform task Y, you hereby transfer title to Z amount of money to me (the employer)." Of course, additional clauses similar to the ones delineated in the defaulting debtor case may be applied to the case of a defaulting employee.

Adjacent to discussions of contractual employee obligations are discussions of voluntary slavery. Kinsella notes the difference between owning a body and owning external goods:

> ...the modified title-transfer theory proposed here [Kinsella's modifications on Rothbard's title-transfer theory] recognizes that the body is 'owned' only in the sense that a person has the sole right to control the body and invasions of its borders. But the body is not homesteaded and acquired, and cannot be abandoned by intent in the same way that homesteaded property can.[58]

The act of originally appropriating a scarce good or receiving it through voluntary exchange creates a superior, objectively ascertainable link with the owner that enables him to demonstrate his claim to said good to any third party. This is the practical condition required to put the private property norm into practice, and to enable a third party to enforce it. If one claimed to be the owner of a good, but had no demonstrable evidence of ownership, then a third-party arbiter would have no objective basis from which to render a verdict. *A superior, objectively verifiable link to specific scarce resources is what grounds legitimate ownership claims and separates them from baseless decrees or declarations.*

Currently, one can only *indirectly* control external goods. Manipulation of an ax first requires the usage of muscles, tendons, and appendages; control of the ax is *indirect* because one integrates it into his plans only through an intermediary – the muscled arms of his physical body – which he directly controls with his will. Once an external good becomes homesteaded, it can only be assigned a new owner through voluntary exchange or abandonment of the good and a re-appropriation before

---

[58] Kinsella, ibid, 32.

84

another may legitimately claim to have a superior, objectively verifiable link and therefore title. Despite being a self-owner, however, it is impossible for one to relinquish ownership of his body. What marks one's ownership over his body is his uniquely *direct* control over it, which itself constitutes a superior objective link. This *direct* control is evidenced by his ability to physically animate his body by will alone – that is, without the assistance of a separate, physical medium. Because one cannot alienate this *direct* control, one cannot create in another a superior objective link to his body, and therefore it is impossible for him to legitimately transfer title over his body to another person via contract. For this reason, one cannot sell himself into slavery. Hoppe elaborates on the issue of body-ownership:

> The answer to the question what makes
> my body "mine" lies in the obvious fact
> that this is not merely an assertion but that,
> for everyone to see, this is indeed the case.
> Why do we say "this is my body?" For this
> a twofold requirement exists. On the one
> hand it must be the case that the body
> called "mine" must indeed (in an
> intersubjectively ascertainable way) express
> or "objectify" my will. Proof of this, as far
> as my body is concerned, is easy enough to
> demonstrate: When I announce that I will
> now lift my arm, turn my head, relax in my
> chair (or whatever else) and these
> announcements then become true (are
> fulfilled), then this shows that the body
> which does this has been indeed
> appropriated by my will. If, to the contrary,
> my announcements showed no systematic
> relation to my body's actual behavior, then
> the proposition "this is my body" would
> have to be considered as an empty,
> objectively unfounded assertion; and
> likewise this proposition would be rejected
> as incorrect if following my announcement
> not my arm would rise but always that of
> Müller, Meier, or Schulze (in which case
> one would more likely be inclined to
> consider Müller's, Meier's, or Schulze's
> body "mine"). On the other hand, apart
> from demonstrating that my will has been
> "objectified" in the body called "mine," it

must be demonstrated that my appropriation has priority as compared to the possible appropriation of the same body by another person.

As far as bodies are concerned, it is also easy to prove this. We demonstrate it by showing that it is under my direct control, while every other person can objectify (express) itself in my body only indirectly, i.e., by means of their own bodies, and direct control must obviously have logical-temporal priority (precedence) as compared to any indirect control. The latter simply follows from the fact that any indirect control of a good by a person presupposes the direct control of this person regarding his own body; thus, in order for a scarce good to become justifiably appropriated, the appropriation of one's directly controlled "own" body must already be presupposed as justified. It thus follows: If the justice of an appropriation by means of direct control must be presupposed by any further-reaching indirect appropriation, and if only I have direct control of my body, then no one except me can ever justifiably own my body (or, put differently, then property in/of my body cannot be transferred onto another person), and every attempt of an indirect control of my body by another person must, unless I have explicitly agreed to it, be regarded as unjust(ified).[59]

One can, however, forfeit a portion of rights over his own body if he commits aggression against the person or property of another. According to Kinsella's estoppel theory, aggressors are unable to coherently object to force applied against them. By their committing a tort, they implicitly have accepted the premise that initiatory force is acceptable. Of course, there is a limit to what degree of force used for retribution may be

[59]   Hans-Hermann Hoppe, *Eigentum, Anarchie Und Staat: Studien Zur Theorie Des Kapitalismus* (Opladen: Westdt. Verl., 1987).

justly applied.[60]

Whenever physical interference is involved with the bodies of others, it is crucial to determine the target's most recent consent or refusal prior to the interaction. Barring the objections of aggressors, this criteria determines whether force applied was just or not (whether aggression has been committed). For instance, all gentlemen understand the difference between rape and seduction; it is the lady's most recent act of consent or refusal. Should either party change their mind, the most recent decree would override the earlier approval. Ownership over things, including bodies, implies the right to change one's mind as to how it is to be employed in the immediate or remote future. Unlike bodies, which we are, for better or worse, stuck with, external goods can be relinquished and a property title ultimately dispensed for them. Either party's consent to sex earlier in the night is not tantamount to a transfer of title, partial or otherwise, of one's body. Once again, one is *unable* to make such a binding transfer of title over his body to his partner or to anyone else. Indeed, the very fact that someone is unable to transfer title to his body explains why mere promises of performance are unenforceable. This is because they would imply, to some degree, a transfer of title over one's body to another. Only if it were possible to alienate the direct control of one's body and furnish a title for it could one be able to justifiably initiate uninvited force against another, or make threats thereof, as a means to compel him to perform a given act or service.

From this, we may be able to conclude that contracts only pertain to the transfer of title to external goods. This does not preclude selling one's own body parts, for as soon as they are removed, they would then naturally become 'external' goods. Finally, this reaffirms the fact that the only justifiable inter-human force is force that is either invited or responsive to uninvited physical interference initiated against one's person or property.

Now, let us deal with the issue of fraud. Fraud is, quite simply, another form of theft. For example, let's imagine that I decide to enter into a trade with a friend whereby I agree to transfer title of my five dollars to her on the condition that she transfer title to a basket of edible apples to me. If I proceed to give her the five dollars and she hands over to me a basket of wooden apples, then she has stolen from me.

The transfer of title over the five dollars was conditional on her providing me with edible apples. So, because she failed to uphold her end of the contract, I would remain the proper owner of the five dollars, and she would be in possession of my property without my consent. Acquiring possession of someone else's property without their consent is the very definition of theft; in the preceding scenario, such theft happened to take

---

[60] See Stephan Kinsella's essay on 'Punishment and Proportionality: The Estoppel Approach' http://mises.org/document/1864/Punishment-and-Proportionality-the-Estoppel-Approach.

the form of a fraudulent transaction. Suppose, however, I manifested my intent to purchase my friend's ornate, painted apples under the impression that said apples were edible, yet in reality they were wooden. In this scenario, the transfer would not be fraudulent as the content of the contract, as evidenced purely by demonstrated preference, expressed merely a desire to exchange my five dollars for my friend's apples. Nothing in this act alone would indicate in any objectively verifiable manner that a condition of this title transfer be that the apples are edible, sweet-smelling, durable, or have any particular attribute. My action of purchasing an apple, without any mutual understanding of context or purpose, only demonstrates a preference for a particular, individual item as-is. As such, I would have to bear the costs of my faulty assumption.

One final and perhaps obvious component to any just contract is that the titles to whatever is being transferred must legitimately be owned by the parties engaged in the contract. For instance, if I stole Johnny's model train and traded it to Debra for a pack of bubble gum, then this would constitute an illegitimate transaction. Johnny would have every right to approach Debra and demand his train despite the fact that she exchanged with me in good faith. Of course, Debra would then be able to retrieve damages from me, as I would have fraudulently taken her bubble gum. This is because her transferring of the bubble gum to me was conditional upon my transferring title of the train to her. Because I never acquired legitimate title to it and yet proceeded to take her bubble gum, my act would be considered theft.

Lessons from the Title Transfer Theory of Contract can also be applied to the "social contract." For the same reasons my exchange with Debra was illegitimate because it involved Johnny's stolen property, so too can the State's "social contract" be deemed illegitimate. Social contract theorists argue that utilization of State-provided resources, such as roads, defense, education, law, etc., gives agents of the State the right to impose laws and command obedience to them by physical force or threats thereof. Beyond this, States claim the right to compel performance of services; such is the case with taxation, conscription, compulsory education, etc. Should one fail to surrender property to the State in the form of taxes, or fail to abide by the laws created by it, then this entity claims the right to kidnap and detain the offender in a cage. Should one resist such an arrest, the State grants its agents the authority to end his life with overwhelming force. This behavior does not generate public outrage, for nearly everyone to some degree believes agents of the State are morally exempt from laws that govern our own behavior. They are given a superior status over normal members of society. Acts such as extortion and murder become euphemized into "taxation" and "execution of the law."

Most people are complicit with this paradigm, as they see the State providing much-needed services to the general public, including the building of infrastructure, national defense, public education, adjudication of disputes and more. However, all of the resources the State and its agents use in order to provide these services are paid for with stolen funds, i.e., the revenue acquired from taxes. The act of taxation constitutes *aggressive interference* with others as a means to compel them to relinquish their property to the State. This is institutionalized robbery. The State must acquire funds before it can provide services. Thus, the State's act of providing "public services" on social contract grounds cannot be supported as it *begins in naked robbery*. Because all of the State's services and functions are only made possible by first committing mass theft against its "citizenry," we can readily judge "social contract" justifications for the State to be invalid. No contract which involves robbery and the transfer of stolen property is just or legitimately enforceable, yet the "social contract" appears to be exactly that: a contract involving the transfer of expropriated goods.

Chapter Four

MONEY AND BANKING

THIS CHAPTER WILL examine the indispensable role that money and banking play in society. Scarcely any other concept is more important to understanding the nature and beauty of economic spontaneous order than money and banking.

Money allows us to protect ourselves against unpredictable contingencies. Holding cash balances is an attempt to mitigate an uncertain future by commanding purchasing power in the maximum number of possible situations. This is the purpose of liquidity: to provide immediately salable goods to trade for anything else one might want. Money prices serve as an indispensable guide in our daily economic decisions, be they as simple as deciding which toothpaste to purchase or as complex as which production method to use for assembling a series of automobiles. Finally, and perhaps most fundamentally, money facilitates cooperation with our fellow man through the harmonization of each of our unique self-interests. Money and money prices weave our interests together in voluntary and mutually beneficial ways. Money that emerges naturally from a state of barter is organic and promotes harmony in much the same way harmony or equilibrium is achieved in nature. This phenomenon of spontaneous order manifests a sustainable and enriching environment for all of its participants, perpetually reorienting itself according to the infinite number of constantly changing variables in a manner that no central planner(s) could ever hope to parallel.

Economic Fundamentals

Many references have been made toward "goods," however, this term has not been explicitly defined. Economic goods are simply any scarce means that a person sees as having the capacity to achieve a certain desired end. Thus, undiscovered or ubiquitous resources are not considered economic goods. For example, a deposit of gold that has been undiscovered in the Ozarks would not be considered a good, because no one would be aware of its existence, and therefore could not see it as a means to a desired end. Homesteading (original appropriation), as discussed earlier, is the

90

process by which scarce non-goods are transformed into goods. Additionally, something like oxygen would generally be considered a "free good/general condition," because it is virtually ubiquitous at sea level on Earth. In other words, one can use as much oxygen as he wants without limiting his own or any other person's access to it. It is important to keep in mind that property rights are only applicable to *scarce* goods, not non-scarce or free goods.

Value is subjective; even in similar situations, opportunity costs may vary from person to person. If both Victor and Bobby go out for lunch, Victor's opportunity cost may be skate boarding while Bobby's opportunity cost may be spending time with his girlfriend.

Economic decisions are those involving the use of scarce, rivalrous goods. "Economizing" goods simply refers to the act of treating them with the understanding that they are scarce and can only satisfy a limited number of desires. This concept may also refer to using/allocating goods in such a way that the greatest number of desires are satisfied to the greatest degree.

There are three types of economic goods: consumer goods, producer goods, and money. Consumer goods are those which directly satisfy desires. The drinking of water as a means to quench one's thirst puts the water into the category of a consumer good. One has a desire to quench his thirst, and consuming the water directly satisfies this desire.

Producer goods, on the other hand, are those goods used to indirectly satisfy desires. Depending on how it is used, the same good could act as a consumer or producer good. Water, used to boil food, serves as a producer good as its usefulness is indirect in that it merely assists in the creation of food – the desired consumer good.

Producer goods – otherwise known as means of production – may be further subdivided into the following three categories: land/natural resources, labor, and capital goods created by the use of land and labor.

Land and/or natural resources refer to any goods that are found in nature. Oil is a natural resource whereas a hammer is not. Only when these gifts of nature are used to indirectly satisfy a desire can they be considered a producer good. Eating a coconut purely to satiate my hunger renders it a consumer good. However, use of the coconut as ammunition in my coconut cannon for the sake of hunting wild game would render it a producer good.

Labor refers to activity emanating from a person's body that contributes to the production of goods or services. If one directs his efforts toward the *indirect* satisfaction of desire, then he is engaging in "labor." Conversely, using his efforts to *directly* satisfy his desires would be considered "leisure." If one's desire is to quench his thirst, then the act of drinking water is considered leisure, however the procurement of this water is considered labor. A related concept is the "disutility of labor," which refers to the fact that people prefer leisure to labor and will only commence in labor if they believe it will produce more satisfaction in the future than the leisure foregone in order to produce it.[61]

Capital goods refer to man-made means of production. Screw drivers and factories are examples of capital goods, since they are used to produce consumer goods and are man-made, i.e., not gifts of nature. In modern society, many capital goods are produced by other capital goods, thus compounding their productive utility (e.g. factories producing screwdrivers). The purpose of capital goods is to make labor more productive, to enable a given amount of labor to generate more goods than it otherwise would.

The third major type of good is "money". Money is any good that serves as a universal or prevalent medium of exchange. It is neither used for direct consumption nor for the production of goods, but is rather used to facilitate the exchange of consumer and producer goods. Rothbard expands upon this definition:

> Money is the medium of exchange, the asset for which all other goods and services are traded on the market. If a thing functions as such a medium, as final payment for other things on the market, then it serves as part of the money supply.[62]

Supply and Demand

The concepts of supply and demand are integral to understanding economic matters and social relations. Often times, they are confused or misunderstood; for the sake of clarity, a quick review is in order.

Supply is a *relationship* between the number of goods held, and at what price sellers are willing to trade them. For instance, Sarah may only be willing to sell two melons at a price of three dollars each, but may be willing to sell five melons at a price of six dollars each. This leads us to the "law of supply" which states "...as the market price of a good or service rises,

---

61   Time preference will also play a role into this value accounting because, other things equal, people prefer to have goods sooner rather than later. Thus, when deciding to engage in labor, one will consider both the value of the object of leisure he/she could have now and the one he/she may expect to gain in the future if labor is resorted to, *along with the cost of having to defer his/her gratification in pursuit of this potentially greater future return.*

62   Murray N. Rothbard, "Austrian Theory of Money" in The Foundations of Modern Austrian Economics, edit. Edwin G. Dolan (Mission, Kan.: Sheed & Ward, 1976), 182.

producers offer the same or greater number of units."[63] To illustrate supply as being a relationship rather than a number, economists will often times construct a "Supply Curve" which is "a graphical illustration of the supply relationship, with price placed on the vertical axis and quantity on the horizontal axis. Sometimes a generic supply curve is drawn as a smooth, curved line or even as a simple straight lie. Supply curves are 'upward sloping,' meaning that they start in the lower left and move up and to the right."[64] Finally, a "reduction in supply" refers to "a situation in which a change other than the price of a good or service causes producers to reduce the number of units they want to sell, at various possible prices." An increase in supply would be the inverse. For instance, if a drought in the Midwest significantly hampers grain production, this event may be said to have caused a reduction in supply, because due to the reduction of salable goods, grain sellers may offer fewer units of grain for a given price than they otherwise would.

Demand is a relationship between how many goods consumers desire, and at what price they are willing to trade for them. Just like supply, demand is not a number but a *relationship*. For example, Harry may only be willing to purchase one game at a price of ten dollars each, but may be willing to purchase five games at a price of seven dollars each. This "demand schedule" is a snapshot in time; in different, more desperate circumstances, Harry may be willing to pay more for the games than if he were in less desperate circumstances. This follows the "law of demand," which states "if other influences stay the same, then a lower price will lead consumers to buy more [or the same number of] units of a good (or service), while a higher price will lead them to buy fewer [or the same number of] units."[65] A common objection given to the law of demand is that a given person may be more drawn to buying a particular hand bag if it were more expensive, due to its reflection as a status symbol. However, this does not contradict the law of demand as the added social status of the hand bag would render it a different good entirely from any mere hand bag. For instance, imagine a card with a typical baseball player on it, and then imagine if this same card were to become a collector's item in the future. Though the physical properties of the card did not change, its perceived status did, thus it went from being a common card to a "collectors card" – an entirely new good. To demonstrate the nature of demand, economists often times construct a "Demand Curve" which is "a graphical illustration of the demand relationship, with price placed on the vertical axis and quantity on the horizontal axis. Sometimes a generic demand curve is drawn

---

[63]   Robert P. Murphy, *Lessons for the Young Economist* (Auburn: Ludwig Von Mises Institute, 2010), 153.

[64]   Murphy, *Lessons*, 154.

[65]   Murphy, ibid, 148.

as a smooth, curved line or even as a simple straight line. Demand curves are downward sloping, meaning that they start in the upper left and move down and to the right." Finally, a "reduction in demand" refers to "a situation in which a change other than the price of a good or service causes consumers to reduce the number of units they want to purchase, at various possible prices." An increase in demand would be the inverse. For example, if there were reports indicating there had been an outbreak of e-coli amongst poultry products, then this may be said to have caused a reduction in demand, because consumers as a whole would not be willing to purchase the same quantity of poultry at a given price as they otherwise would have purchased had the outbreak never occurred.

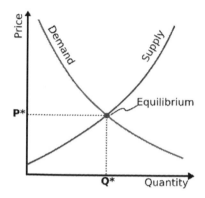

Many economic concepts may be extrapolated from supply and demand mechanics, however we will only cover three: surplus, shortage, and equilibrium prices. A surplus occurs when producers attempt to sell more units of a good or service than consumers are willing to purchase at a given price. For example, if a television salesman offers fifteen units at a price of 1,000 dollars each, but only ten people are willing to purchase them, then the salesman will have a surplus of five units that he is unable to sell. A shortage occurs when consumers want to buy more units of a good or service than producers are willing to sell at a given price. Using the television analogy, suppose the salesman offers his fifteen units for 700 dollars each, but there are twenty people who wish to purchase them at this price. In this case, the salesman will have a shortage of five units. Finally, the equilibrium price (or market clearing price) is "the price at which producers want to sell exactly the number of units that consumers want to purchase. On a graph, the equilibrium price occurs at the intersection of the supply and demand curves."[66] This situation occurs if our salesman prices his fifteen television units at nine hundred dollars each and exactly fifteen people are willing to purchase them at such a price.

---

[66]   Murphy, ibid, 171.

Origin of Money

Money spontaneously rose out of the barter economy, due to its trade facilitating properties. Participants in the economy tend to pick the most salable good on the market as their unit of trade. Silver coins are more salable than horseshoes, and so the former will tend to beat out the latter as a medium of exchange. Users will tend to gravitate towards salable objects as they allow each person the maximum degree of control over future uncertainties. Jörg Guido Hülsmann describes the process individualistically:

> The emergence of money happens through a gradual process, in the course of which more and more market participants, each for himself, decide to use one commodity rather than others in their indirect exchanges. Thus the historical selection of gold, silver, and copper was not made through some sort of a social contract or convention. Rather, it resulted from the spontaneous convergence of many individual choices, a convergence that was prompted through the objective physical characteristics of the precious metals. Money selected in the free market. i.e. money that comes into use by the voluntary cooperation of acting persons, is also called natural money.[67]

Hoppe explains how monies gain inertia:

> By adding a new component to the pre-existing (barter) demand for these goods, their marketability is still further enhanced. Based on their perception of this fact, other market participants increasingly choose the same goods for their inventory

---

[67]   Jörg Guido Hülsmann, "The Origin and Nature of Money" in *The Ethics of Money Production* (Auburn: Ludwig Von Mises Institute, 2008), 22-24.

of exchange media, as it is in their own interest to select media of exchange that are already employed by others for the same purpose. Initially, a variety of goods may be in demand as common media of exchange. However, since a good is demanded as a medium of exchange to facilitate future purchases of directly serviceable goods (i.e., to help one buy more cheaply) and simultaneously widen one's market as a seller of directly useful goods and services (i.e., help one sell more dearly), the more widely a commodity is used as a medium of exchange, the better it will perform its function.[68]

And Mises describes the inevitable tendency of a successful money:

Because each market participant naturally prefers the acquisition of a more marketable and, in the end, universally marketable medium of exchange to that of a less or non-universally marketable one, there would be an inevitable tendency for the less marketable of the series of goods used as media of exchange to be one by one rejected until at last only a single commodity remained, which was universally employed as a medium of exchange; in a word, money.[69]

Characteristics of Money

It is observed that money spontaneously chosen by market dynamics tends to have a certain set of characteristics: homogeneity, portability, divisibility, durability, verifiability, scarcity, and, from all of these, liquidity.

---

[68]   Hans-Hermann Hoppe, "How Is Fiat Money Possible? Or, the Devolution of Money and Credit," in *The Review of Austrian Economics* 7.2 (1994): 50.

[69]   Ludwig von Mises, "The Functions of Money" in *The Theory of Money and Credit* (New Haven: Yale University Press, 1953), 32-33.

1) Money must be homogeneous. The natural process by which money emerges is one in which one good is set up against all others so as to enable simple and accurate economic calculation by means of exchange ratios. "Heterogeneous money" (money units that differed from each other) would undermine the process of economic calculation by requiring multiple exchange ratios. Not only this, but a heterogeneous money would imply that some of its component goods would be more salable than others (given their differing qualities) thus rendering this monetary unit necessarily less efficient than a money comprised of the single most salable good.

2) Ease of transport is highly regarded among monetary units as having to lug around cumbersome and hefty goods for trade incurs unnecessary transaction costs (i.e., the space and energy required to transport it)

3) Divisibility of the unit is of chief importance as this allows the users of money to make small and large purchases of varying degrees.

4) Durability is another important consideration, for money would hardly be useful if it melted in your pocket or disintegrated once touched.

5) The ability to verify the integrity of a money unit is paramount. Units that could be easily counterfeit would not survive long as the most common medium of exchange. If a seller finds it difficult to verify the authenticity of money, he will be less likely to accept it as payment.

6) Scarcity is one of the most important factors, for if a money had an infinite supply, then it would be unable to yield comprehensible prices. Money prices are simply the exchange ratios set up between monetary units and all other goods/services in the economy. Thus, if one side of this ratio was infinite, then it would be impossible to compare and contrast the values of individual goods and services. This would effectively defeat the purpose of a medium of exchange – to enable market participants to more objectively ascertain the costs of their economic decisions.

7) All these criteria fit together and reinforce the marketability of a good giving it liquidity. This is perhaps the most important characteristic of money, as the overall utility of money is primarily measured by how widely it is accepted as payment. Highly reproducible, fragile, and non-divisible goods will seldom become liquid. Liquidity is a state of acceptance. The very purpose of money is to facilitate exchange and the facilitation of exchange is completely contingent upon the desirability of what is being used as a medium of exchange.

A SPONTANEOUS ORDER

There are two different types of money: commodity money and fiat money. Commodity money is a scarce money unit, such as gold or silver, or its redemption is promised in terms of such a good. Fiat money is commonly referred to as "paper money" as it is not "backed by" – or redeemable for – any particular good or commodity. Such money is brought into existence by the coercive dictates of States and is deemed "legal tender" by law (i.e., by central fiat). When the State supports or creates fiat money, it usually does so by means of legal tender laws. This *requires* that all creditors under its jurisdiction accept it as payment of debt under threat of legal action for non-compliance.

Moreover, taxes are generally required to be paid in the form of legal tender. Such legal tender laws are one of the primary reasons that commodity money is not in more prevalent use today. Without the violence and coercion of the State, market actors would utilize sound currency that bears little to no resemblance to today's government fiat. According to Robert Murphy, a sound money is one "...for which the value doesn't bounce around erratically, and doesn't lose its purchasing power over time."[70] In addition, sound money is one in which tight control over the production of the money unit is maintained. This may be due to wise stewardship over fiat production, geological factors limiting production of precious metals, or advanced cryptography securing the scarcity of digital money.

Double Coincidence of Wants

Barter is the act of trading consumer or producer goods directly for other consumer or producer goods. One of the advantages the use of money has over direct barter is that its users are not constrained by the "double coincidence of wants." This is a situation in which both trading partners must desire precisely what the other offers. A double coincidence of wants situation may play out thusly: Suppose that Bob is a strawberry producer who wants to acquire shoes from Joe the shoemaker. Bob decides to offer Joe a bucket of strawberries in exchange for a pair of shoes produced by Joe, but, as it turns out, Joe places little value on strawberries and refuses Bob's offer. Naturally, Bob asks Joe what it is he does want, and Joe replies "one pound of bacon." Bob then proceeds to offer the local butcher a bucket of strawberries in exchange for one pound of bacon, but tragically finds himself in the same predicament because Sam the butcher desires butter, not strawberries. The poor strawberry producer Bob inevitably repeats this process until he finds someone who does desire his strawberries and is willing to trade. For simplicity's sake, assume the local

---

[70]   Murphy, ibid, 338.

dairy farmer does accept Bob's strawberry offer in exchange for butter, which in turn Bob now uses in exchange for the butcher's bacon, and finally uses the bacon to acquire the shoes he originally sought from Joe the shoemaker. This tedious process is clearly inefficient when compared with a monetary economy where Bob can simply sell his strawberries for money – a common unit of account – and then use the money to purchase the shoes directly. This significantly reduces Bob's otherwise high transaction costs involved with executing many exchanges in order to procure one desired good.

Calculation

In addition to being able to trade more easily, Bob realizes he is able to have a much clearer understanding of the costs of any good or service under a monetary system. Prior to the advent of money, Bob had to keep track of a myriad of exchange ratios between various goods. He had to figure out how much shoes were worth in terms of strawberries, pounds of butter, and gallons of milk. A gallon of milk itself would be priced in terms of horseshoes, sheep, leather, strawberries, etc, and every other good likewise would be priced in terms of every other good. Bob would repeat this valuation process for every other good he might desire. Even if he were able to understand or calculate his costs in terms of all of the economy's exchange ratios, by the time he finished, most of them would have become irrelevant and obsolete due to the likely shift in availability and preferences that would have occurred in the interim. Thanks to money, Bob now only has to keep track of the exchange ratios between units of money and all other goods offered on the market. This exchange ratio is more commonly referred to as a good's "price." With money, Bob is also able to make more rational economic decisions in regards to production and consumption, because he is now able to quantify his opportunity costs in terms of monetary units. Bob can compare how much money it would cost to purchase Strawberry producing equipment with how much income he expects to receive from the greater production of strawberries this equipment will yield. If he predicts that the extra income he generates will be less than what the equipment costs, he will likely decide to refrain from purchasing it. If he predicts his additional income would be more than the cost of the equipment, he will likely follow through with the purchase. This is how money facilitates and simplifies entrepreneurial decisions; it allows actors to appraise their costs in terms of one unit – the most popular and salable – instead of maintaining and updating hundreds of exchange rations simultaneously.

Money also simplifies the testing of these predictions. For example, it may be the case that Bob receives much less income than he predicted by incorporating this new machinery. Such erroneous predictions will occur in any economic context because no one can or will have perfect information. However, money and the pricing mechanism it manifests allows entrepreneurs like Bob to more easily recognize when they are generating losses, thus allowing them the insight necessary to modify their production processes accordingly. Without money, it would be much more difficult for Bob to determine whether or not his business was profitable. It would be even more challenging to pinpoint the specific business practices that were succeeding or failing and to what degree they yielded profits or generated losses. This "calculation" process enabled by money can be applied to any economic decision. Of course, the entrepreneur does not *have* to do what is most profitable in terms of money. The availability of money and prices merely provides him with a better understanding of which activities will satisfy the desires of the consumer and to what degree they do so. Such information allows him to make more informed economic decisions regarding where to produce his goods, how to produce them, from which materials to produce them, where and how to distribute them, how many to produce, and so on. The introduction of money informs all these choices.

To further illustrate, consider the case of a furniture producer seeking a location to construct his factory. On the surface, it may seem most sensible for him to place his factory next to the retailers willing to sell his products so as to cut down on transportation costs. However, it may be the case that the land in this area is of even greater value to a computer chip manufacturer who is willing to bid more for it than our furniture producer. Thus, it may make more sense for the furniture producer to locate his factory at a more distant location if he projects that the increased costs in transportation will be less than the additional costs he would otherwise have to pay to secure the location nearest the furniture retailers. The same may be said regarding which materials to use. It may not be profitable to use the "best" or "highest quality" materials as such materials may be valued more for use in other productive processes than in the furniture entrepreneur's plans. Thus, the pricing mechanism takes into account all of the opportunity costs regarding what to produce, how to produce, where to produce, and what materials with which to produce when conveying to the producer what course of action will be most profitable. Without such a mechanism, this entrepreneurial decision making process would be highly arbitrary and comparatively less efficient.

It is only through the private ownership of economic goods that the market is able to produce prices which accurately reflect the relative demand for and supply of the world's scarce resources. To understand this further, simply consider how prices are generated. The seller generally wants to price his goods such that the number of people willing to purchase them equals the numbers of units he is offering. In other words, he wants to price his goods at the highest level possible without having a leftover surplus of his wares or services. Conversely, the consumer wants to spend the least amount of money on a given good that a seller is willing to offer. The buyer and seller have an incentive to negotiate with each other in the presence of competition. If the seller offers a good for "too high" of a price, the buyer may decide to go to his competitor offering the same or similar good at a lower price. If the buyer insists on making offers which are "too low," he may lose out on the opportunity to acquire the given good or service to the next potential customer who is willing to pay a higher price. Thus, opposing desires, in the context of a competitive economy, drive a tendency towards a meeting in the middle (this is also known as the market clearing price). There is always a tendency for such a harmony to be achieved in the free market where economic goods are privately owned.

Most socialist doctrines, however, call for the collective ownership of all the means of production. In light of our understanding of the function of private ownership of goods, let us examine the consequences of this arrangement. Those who employ the means of production in a socialist economy are not as able or incentivized to experiment in novel ways to make profit – that is, to continually search for new ways to reorient or modify their employment so as to increase productivity – as private owners of means of production would have in a competitive economy.

Patronage for the services of such productive means is guaranteed; as all means of production would be collectively owned, no counterpart providing competitive disruption may exist. Without competition, wasteful and/or undesirable enterprise abounds because its survival is shielded from market pressures. Socialist enterprise is not guaranteed to experience the consequences otherwise faced in a free market for poor performance: loss of business and money.

Let us assume, however, that the workers and managers of such collectively owned producer goods are saints and angels and wish to maximize production owing to their altruistic love of mankind and of achieving the "greater good." Even with such magnanimity, without prices amongst the means of production, it is virtually impossible to determine the way in which they may be economized. With market prices, entrepreneurs have quantifiable and objectively comparable indicators of the demand for varying arrangements of the means of production. For instance, without market prices for the means of production, there is no way to objectively determine the true production costs of any particular good, and therefore whether its production (or the method used to produce it) is profitable. Knowledge of market prices for the means of production enables entrepreneurs to structure their capital or productive projects in a manner that yields the lowest opportunity costs. Another way of saying this is that competitive pressures continually exert on the entrepreneur to provide the most valuable products and services while using those resources which have the least relative demand for alternative applications. However, if such factors of production are collectively owned, it is comparatively much more difficult, if not impossible, to determine their opportunity costs (as no money prices can emerge for them), thus rendering the productive infrastructure in such a socialist paradigm comparatively less efficient than its counterpart in a free market economy. Economic actors in a fully socialist economy cannot engage in rational economic "calculation" – the process of reducing opportunity costs by discovering less valued means of production. Centrally planned industries bear only superficial resemblance to competitive markets, for they operate with workers and managers and sell products at certain money prices. However, in socialist economies, production processes are given down from government fiat. Planning boards determine all the relevant economic details of a firm – what supplies to be used and from where to acquire them, how many laborers must be hired and to what employments they will be put, even down to the products and the prices at which they are to be sold. In such a society, there are no entrepreneurs, merely managers. Heads of industry simply obey the production diktats given from on high. For every production process chosen, they must operate in the dark. *Therefore, to the extent market prices are perverted through measures which infringe on the private ownership of any scarce good, entrepreneurs are hindered in discovering efficient means by which to produce goods, resulting in the economy's departure from its optimum productive potential.* Murray Rothbard explains the importance of Mises' calculation insight and the need for money prices to translate opportunity costs:

> ...Mises was one of the very first to realize that subjective valuations of the consumers (and of laborers) on the market are purely ordinal [they are expressible by preference rankings only], and are in no way measurable. But market prices are cardinal and measurable in terms of money, and market money prices bring goods into cardinal comparability and calculation (e.g., a $10 hat is "worth" five times as much as a $2 loaf of bread). But Mises realized that this insight meant it was absurd to say (as Schumpeter would) that the market "imputes" the values of consumer goods back to the factors of production. Values are not directly "imputed"; the imputation process works only indirectly, by means of money prices on the market. Therefore socialism, necessarily devoid of a market in

land and capital goods, must lack the
ability to calculate and compare goods and
services, and therefore any rational
allocation of productive resources under
socialism is indeed impossible.[71]

Profits

One of the most incredible attributes of free markets is the ability
to harmonize our self-interests with the interests of greater society.
Contrary to the popular demonization of profits as extraction of surplus
value, profits in freed markets actually represent the adding of value to
society. Making a profit in free markets requires one to combine or
transform some good(s) in such a way that its resulting configuration is
valued more by the consumer than the cost of labor and original materials,
including time, used to produce it. In other words, a profit is the positive
difference between the total costs of production and the resulting price paid
for a good or service by the consumer. If Joe constructs a bench that costs
fifty dollars in materials, twenty dollars in labor, and ten dollars in overhead
costs (the fixed cost of the facility, utilities, etc.), then the total production
cost would be eighty dollars. Assuming Joe is able to sell the bench for one
hundred dollars, this would indicate that he would have added over twenty
dollars of value to society. Remember, prior to Joe's efforts, the sum value
of the resources and labor used only amounted to eighty dollars. However,
through his entrepreneurial insight, Joe was able to combine all these
resources in such a way to create a product that was worth more than the
sum of its individual components. Moreover, the trade is mutually
beneficial. Joe benefits because he gets to pocket twenty more dollars than
he originally possessed, and the consumer benefits by receiving a product
that he/she must necessarily value more than one hundred dollars. All
parties to any voluntary trade must necessarily expect to be better off after
conducting the trade, otherwise the trade would never have occurred. In
unhampered economies, profits are always and necessarily a win-win. Thus,
the quest for profits by way of voluntary exchange – and not political
entrepreneurship – is surely a humanitarian one.

It should also be noted that profits need not be monetary; they may
also be psychic. For instance, if one were to decide to give a homeless man
on the street five dollars, this would not yield the benefactor a monetary
profit, however, the psychic pleasure he receives from the gesture is more

---

[71]   Murray N. Rothbard, "The End of Socialism and the Calculation Debate Revisited"
in *The Review of Austrian Economics* 5.2 (1991): 65.

valuable to him than the five dollars he surrendered. Once again, such an act would be considered one whose aim is profit. It is through this concept of psychic profit that economists are able to explain actions taken by actors in the economy that deliberately result in monetary losses. Monetary profits are merely a subset of all possible motivations.

Money As Protector Against Uncertainty

Because money can be employed for the *instant satisfaction of the widest range of possible needs*, it provides its owner with the best economically possible protection against uncertainty. In holding money, its owner gains in the satisfaction of being able to meet instantly, as they unpredictably arise, the widest range of future contingencies. The investment in cash balances is an investment contra the (subjectively felt) aversion to uncertainty. A larger cash balance brings more relief from uncertainty aversion.[72]

As money is by definition the most salable good in the economy, it can be exchanged against any resource that is "for sale" that one may need at a moment's notice. Unlike insurance, however, it has the capacity to protect against all possible contingencies. In contrast, insurance requires that one have some degree of certainty as to the particular nature of the risk he expects to encounter. Thus, uninsurable risks, otherwise known as uncertainties, may be mitigated by adding to one's cash balances or savings. In this way, money behaves as the best possible guarantor in ensuring one that his unknown future needs may be fulfilled as they spontaneously arise.

Some economists consider additions to one's cash balance as a form of savings. Nearly everyone – at all times – holds some quantity of cash on them, whether in a bank account or in a wallet. This is done to protect oneself from as many unforeseen contingencies as possible by retaining the most salable good in society. This utility of money proves it is not "barren" or "sterile" -- an unproductive asset that hamstrings economic activity in the Keynesian view. In order to retain cash holdings, however, one must have earned some prior income. One cannot have exhausted all his possible consumptive options if he still carries cash. Cash's consumption power is a potential. While assets remain, there is as of yet unconsumed income. The cash-holding actor has invested this retained savings *in the form* of cash. As William Hutt noted, money held serves a yield. It is a productive asset that serves the one who holds it by best preparing him for the greatest number of possible outcomes in which he might want to consume or invest

---

[72]   Hans-Hermann Hoppe "'The Yield From Money Held' Reconsidered," (lecture presented at the Franz Cuhel Memorial Lecture, Prague, Czech Republic, April 24, 2009).

further in any number of ways.[73] If all this is true, then assets retained in the form of cash holdings are savings just as certificates of deposit or a stock of food. Money is different in that its yield is expressed only in psychic terms (the peace of mind that comes from being able to fulfill unforeseen future desires) and never in nominal terms, contrary to typical savings vehicles such as equity or bonds. While the total volume of savings is determined by the level of one's time preference (the degree to which it is high or low), the proportion between our cash holdings and other saved assets is determined by our subjective valuations regarding the uncertainty of the future.

Division of Labor and Specialization

The concept of the division of labor simply refers to the economic arrangement whereby participants *specialize* in different tasks and exchange the products of their efforts with one another. The result of this specialization and cooperation yields an output that is greater than what would be achieved if each individual attempted to produce the entire array of his own goods himself. To illustrate this, suppose Bob decides to specialize in shoe production, dedicating a majority of his labor toward this end. In doing so, he expects to exchange the excess production of shoes with the products or services of others (e.g. for food, medicine, housing, etc.) Bob has essentially decided to engage in the division of labor. The only way for Bob to abstain from the division of labor would be for him to make his own food, produce his own medicine, build his own housing, and even create his own clothing and shoes. However, this would not be very practical for a variety of reasons. First, Bob may not have ready access to the resources requisite to produce the entire set of goods or services he desires. Perhaps Bob wants Alaskan Crab, but lives in Florida. Perhaps Bob doesn't have the necessary tools to build the type of house he wants, or maybe he does not currently have the necessary skills or physical ability to do so. The quality of housing or seafood he could create will inevitably be lower than if he simply traded with those who are gifted and practiced in the creation of such goods. One may see how quickly Bob's standard of living would plummet if he was in a position where he was required to produce all the goods he desires himself.

One can now easily recognize the distinct advantages of the division of labor. Under the division of labor, one may be able to focus on one task or a limited set of tasks geared towards producing a particular good/service as opposed to the entire spectrum of tasks required to fulfill

---

[73]   William H. Hutt, "The Yield from Money Held," in *Freedom and Free Enterprise: Essays in Honor of Ludwig von Mises*, edit. M. Sennholz (Chicago: Van Nostrand, 1956), 196-216.

all his needs. The fact that, under such an arrangement, people are able to focus on a more limited set of tasks allows them to increase their proficiency at these tasks and thus become more productive, i.e., to be able to produce more with the same amount of labor. Moreover, because they can choose to specialize in one field or another, they now have the opportunity to engage in that which they have the "comparative advantage" at doing. In other words, they may choose to do that which offers them the greatest amount of profit. Without money, it would be quite difficult to determine such profits due to calculation limitations. Who is to say producing twenty bananas a month is more or less productive than producing ten shoes in the same span? However, in the context of a monetary based economy, one may compare the profits yielded from producing the twenty bananas with the profits yielded from producing the ten shoes. It may be the case that producing ten shoes/month yields a profit of fifty dollars whereas producing the twenty bananas only yields a profit of twenty five dollars. Of course, this doesn't mean our hypothetical producer is prohibited from producing bananas, it simply means he now has an additional piece of information that allows him to more accurately determine his opportunity costs associated with each task. Moreover, there are large costs associated with having to switch from the task of making shoes, to growing food, producing medicine, and constructing a house when compared with specializing in one of those activities and contracting out the rest. Thus, specialization and the division of labor enable people to more easily do what they want and what they excel at doing, while at the same time enjoying a higher standard of living afforded by the more efficient hands of others.

Money enables economic actors to engage more deeply and more effectively in the division of labor due to its trade facilitation properties. For instance, if a cobbler desires bacon, but is unable to find a bacon producer willing to trade him bacon for his produced shoes, then the cobbler must resort to either producing the bacon himself, producing (or procuring) that which the bacon producer does want (and what he likely does not have the desire or comparative advantage at producing), or go without. In contrast, the bacon producer is much more likely to accept money in exchange for his bacon, thus allowing the cobbler to produce shoes and sell them for cash to ultimately attain the bacon he desires.

One more example will suffice to explain the idea of "comparative advantage." Suppose that Molly is a surgeon who also owns a bakery and that Louis manages the bakery for her. When Molly manages the bakery, she is able to turn $300 per day in profit. However, on the days she performs surgery, she is able to create $1,000 per day in profit. When Louis manages the bakery, he only generates $250 per day in profit. In this case Molly has what is known as the "absolute" or "all-around advantage". Seeing that Molly is able to generate more profit than Louis at the bakery, would it behoove her to quit her surgical practice in order to manage the bakery full time? Of course not, because even though she can generate more profit than Louis at the bakery, she would be giving up her performance at her surgical practice in order to do so. In other words, she would be relinquishing $1,000 in profit at her surgical clinic for the sake of recouping fifty dollars extra profit at the bakery. The monetary opportunity cost of managing the bakery is $1,000. Should she commit to baking full time, this decision will leave her $950 poorer per day than she was prior. Even though Louis is less apt at managing the bakery than she is, she will realize greater profits overall if she performs the role at which she excels – surgery – than if she managed the bakery herself.

The Money Supply

Reliability in the scarcity of the money unit is one of the chief criteria granting it value. An easily duplicated or produced money unit hurts the integrity of that unit's exchange value. Central bankers or advocates for economic central planning often claim that contracting or expanding the money supply can be a great method to regulate and "stabilize" the economy in comparison to the spontaneous twists of free markets. However, such a claim is nonsense, for to increase or decrease the amount of monetary units does absolutely nothing to increase actual wealth in society as expressed by the presence or lack of goods and services. Once a good has achieved a large scale or universal consensus regarding its "moneyness," *any amount* of it is sufficient to optimally perform its role. An increase in the money supply without a corresponding increase in the total number of goods will only serve to dilute the purchasing power of money, whereas decreasing the monetary units will accomplish the opposite. Tampering with the money supply only serves to *redistribute* wealth. In the case of inflation or monetary expansion, wealth is transferred from later users to earlier users, as the first users of this "newly created money" will be able to enjoy spending it in an economy where the prices have yet to adjust to the new increase in money supply. By the time this money makes its way down to the last recipients, market prices will have adjusted to this larger money supply in the form of higher prices. Thus, the last users may have the same nominal amount of money, but would have comparatively less wealth than they did before the additional monetary units were injected into the economy. This redistributive effect of inflation is known as the Cantillon effect. Thus, someone's wealth in a monetary economy may be determined by the proportion of the money supply he wields (along with the market value of all of his assets). In other words, the number of monetary units in itself means very little. Population growth in excess of the growth of the money unit will simply increase the purchasing power of the unit; no new units need be introduced. Rothbard addresses the unique category of good money plays:

> With respect to the supply of money, Mises returned to the basic Ricardian insight that an increase in the supply of money never confers any general benefit upon society. For money is fundamentally different from consumers' and producers' goods in at least one vital respect. Other things being equal, an increase in the supply of consumers' goods benefits society since one or more consumers will be better off. The same is true of an increase in the supply of producers' goods, which will be eventually transformed into an increased supply of consumers' goods; for production itself is the process of transforming natural resources into new forms and locations desired by consumers for direct use. But money is very different: money is not used directly in consumption or production but is exchanged for such directly usable goods. Yet, once any commodity or object is established as a money, it performs the maximum exchange work of which it is capable. An increase in the supply of money causes no increase whatever in the exchange service of money; all that happens is that the purchasing power of each unit of money is diluted by the increased supply of units. Hence there is never a social need for increasing the supply of money, either because of an increased supply of goods or because of an increase in population. People can acquire an increased proportion of cash balances with a fixed supply of money by spending less and thereby increasing the purchasing power of their cash balances, thus raising their real cash balances overall.[74]

Free Banking

Banks serve two distinct functions: as safe warehouse of funds and as intermediaries between borrowers and savers. On the one hand, banks come forward to meet the increasing demand for the safekeeping, transporting, and clearing of money. On the other hand, they fulfill the increasingly important function of facilitating exchanges between capitalists (savers) and entrepreneurs (investors), actually making an almost complete division of labor between these roles possible. As institutions of deposit and in particular as savings and credit institutions, banks quickly assume the rank of nerve centers of an economy. Increasingly the spatial and temporal allocation and coordination of economic resources and activities takes place through the mediation of banks; in facilitating such coordination, the emergence of banks implies still another stimulus for economic growth.[75]

As Hoppe mentions, banks are absolutely crucial in not only protecting one's wealth, but also in coordinating resources throughout the economy. Banks enable entrepreneurs to pursue the most economical ends with resources that would otherwise be unemployed. However, unlike banking in societies dominated by fiat money and ubiquitous State intervention, a free market banking system will be segregated into two distinct roles: deposit banking and loan banking.

Deposit banking refers to the safeguarding services provided by a bank. People generally feel their money is better protected behind a heavy vault as opposed to under their mattresses. Thus, many people would happily pay a fee in exchange for a bank's warehousing services. The bank

---

[74]   Rothbard, "Austrian Theory of Money," 310-311.

[75]   Hoppe, "Banking, Nation States, and International Politics" in *The Economics and Ethics of Private Property*, 79-80.

benefits by being paid for its services and the customer benefits by having the peace of mind of knowing his bank is professionally protected. Competition amongst different banks offering these services will tend to keep prices at a minimum and ensure that various banks distinguish themselves by offering more locations to conveniently withdraw or deposit funds, and other important functions. In the case of a gold standard, such banks may offer bank notes or electronic credits redeemable in gold to be used by its customers in lieu of them physically carrying metal in their pockets, or as an additional form of security backstopped by the bank's digital security practices. When the number of bank notes or electronic credits offered directly corresponds with the amount of money (in this case gold) in the vaults, such an arrangement is referred to as "100% reserve banking."

The second type of banking is "loan banking." Under loan banking, savers lend their money to the bank so that it can lend this capital to borrowers. The saver lends these funds with the expectation of receiving interest payments from the bank, and the bank proceeds to lend this saved money in the hopes of earning more interest than it must pay. This division of labor benefits the saver by delegating to the bank the task of successful forecasting – in which the saver may have no skill or desire to perform. Delegating the lending to the bank would in most cases provide the customer with a more secure investment than if he were to lend the money out himself on the basis of his own judgments of entrepreneurial success. The bank benefits from this arrangement by having access to capital from which it can now earn interest. Interest payments primarily are paid for the service of acquiring access to capital sooner rather than later. Competition between various banks will tend to minimize the differential between what the banks charge borrowers in terms of interest and what the bank provides to savers in terms of interest paid. This is due to the fact that savers have the incentive to select those banks which pay out the highest interest rates. Conversely, borrowers have the incentive to patronize those banks which charge the lowest interest rates for borrowing. Along with the interest rates themselves, such customers will also be interested in the bank's track record, that is to say, how often it has defaulted on its debt obligations and how well it is capitalized. This tempers a given bank's propensity to engage in high risk lending practices.

What distinguishes loan banking from deposit banking is that customers cannot expect to be able to withdraw their money at *any* time. When they loan their money, the banks are only obliged to return the whole of their money plus interest at a predetermined point of time in the future. Banks could hardly be expected to maintain interest payments on funds that savers could withdraw on demand. The bank is only able to pay savers' interest because it was first able to procure interest from borrowers which exceeds the interest payments promised to the saver.

110

For example, suppose Bob deposits one hundred dollars in a loan banking institution. In exchange for letting them borrow his money, the bank offers Bob a five percent quarterly interest rate in return. Now, imagine that Joe wishes to borrow that same $100 from the bank so that he may start a small business. The bank will proceed to review Joe's credit which includes his assets, his history of timely payments, his current income, etc. After his credit has been evaluated, the bank may also evaluate his business plan and determine its likelihood for success. The bank will then offer Joe the loan with an interest rate that corresponds to his "appraised risk" as determined by the bank's investigative process. Suppose the bank offers Joe one hundred dollars with a ten percent interest rate to be paid in two months. Joe accepts the funds and two months transpire. Joe has responsibly paid the bank the principal of his loan (one hundred dollars) along with the ten percent interest (ten dollars). The following month, Bob arrives to collect his investment, at which point in time, the bank may return to Bob his principal and interest or offer to keep the funds and renew the lending agreement. Even if Bob refuses the offer to continue and decides to collect his funds, both parties benefit as both parties become five dollars richer. Even Joe the borrower benefited by gaining access to capital needed to start his small business sooner as opposed to his waiting later. Perhaps starting the business at that current point of time was crucial to its success. This is one example of how banks efficiently coordinate the allocation of scarce resources. Their specialization in lending and risk management benefits both parties through a division of labor.

Money in a free market system represents real resources. In order for Joe to borrow money (claims to resources) *now*, Bob had to refrain from claiming said resources until *later*. Thus, the monetary supply remained unchanged during the course of this lending/borrowing process.

Fraudulent Banking Practices in the Free Market

With the advent of bank notes comes the temptation for banks to engage in inflationary practices and to print more notes than assets they've accepted in deposit. This is tantamount to the bank providing multiple titles to the same set of goods. If the bank has one hundred ounces of gold in its vaults, but issues one hundred ounce bank notes to both Sam and Juliet, then both Sam and Juliet essentially have conflicting titles over the same set of goods despite the promise issued by the bank for instant redemption. In other words, the bank is handing out titles for non-existent goods (promised assets which do not exist). The bank hopes to gain from this by relying on its customers, Sam and Juliet, not to ask for redemption before it is able to replenish its reserves to the point where it may be able satisfy both of their requests. By engaging in this practice, the bank will be able to earn interest on double the assets it actually holds. This practice is risky, however, for in a free banking system, if Sam and Juliet redeem their notes simultaneously, the bank must default on its obligations and suffer reputational damages which directly impact its future business prospects. If it is true that a bank cannot make good on its outstanding obligations, it is insolvent. The insolvency is only revealed at the time it fails to honor depositor agreements. The risk of this situation occurring would serve as a serious deterrent against this practice. The issuance of extra, unbacked notes is more commonly referred to as "fractional reserve banking," which is the practice of holding only a fraction of what one has obliged himself to redeem instantly and at any time.

If depositors learn that their bank is engaging in fractional reserve practices, they will be more inclined to redeem their notes as soon as possible so as to avoid default on part of the bank. Jörg Guido Hülsmann elaborates on the necessary discount between holding money proper and holding bank IOUs with redemption promise.[76] Bank runs can be extremely disruptive to an economy as many savers, having trusted banks to be excellent stewards of the funds, lose their deposits and a cascading set of systemic defaults ensue,[77] hurling the economy into a recession or depression.[78] Such bank runs could not occur in a 100% reserve banking system where all deposits are held securely without claims to them given to third parties. Thus, only loan banking institutions would be at risk for default, and even this would be minimal due to competition and consumer preference as savers have a vested interest in lending their money to reputable institutions. High rates of return might indicate that the institutions offering such rates would be engaged in high risk lending practices. In any case, such defaults would be more limited and predictable in a free banking system, where banks are separate, competitive enterprises and not shackled to each other by central bank operations. Thus, the risk for systematic economic distress would be virtually nil when compared to its fractional reserve banking system counterpart. Hoppe explains how competition between banking institutions may serve as an additional fraud deterrent under a free banking system:

---

[76] Jörg Guido Hülsmann, "Has Fractional Reserve Banking Really Passed the Market Test?" in *Independent Review* Winter VII.3 (2003): 399-422.

[77] Irving Fisher, "The Debt-Deflation Theory of Great Depressions." *Econometrica* 1.4 (1933): 337.

[78] Hülsmann makes the argument that debt deflation cycles promote long-term economic health by reorienting the structure of production along more sustainable monetary foundations: an economy structured purely on commodity money and credit, without fiduciary media. Jörg Guido Hülsmann, *Deflation and Liberty* (Auburn: Ludwig Von Mises Institute, 2008).

> Under a system of free banking, ...with no
> legal tender laws and gold as money, an
> additional constraint on potential bank
> fraud arises, for then every bank is faced
> with the existence of non-clients or clients
> of different banks. If in this situation
> additional counterfeit money is brought
> into circulation by a bank, it must
> invariably reckon with the fact that the
> money may end up in non-client's hands
> who demand immediate redemption,
> which the bank then would be unable to
> grant without at least a painful credit
> contraction. In fact, such a corrective
> contraction could only be avoided if the
> additional fiat money were to go
> exclusively into the cash reserves of the
> bank's own clients and were used by them
> exclusively for transactions with other
> clients. Yet since a bank would have no
> way of knowing whether or not such a
> specific outcome could be achieved, or
> how to achieve it, the threat of a following
> credit contraction would act as an
> inescapable economic deterrent to any
> bank fraud.[79]

A sophisticated critic may retort that banking cartels may form to help
circumvent this limitation. However, Hoppe addresses this as well:

> With no restrictions of entry in existence,
> any such bank cartel would have to be
> classified as voluntary and would suffer
> from the same problems as any voluntary
> cartel: Faced with the threat of non-
> cartelists and/or new entrants, and
> recognizing that like all cartel agreements,
> a banking cartel would favor the less
> efficient cartel members at the expense of
> the more efficient ones, there is simply no
> economic basis for successful action, and
> any attempt to cartelize would quickly

---

[79] Hoppe, ibid, 83.

break down as economically inefficient. Moreover, insofar as the counterfeit money would be employed to expand credit, banks acting in concert would set off a full-scale boom-bust cycle. This, too, would deter cartelization.[80]

The State's Involvement in Money and Central Banking

....the state's position regarding money and banking is obvious: Its objectives are served best by a pure fiat money monopolistically controlled by the state. For only then are all barriers to counterfeiting removed (short of an entire breakdown of the monetary system through hyperinflation) and the state can increase its own income and wealth at another's expense practically without cost and without having to fear bankruptcy.[81]

Before the state can reach its ultimate goal as stated by Professor Hoppe, it must first gain public support for its actions. The first step in the process of the State gaining ultimate control over money and banking is to establish legal tender laws which demand tax debts and private payments to be settled in units of a specified medium of exchange. Other institutions may still create gold or silver coins, or other private monies, however, the money produced by the State is mandated to be accepted by any creditor (lender) as repayment for debts. Taxes are also required to be paid in such legal tender, usually its own, designed fiat money. This gives the government issued money an artificial advantage over private monies as its perceived "acceptability" is increased through coercive mandate. Initially, the currency begins with promises of redemption into certain portions of gold or silver. However, the State and central bank will inevitably begin issuing extra, unbacked notes. The bank notes in such a scenario are identified by Mises as "fiduciary media." The consequence of producing fiduciary media is inflation, which favors the earlier receivers of this newly-printed, fiat money at the expense of the later receivers, triggering Cantillon effects. The early receivers tend to be government agencies themselves,

---

[80] Hoppe, ibid, fn. 18, 83.
[81] Hoppe, ibid, 89.

government contractors, large commercial banks, and major industrial leaders thus giving this class of society the incentive to support such fractional reserve practices. The government engages in these banking practices because doing so makes it far easier to finance its operations. In contrast to taxing or borrowing, inflating the currency achieves a far more covert pattern of wealth redistribution in the State's favor. John Maynard Keynes identified the benefit of inflation's obscurity when he remarked:

> Lenin is said to have declared that the best way to destroy the capitalist system was to debauch the currency. By a continuing process of inflation, governments can confiscate, secretly and unobserved, an important part of the wealth of their citizens. By this method they not only confiscate, but they confiscate arbitrarily; and, while the process impoverishes many, it actually enriches some. The sight of this arbitrary rearrangement of riches strikes not only at security but [also] at confidence in the equity of the existing distribution of wealth. ...Those to whom the system brings windfalls, beyond their deserts and even beyond their expectations or desires, become "profiteers," who are the object of the hatred of the bourgeoisie, whom the inflationism has impoverished, not less than of the proletariat. As the inflation proceeds and the real value of the currency fluctuates wildly from month to month, all permanent relations between debtors and creditors, which form the ultimate foundation of capitalism, become so utterly disordered as to be almost meaningless; and the process of wealth-getting degenerates into a gamble and a lottery. ...Lenin was certainly right. There is no subtler, no surer means of overturning the existing basis of society than to debauch the currency. The process engages all the hidden forces of economic law on the side of destruction, and does it in a manner which not one man in a million is able to diagnose.[82]

The institution that is used to mediate this process is the central bank. The central bank is sold to the public as a "lender of last resort" endowed with the purpose of eliminating the threat of bank runs as banks are now given the ability to borrow from the central bank whatever amount is needed to maintain immediate solvency. In addition to this role, the central bank is also responsible for setting monetary policy for the ostensible purpose of stabilizing the value of the money it issues as well as the growth of the economy. In the eyes of its proponents, the central bank is to be used to depress an "overheating" economy by taking measures to contract the money supply, as well as to stimulate the economy during times of low market activity by expanding the money supply through inflation. In practice, the central bank will almost always resort to inflationary procedures, and will seldom take measures to contract the amount of credit in the economy.

The central bank's *true* purposes are to finance government operations, cartelize the banking system, and win over support from the financial elite by allowing them access to newly created money before the rest of society, thus concentrating ever more wealth into the hands of a select privileged few at the artificial expense of the many. Wealth accrued in this way is destructive of the market process as it is achieved through expropriation and not the production and voluntary exchange of genuine goods and services. In order to mask its true purposes, the central bank will generally employ obscure and clandestine means to counterfeit money and expand credit. Of these means, the three most common are:

1) *Purchasing Government Securities* is the most direct way in which the central bank is able to finance government operations, i.e., by buying debt from it directly in the form of treasury bonds. To provide the funds to purchase government debt on the open market, the central bank will print or create the money out of thin air. It is able to acquire treasury bills without expending any resources of its own. This is modern alchemy and by its very nature counterfeiting, but what separates the central bank from any other unscrupulous counterfeiter is that the government has given it the exclusive legal privilege to perform these acts. In other words, the government has granted the central bank a monopoly over the production of legal tender. Because the central bank buys government debt with newly created money, all those holding the fiat money must tolerate a reduction in their purchasing power to finance the principal of this loan. Because only the central bank is

---

82 John Maynard Keynes, "Europe After the Treaty" in *The Economic Consequences of the Peace* (New York: Harcourt, Brace and Howe, 1919), 235-36.

permitted to counterfeit in such a way, it is able to reap the concentrated benefits of such an expropriating practice whereas all others in society are required to produce in order to make money. Thus, the central bank produces nothing but paper or digital entries, and in return receives real wealth.

2) *Setting Reserve Requirements* is another arm of conventional monetary policy. Unlike in a competitive banking scenario, commercial banks are now able to engage in fractional reserve practices with virtually no risk due to the oversight of the central bank. Any amount of money lent to commercial banks by the central bank is itself multiplied as commercial banks do not hold full reserves, but instead create additional credit from the deposit. Fractional reserve banking systems are, by their very nature, unstable. To combat the alleged evils of "wildcat banking," central banks will often require minimum reserves in the vaults of their commercial bank clients. To illustrate how a 10% reserve requirement would play out suppose the central bank deposits $1,000 in bank A, of which it is now able to lend $900. Let's assume that Jerry borrows this $900 and deposits it in bank B. His bank, due to the reserve requirements, may lend out $810 of those dollars. Once the $810 is lent out to Max, he'll deposit this money into bank C which will now be able to lend out $729 of his deposit. This process will continue until the original $1,000 deposited into bank A has turned into $10,000 of newly created credit now injected into the economy. The fractional-reserve tactics of commercial banks multiply the amount of money they receive from the central bank through its "discount window."

3) *Setting the Discount Rate* is another tool by which central banks use to expand the money supply. The discount rate is the interest rate by which various commercial banks may borrow money from the central bank during the "discount window." If the central bank decides there has been a significant disruption in the economy that has caused the banking system to experience a shortage of liquidity, it will allow the affected banks to borrow from its own holdings as a lender of last resort. Thus, the lower the central bank sets the discount rate, the more commercial banks will be encouraged to borrow. Once again, in order to acquire loanable funds, the central bank simply creates them from nothing. However, this fact in no way lessens the obligations for the borrowing banks to repay the loan in full with real wealth and savings plus interest. Once again, if depositors start withdrawing all their funds and a particular bank becomes insolvent, all it must do is take a "bank holiday" and borrow the discrepant amount of funds from the central bank, effectively eliminating the possibility of default. Fractional reserve

117

practices multiply this expansion of the monetary supply. Suppose the central bank sets the reserve requirement at ten percent, meaning, of all the demand deposits in a given bank's ledger, i.e., the sum of all the money in all of its clients' bank accounts, only ten percent of this needs to remain in the vault. Now, suppose Joey and Mark each deposit $500 in bank A leaving it with $1,000 on the books. Due to the reserve requirements set by the central bank and the promise of a bailout if it becomes insolvent, a moral hazard manifests which prompts the bank to lend out 900 of those demand deposit dollars. Economists call this a moral hazard, because if the bank were not guaranteed a government bailout in the case of insolvency, then it would operate much more conservatively. In other words, moral hazard occurs when one party assumes riskier behavior because others have promised to bear the costs for them.

Insofar as a market's currency is backed by a scarce commodity, there is a concrete limitation to a bank driven inflationary process. Initially, the central bank may, as was done in the United States by its central bank The Federal Reserve, require its member banks to deposit gold in its own vaults and issue the member banks receipts or notes in return. Though an expansion of credit is possible in such a system through fractional reserve banking, it is still ultimately constrained by the supply of gold specie. For example, the central bank may itself have to keep a set proportion of gold specie deposits made by its member banks in the vault due to reserve requirements. Thus, the gold would serve as the non-expanding and concrete base to this inflationary pyramid. However, as the circulation of notes becomes more normalized and the people tend to less and less associate gold with real money, the State will gradually debase the currency until the point where it becomes pure fiat, i.e., pure paper notes without redemption. Thus, when the central bank's issued paper notes become the new currency, there is no more physical limitation to inflation and by extension to its power over the economy. The United States is under such a pure fiat money system today, along with virtually the entire civilized world.

Austrian Business Cycle Theory

In addition to the redistribution of wealth from late to early comers, the above inflationary process precipitates artificially severe and economically destructive business cycles. Insofar as prices are distorted through central bank inflation, their utility as guides for rational economic calculation is diminished. In a free banking system, higher interest rates indicate that consumers as a whole have higher time preferences; they prefer to consume now as opposed to later despite the fact that foregoing said consumption may lead to an enhanced capacity to produce consumer goods in the future. Conversely, lower interest rates indicate that consumers have a lower time preference as a whole; they prefer to forgo consumption now so they may enjoy a greater amount and/or quality of goods at some future time. In the former case, where higher interest rates are predominate, entrepreneurs will tend to invest in comparatively less efficient and shorter production processes which correspond more appropriately with a prevailing high time preference on the part of consumers. In the latter case, where lower interest rates are predominate, entrepreneurs will tend to invest in more efficient and roundabout production processes that require a comparatively longer and/or greater degree of consumption forbearance in order for the consumer goods to manifest.

In a competitive economy, banks harmonize the profit motive of these entrepreneurs with prevailing consumer time preference (as indicated by the supply of available savings). As all savings in a 100% reserve banking or free banking system are *real* savings, they represent actual resources in the economy. When there are higher savings, this means there are more actual resources available to be employed in productive investment channels, thus, the low interest rates enables a larger amount of resources to be used for productive ends. Conversely, when there are lower savings, this implies there are fewer available unemployed resources present, and thus the higher interest rates ensure that these relatively scarcer resources will only be used by those entrepreneurs who project the return on their investments to be high enough to warrant paying such rates. It is in the banks' interest to only loan money out to borrowers that they expect to be capable of repayment at the designated time in the future, thus adding an additional mechanism to ensure that such resources are used efficiently. Furthermore, should these borrowers default on their debt obligations to the bank, this will be reflected on their credit which will deter lending institutions from loaning money to them in the future without adjusting their interest rates to account for the added default risk. It is in this way that competitive markets are able to efficiently and organically allocate scarce resources to their optimally productive ends.

In distinct contrast, the central bank's involvement in the economy produces an entirely different result. When new money is injected into the economy via open-market operations (bond purchases) and manipulation of reserve requirements and the discount rate, an illusion of greater savings is created, which, in turn, prompts greater levels of borrowing and investing. This artificial stimulation produces a temporary "boom" period where consumers have not changed their consumption habits and yet a simultaneous surge in investments takes place. So, at least for a while, it may be possible for one to have his cake and eat it too. This illusion of greater savings pushes down interest rates, which misleads entrepreneurs into thinking there are more available unemployed resources than actually exist. Incentivized by lowered interest rates, entrepreneurs begin to engage in longer term and/or more risky investment projects than they otherwise would. These investments then bid up the prices for labor, capital goods, and natural resources required for their completion. Because these entrepreneurs are acting in a way that is consistent with the illusion of a larger quantity of resources available than there actually are, not all of them will be able to finish their investment projects. The prices for the goods and labor will increase over their originally projected amount, requiring entrepreneurs to borrow more money than originally intended in order to complete their projects. Eventually, in order to prevent a full-blown currency crisis, the banks will cease lending out more money to all of these investors at the interest rate they are seeking thus forcing liquidation and the abandonment of their projects. This will create a ripple effect throughout the economy as the sudden decrease in demand for laborers and "early stage capital goods" in these projects generates even more losses. Such decrease in demand for labor will take the form of layoffs. The unemployed workers – who may have otherwise been actively used for more productive and sustainable ends – are now unable to produce for the period of time it takes to find new employment. The preceding investments made under the illusion of greater savings are what are known as "malinvestments." It is at this time that the malinvestments will have to be "liquidated," i.e., halted and their components sold off or freed up to be used by others willing to purchase and put them to more productive use, usually at a substantial loss to the entrepreneur. Mass unemployment and capital liquidation is recognized as the "bust" period in the business cycle.

As opposed to allowing this market correction or liquidation of malinvestment to occur, the central bank will often times inject even more money and credit into the economy, attempting to rebuild an uneven structure of production, prolonging the boom, and setting the stage for an even more severe bust in the future. In the long run, this is much more wasteful than allowing the banking system to operate organically, as many hours of labor and resources are used up during the boom cycle that are ultimately destined for bust which could have instead been used for more productive and sustainable ends. Additionally, more labor, time, and resources will be used to "liquidate" these projects so that their component resources may be freed up for use elsewhere (an expenditure only made necessary by central bank interference). Hoppe summarizes this process:

> Yet in addition, this time a boom-bust cycle is also set in motion: Placed at a lowered interest rate, the newly granted credit causes increased investments and

initially creates a boom that cannot be distinguished from an economic expansion; however, this boom must turn bust because the credit that stimulated it does not represent real savings but instead was created out of thin air. Hence, with the entire new and expanded investment structure under way, a lack of capital must arise that makes the successful completion of all investment projects systematically impossible and instead requires a contraction with a liquidation of previous malinvestments.[83]

In truth, the only thing that must be done to ensure a tendency toward efficient and ethical banking systems is to ground the legal system in the private property ethic. This naturally entails abolishing the State and allowing the organic governance of the free market to reign. The spontaneous order that is derived from this bottom-up approach produces greater harmony between self and societal interests than any central planner could possibly achieve.

---

[83] Hoppe, ibid, 82.

Chapter Five

MONOPOLIES AND CARTELS

THE NOTION OF a "freed market" or an "unhampered market" is a conception of a market operating quickly, spontaneously, and unpredictably. It is a market where every person can negotiate the terms of every exchange he makes and fully owns every good he intends to trade. It is a system of maximally free trade. Taxes, tariffs, quotas, price restrictions, mandated licensure, labor regulation, and intellectual property never exist in this market. Everyone is free to copy and remix others' work, acquire cheaper materials, and produce a good in any industry. With the absence of aggressive barriers to entry into any industry, competition becomes fierce and unrelenting. Without occupational licensing or securities regulations or taxes by which to abide, even small discrepancies in customer satisfaction can allow newcomers to instantly topple an established giant. Operations that produced the same service indefinitely would be rare and unsuccessful. These dynamic markets organically emerge from the free, spontaneous interplay of people.

This environment is vastly different from what exists today, thus one must relieve himself of prejudice generated by his experience of the current reality if he wishes to fully comprehend the contrasting merits of truly freed markets. The salient characteristic of such markets is the absence of systemic aggression. Such aggression is what enables consumer and worker exploitation, and is indeed worthy of vigorous opposition. Surprisingly, the most powerful and destructive perpetrator of systemic aggression is the State itself. To mask this ugly truth, the State has cleverly disguised itself as the protector of the weak, poor, indigent, and disenfranchised. Moreover, it claims to be a *necessary*, if not sufficient, institution to carry out this purported role. To complete this deception, the State and its sympathizers have taken great strides to indict the unfettered market as the primary culprit of the commoner's tribulations, though the truth is quite the contrary. One manner in which the State inflicts great harm upon us is by its manipulation of competitive markets.

MONOPOLIES AND CARTELS

Competition

In a free market, *all* businesses are competing for consumer patronage. Competition exists between all firms in every industry. For example, one who sells ice cream competes not only with Ben and Jerry's, but also with movie theaters, as one can always choose not to purchase ice cream and instead attend the movies.

This is the true meaning of cost: the foregone next most-favored course of action. Should one choose to spend the afternoon having a sundae at an ice cream parlor, he cannot also spend it at the cinema. One cannot be at both places at the same time. Hence, the price and attractiveness of the movie is relevant to one's decision when choosing to buy ice cream, not merely the price and attractiveness of the ice cream. There are two types of competition: active and potential. Active competition is the businesses or competitors that actually exist today. Potential competition, on the other hand, consists of those businesses or competitors which may manifest should a given business' services or products satisfy consumer demands less and less.

Defining Monopoly

There is much confusion over what constitutes a monopoly. A common definition of monopoly is "a firm that is the single provider of a particular good or service." This definition, however, is useless for a number of reasons. Defining a monopoly as a single provider implies the smallest differentiation of a product or service could, in turn, bestow upon the creator a monopoly over its provision. For example, Jackie may have a monopoly on purple polka dotted peppermints or Joe on magnolia-flavored popsicles. Even with regards to homogeneous goods such as wheat, one could still hold a monopoly on "Robinson Wheat" and Joe could hold a monopoly on "Joe Wheat," as the wheat produced could be differentiated by how it was grown, what fertilizers or nutrients were added, etc. This definition of monopoly does not yield us any pertinent or useful economic information as it virtually renders everyone a monopolist. Nobody else can offer the unique labor contributions of other people; we are all monopolizing our skillsets.

The term "monopoly" itself evokes negative feelings, but to what did the term "monopoly" originally refer? A monopoly originally meant an exclusive privilege to produce or sell a given product or service, granted by the King. It was a privilege given to favored producers or guilds for them to produce without any competition. Should any upstart break from the privilege, the King's might would be summoned. Thus, a monopoly is a creation of the State. Murray Rothbard explains:

> Monopoly is a *grant of special privilege by the State, reserving a certain area of production to one particular individual or group.* Entry into the field is prohibited to others and this prohibition is enforced by the gendarmes of the State.[84]

Using this definition, consumers are justified in opposing monopolies as they imply the threat or use of aggression to uphold and maintain, and therefore constitute a distortion of natural market dynamics. Without the Statist apparatus of compulsion, there could be no special grants given to certain businesses. Free entry is the default condition for all industries, and, as such, monopolies created by the power of the State *could not exist in a truly free market.*

Natural Monopoly

In the words of Thomas Di Lorenzo:

> A natural monopoly [a single service provider] is said to occur when production technology, such as relatively high fixed costs, causes long-run average total costs to decline as output expands. In such industries, the theory goes, a single producer will eventually be able to produce at a lower cost than any two other producers, thereby creating a 'natural' monopoly. Higher prices will result if more than one producer supplies the market.[85]

Some commonly cited examples of these "natural monopolies" include utility providers such as gas, water, or electricity companies. The

---

[84] Murray N. Rothbard, "Monopoly and Competition" in *Man, Economy, and State: A Treatise on Economic Principles ; with Power and Market: Government and the Economy* (Auburn: Ludwig Von Mises Institute, 2009), 669.

[85] Thomas J. Dilorenzo, "The Myth of Natural Monopoly" in *The Review of Austrian Economics* 9.2 (1996): 43-58.

concern regarding the manifestation of such "monopolies" is that they may charge exorbitant prices with economic impunity. Should they take advantage of their position, however, there always exists potential competition which may serve to temper their behavior. For the sake of argument, however, let us assume that a single provider of a given good or service does arise. As the absence of aggressive barriers to entry into any industry is inherent in free markets, the threat of a potential competitor will be much stronger relative to the case in which the State imposes artificial barriers, and sometimes even prohibitions, on competition in various industries.

Let's entertain the worst case scenario: A water company decides to triple its rates without a corresponding increase in the cost of production, how do market participants respond? In the first place, future, potential customers would be deterred from moving to this town due to these exorbitant rates, and current residents are incentivized to move elsewhere. This would, of course, result in a loss of business for the water company. Moreover, the consumer will be incentivized to act more conservatively with his water. Perhaps husbands and wives will take showers together, decrease how often they water the lawn, or install rainwater collectors in their backyard. How the conservation is accomplished is irrelevant. Less water will be used, and a decrease in the usage of water translates into a decrease of revenue for the water company. Worse yet, even if the water company decides to revert back to its original rates, its customers may have grown fond of these water conservation efforts and continue their practices nonetheless, thereby permanently lowering the income of this water company. However, if the water company maintains these exorbitant prices despite the preceding events, then a competing water company from the next town over may decide to move in and start operations if the benefit of an alternate provider outweighed the costs and inefficiencies of establishing redundant infrastructure. If, in response to the presence of a new competitor, the old water company decides to return to its lower rates, the customers' trust in it will have nevertheless been undermined. Consumers may choose to switch over their services to the new water company even if it does charge marginally higher prices, so long as it can demonstrate a long history of stable and predictable prices. Furthermore, a common practice before developing any land in an area is to make contractual agreements with surrounding utility companies regarding fixed pricing. This type of reassurance will incentivize prospective developers to build homes and businesses on this land. Finally, for a water or electric company to have achieved a "monopoly" status in the first place, it would have first been required to gain the trust of their customers and to have provided a more satisfying service than their actual or potential competitors. The likelihood of this company fundamentally changing business practices that made it successful in the first place is relatively low. This is all, of course, speculative to some degree, but hopefully the hypothetical may demonstrate the means by which men and women in the market may effectively deter, prevent, and mitigate all activity that is harmful to the consumer. This same line of reasoning may be applied to any other firm that enjoys a large share of a given industry.

Cartels

A cartel is a group of individual firms in like-industries which decide to coordinate their practices as a means to maximize profits. These coordinating efforts can take the form of setting production quotas or "fixing" prices. From this definition, one may surmise a few inherent weaknesses of a cartel and why such an arrangement, if intended to secure extra profit by maintaining prices above the market rate, is almost assured to be temporary and tenuous in a purely free market.

The first and most obvious complication in any cartel is determining unanimously amongst the individual members exactly where the prices for their goods or services should be set and/or how much each member firm should be permitted to produce. Of course, the more efficient members are likely to be the most uneasy about such an arrangement as they would likely resist any restrictions on their own production for the sake of the less efficient member firms. Thus, at the soonest feasible opportunity, it is likely that these more efficient members will emancipate themselves from the cartel. Further, under such an arrangement, all the members will be tempted to "cheat" by either lowering their agreed upon prices or increasing their agreed upon production as a means to secure a larger share of the market outside of officially established lines. Finally, even assuming a cartel is able to successfully coordinate the actions of its members and to reconcile all of their disparate interests, there would still be the issue of potential outside competition. The main purpose of a cartel is to coordinate with other firms in the same industry so as to generate greater revenue for their services than they could otherwise earn. However, the higher the prices – or the lower the production limit the cartel sets for its members – the more vulnerable the cartel becomes to outside competition undercutting the cartel's prices and taking away its valuable customers.

The difficulties of coordinating efforts among independent firms, combined with the potential for outside competition, renders the consumer-unfriendly cartel an unlikely market arrangement. It is important to remember that cartels today do operate outside market forces in an exploitative capacity, but they are only able to do so by purchasing and acquiring influence over the State. Only through the application of State-mandated price ceilings, price floors, regulations, occupational licensure, minimum wages, taxes, and even explicit grants of monopoly over certain industries, can a given firm or cartel exploit the consumer. Exploitation of the consumer only exists in this arrangement because the State is able to insulate a given business from market forces via legislation. Conversely, in a purely free market, the survival of these businesses would be predicated on how well they could satisfy the desires of the consumer relative to existing and potential competition. Where there is choice and an absence of coercive barriers to entry, there can be no exploitation. Finally, there are no rights violations associated with cartelization, as it merely represents the pooling of resources on an inter-company scale. Having property rights over resources entails the right to pool them with the resources of others in a voluntary manner.

Cartel Production Restriction

One danger often pointed out as being possible in an unfettered market is the act of a cartel restricting production as a means to keep the price of a given good higher than it otherwise would be. The critics of this method are correct insofar as the purpose is concerned: to maximize profits. However, this is no different than any other market activity.

Take rice, for example. If a cartel of rice producers in combination creates two hundred tons of rice in a year, but comes to learn that one hundred tons would yield the greatest profit, then it will naturally begin to release only one hundred tons of rice into the market. This sort of "collusion" is deemed as predatory by many mainstream economists, for had the cartel released all two hundred tons, presumably the larger supply would have translated into lower prices per unit for the consumer, leaving him ostensibly better off than had the cartel restricted their production to one hundred tons.

If one hundred tons is more profitable, the rice producers will decrease their production in the future accordingly. The materials and/or labor required to produce two hundred tons will exceed the materials and/or labor required to make the one hundred tons. The excess resources will now be freed up and available for use in the production of other demanded goods or services. The influx of these additional resources being funneled into more valuable sectors of the economy, all other things equal, will cause a rise in the overall standard of living. Therefore, on *net* there is no restriction of production. In fact, the act of the rice cartel reducing its overall output will have resulted in a *greater* net production of wealth, as this would permit the excess resources to be allocated to more profitable ends. This same line of reasoning is equally applicable to a single large firm which decides to lower its production.

A SPONTANEOUS ORDER

Potential Benefits of Mergers or Cartelization

It should be noted that large firms or cartels in freed markets are likely to yield a positive effect for the consumer, otherwise they would either dissolve or be out-competed by more agile newcomers. One major benefit to consumers is due to economies of scale. This is the principle that suggests that with more resources and capital goods at one's disposal, the easier it becomes to maximize the efficiency of productive output.

This is true for a number of reasons, the first of which is the possibility of bulk purchasing. Typically, buying in bulk yields a lower price per unit of whatever it is being bought, because the seller of said bulk good is typically happier with a larger guaranteed purchase at a lower price than he is with taking the risk and the extra time of making more sales of smaller quantities at higher prices. Moreover, the larger the firm, the more it is able to benefit from the division of labor, specialized machinery, lower overhead costs per unit of output, advertising, access to cheaper credit, established lines of transportation and logistics, etc.

Further, with access to greater amounts of capital, a cartel or recently-merged firm can afford to invest in more productive capital goods which were once prohibitively expensive. Once this firm is able to enjoy the benefits of greater production afforded by the newly acquired capital goods, the employees will in turn be able to produce more with the same amount of resources, increasing their labor productivity. This would create the tendency to command higher wages for employees and/or to offer the consumer lower prices without negatively affecting one's profit margin.

The difficulty for any one person to enter into a given industry is diminished insofar as the current provider(s) are not sufficiently satisfying consumer demands, by either producing faulty (or undesired) products/services or by charging prices that are "too high." If this is the case, there will be a large demand for an alternative. If the number of unsatisfied consumers becomes substantial, it would become clear that an alternate provider could make a great deal of money and potentially take many customers from the incompetent, ossified firms.

To overcome the difficulties of breaking into established markets, an entrepreneur who has a spectacular and compelling business model may seek "venture capital." There are many wealthy investors who are looking for ways to earn a positive yield as opposed to having financial capital sit idle. In such an environment, investing in an entrepreneur with a solid business plan could prove to be an enticing and lucrative option. Alternatively, an entrepreneur may take out loans or sell shares of his company as a means to raise the funds required for its creation.

In many cases, entrepreneurs are competing with the current incompetent firm or cartel in the same industry. However, it may very well be the case that the overall dissatisfaction of how this product or service is being offered would generate an impetus for someone to invent a technology that renders it obsolete. For instance, the invention of a hydro-powered hover car may render fossil fuel-based automobiles obsolete due to lower maintenance costs, cheaper fuel, and shorter transit times.

Technological developments, however, do not necessarily have to be in the form of different products which make the former obsolete. They could very well be developments that permit alternate means of production which prove to be far cheaper. There are truly a myriad of ways in which one may take on an incompetent firm in a capital-intensive industry. In a free market where there are no aggressive barriers to entry in any industry, the threat of economic exploitation via business practices is virtually nil. In fact, it is complete economic liberty that is the greatest defense against exploitation and predation. Take, for example, the notion of "predatory" price cutting. The idea that any form of price cutting could be "predatory" is absurd from the start, because it implies that some sort of injustice can be committed by a firm deciding to lower the prices of its goods or services relative to its competitors. The owner of any given good, or the provider of any service, has a right to charge whatever price he wants for whatever it is he is selling, and likewise the consumer has the right to either purchase or not purchase whatever is being sold.

The common claim is that a large firm will take advantage of its economies of scale and lower its prices to a level that its smaller competitors cannot afford to maintain, thereby running them out of business. This "cutthroat" firm will then proceed to raise its own prices to exorbitant levels that were previously tempered by the presence of competitive forces. Without State support of monopoly privileges, however, there is always competition, whether between firms in other industries or from potential future competition. It is never possible to price one's goods or services without taking into consideration, at the very least, the potential of future competing producers being attracted by higher selling prices.

Furthermore, the smaller businesses who can't afford to sell their goods or services at such a low price, even temporarily, could cease operations and buy up its competitors' now cheap goods. A smaller firm could then sit on the inventory until the larger firm decides to raise its prices back to normal levels, thus defeating the purpose of starving the small firms. This "predatory price cutting" would also allow the consumer, at least temporarily, to enjoy a discount bonanza. The money the consumer saves could then be used to satisfy various other desires, increasing his standard of living. This large "predatory" firm would, in the long run, be shooting itself in the foot by using such a foolish method to attempt to secure a greater share of the market. Moreover, even if the firm is able to offer these prices without suffering any losses then so much the better. The other businesses which fail and liquidate will free up resources to be used by more efficient firms, in either the same or a different industry. Once again, the result of this would be an overall increase in the standard of living for all consumers.

The State as Ultimate Monopoly

Anyone who would advocate for State intervention as a means to break-up and prevent the formation of monopolies (whether defined as "single provider" or "exclusive privilege") would be caught in a contradiction, as the State itself is the greatest and most exploitative monopoly of all.

The State has a legal monopoly on the right to use aggression against others in the form of taxation and compulsory edicts (legislation). Not only must "customers" pay into its operation without regard to their consent, but they must surrender to the rules its internal processes determine at all times. Additionally, the State has a monopoly on the provision of security, and has anointed itself as the ultimate arbiter in all conflicts, including those conflicts which involve its own agents. It maintains this monopoly by the threat and application of aggressive force, and thus meets Rothbard's criteria for monopoly.

Agents of the State are motivated by profit and self-interest just like any given businessman. However, what separates the businessman from the State is that the former has to persuade you to pay for whatever is being offered, whereas the latter *demands* its citizens pay for its "services," and unilaterally alters the price and scope of the "services" offered. Moreover, if payment towards an institution (the State) is guaranteed, then its services will tend to diminish in quality and increase in cost. The only thing that tempers the power of the State is its need to maintain perceived legitimacy. Thus, if one's aim is to eliminate systemic, monopoly exploitation, then the perceived legitimacy of the State must be undermined. Various means may be employed to this end, including widespread education, social outreach, peaceful parenting, the development of the counter-economy, the use of strong encryption, and the formation of free enclaves outside the grip of the State.

Chapter Six

INSURANCE

IN A FREE market society, insurance may play a central role in the operation of many services ranging from security, title dispute resolution, the alleviation of the devastating effects of natural disasters, and more. However, there is a large amount of misconception present in the current environment as to the nature and proper scope of insurable events due to massive interference and misinformation propagated by the State. This chapter will focus on the general nature of insurance, and its corresponding power and limitation in free markets. With this insight, it will become markedly easier to understand exactly how other services may be feasibly provided by individual actors, through the use of insurance, in a free market. A natural starting point for this topic will be to examine the nature of insurance itself. Hoppe describes the incentives each person faces in an insurance pool:

> Any insurance involves the pooling of individual risks. Under this arrangement, there are winners and losers. Some of the insured will receive more than they paid in premiums and some will pay more into the system than they ever get back. This is a form of income redistribution from the healthy to the sick, but the characteristic mark of insurance is that no one knows in advance who the winners and losers will be. They are distributed randomly or unpredictably, and the resulting income redistribution within a pool of insured people is unsystematic. If this were not the case — if it were possible to predict the net winners and losers — the insurance losers would not want to pool their risk with the insurance winners; they would seek to pool their risk with other "losers" at lower premiums.

... Now even if the insured themselves do not recognize that there are systematically predictable winners and losers, free competition in the insurance market would eliminate all systematic redistribution among the insured. In a free market, any insurance company that engaged in any systematic income redistribution (mixing people with objectively different types of risks into one single group) would be out-competed by any company that did not engage in this type of practice. Another insurance company might realize that there are people who sit behind desks and rarely fall off their chair and injure themselves. They would recognize that they could profitably offer a lower premium to desk jockeys and insure them in a separate pool from the professional athletes. And by offering lower premiums, they would of course lure away those people who had previously been mis-insured. As a result, the various companies that had mis-grouped people (by mixing their low-risk clients in the same pool with their high-risk clients) would have to raise the premiums for their higher-risk clients to their naturally higher level.[86]

"Winners" and "losers" in this context simply refers to those clients who received more (winners) or less (losers) in reimbursements than he/she paid into the system. This should not be confused with someone who comes down with cancer which his insurance covers as being a winner in the general sense of the term. Furthermore, when Hoppe references income redistribution from the "healthy" to the "sick," he is referring to those who didn't experience the occurrence of a covered risk to those who did. This clarification may seem obvious. It is important, however, to make clear that the above description applies to all forms of insurance. The most efficient way to pool clients, given the goal of insurance is to bear risk, is by grouping together those who have like or homogeneous risks (at least to the extent of which may be objectively determined). If clients with different or

---

[86] Hans-Hermann Hoppe, "The Economics of Risk and Insurance" (lecture presented at the annual Mises University, Auburn, Alabama, July 2001.

heterogeneous risks were to be pooled together, then the less at-risk clients would be effectively subsidizing the more at-risk clients in the form of higher premiums. As a consequence, these lower at-risk clients would be incentivized to relieve themselves of this coverage in the pursuit of a company that charged premiums which corresponded more closely to the actual risk they present. Finally, for a risk to be "insurable" at all, one must be *unable* to predict with relative certainty those clients who will be "winners" or "losers" as defined above. If the winners or losers were able to be identified in such a way, then insurance companies would likely refuse to insure the would be "winners" and the would be "losers" would likewise refuse to purchase insurance.

A delicate balance is sought in the insurance industry, where the upper limit of what may be charged is tempered by the presence of other competitive industries willing to lower their premiums offered, and the lower limit is tempered by the desire to avoid negative cash flows, or losses. To more effectively determine optimal pricing at any given point in time, insurance firms will be compelled to engage in continual in-depth research regarding the field covered. Determining the premiums for natural disaster occurrence, for instance, will largely be based upon a given client's geographical residence. In order to determine a price figure for this client, the insurance agency in question will have to invest in research that reveals the risk of such an event occurring in the proximity of the client's residence. Naturally, those companies that attain more accurate data on such risks will be at a relative advantage to their competitors as such information will reveal more precisely the potential risk and frequency of its payouts to clients. This information will allow an insurance agency to ascertain the "lower limit" of what it is willing to charge its clients with greater precision.

The incentives mentioned above will drive these insurance companies to determine ever more refined groupings and sub-groupings for their clients. This process of discrimination will likely be based off of objectively verifiable criteria and not subjective bigoted prejudice – as the former will result in greater market share and profits and the latter in a loss of market share and losses. In other words, if a company uses poor data (or unverifiable prejudice) to determine prices, it will either overcharge for its services driving clients away to lower cost alternatives or undercharge relative to actual risks, resulting in losses, which will either cause the company to alter its practices or go broke, thereby freeing up the resources it once commanded to more efficient and profitable firms in the marketplace.

Risk and Uncertainty

Risk and uncertainty are categorically different phenomena. Risk refers to a chance occurrence in a knowable long-run probability distribution. Uncertainty refers to a chance occurrence in which no information regarding probability is known. Mises introduces the terms "class probability" and "case probability" to refer to measuring the probability of repeatable events and unique events, respectively. Those events whose approximate likelihood can be known from repeated testing, such as the odds of a coin flip, can be mitigated by the use of insurance. The likelihood of one's property catching fire can be predicted on the basis of long-run frequency distributions and thus, by acquiring insurance, one can defend himself from the consequence of a fire. It is only possible to determine risks for classes of people or events, but not for singular events or people. Mises affirms this point "We know or assume to know, with regard to the problem concerned, everything about the behavior of a whole class of events or phenomena; but about the actual singular events or phenomena we know nothing but that they are elements of this class."[87] The danger presented to someone without insurance is quantifiable; the risk of one's property catching fire in the future can be extrapolated from the whole set of past fires. Because the probability of one's house catching fire is determinable, it is considered a member of "class probability."

Conversely, those events whose probability cannot be determined by any past outcomes are uncertainties, and have no determinable probability of occurrence. Suppose Billy the Kid and Jesse James enter into a duel. In such a case, it would be impossible to determine the probability of a given outcome, as each of their prior duels would have involved a unique context and environment. For instance, their prior opponents may have had different skill sets, felt ill, carried a different fire arm, or maintained it differently. Perhaps the humidity was higher, the sun brighter; there may have been a distracting member in the audience, either The Kid or James may harbor emotional attitudes about each other, perhaps the landscape offers greater/lesser cover, etc. All of these contingencies affect the circumstances of the current duel, and it would thus not be an approximate replica of past duels. The outcome of a duel is uncertain, not risky. Risky implies knowledge of the probability of occurrence. Other uncertain events include the presidential election of 1944, the performance of athletes, the creation of art, the emergence of social movements and revolutions, entrepreneurial activities, and many more. These events have uncertain outcomes as they all occur within heterogeneous circumstances. These are not insurable events. The best way to prepare for such

---

[87]   Mises, "Class Probability" in *Human Action*, 107.

uncertainties is to accrue savings in the form of money. This is because money, in contrast to any other good, allows its holder to acquire the maximum amount of uncertain goods at uncertain times/locations in the future. Should one of our duelists take on injuries, it would be far easier for him to acquire medical care by paying the asking monetary price, as opposed to attempting to barter for it.

Events that fall within the category of "class probability" are those which are known to occur at relatively constant frequencies within a given set of parameters. An example of an event that falls into the category of class probability is coin flipping. The circumstances behind coin flips are approximately the same, and it has been demonstrated through repeated testing that the odds of a given coin falling on heads or tails is 50/50. In other words, because fair coin flips are nearly identical, one may extrapolate the probability of an outcome for a particular coin flip based on trends observed from the results of numerous past coin flips. Another example of a repeatable event is a lottery. One knows from the outset that there *will* be a lottery winner, however this knowledge does not reveal to him *whom the particular winner will be.* Thus, because it is known that there will be only one winner of a lottery, the likelihood that any one person may be the winner can be appraised and quantified based on the proportionate amount of tickets he purchases with the total number of tickets available. The ability to appraise and quantify the risk of such an event occurring, along with the inability to definitively determine who the particular winner will be, renders it viably insurable.

If it were possible to determine or predict the occurrence of a particular event with a high degree of certainty, then insurance would be unnecessary. Insurance is only valuable insofar as the various particular occurrences of events are unable to be predicted with relative certainty. If an insurance company were to attempt to cover a highly predictable occurrence, then the presence of competition in the insurance market would render coverage for the event unprofitable. In such a situation, it would be cheaper for one to save up money oneself, as the insurance company would not be willing to charge less than what it knows it would have to pay out in the future. In addition, it would also have to charge more to cover its operating costs, rendering its service more expensive than merely saving up for this impending disaster oneself. An example of something an insurance company may be unwilling to cover is the purchasing of glasses, contacts, or laser eye surgery for a client who is known to have deficient eyesight prior to being covered. The insurance company would understand that it is highly likely that this client would need to purchase some good or service which treats deficient vision. Thus, in order to be profitable, the rate the agency would have to charge for this coverage would cost the prospective client more than if he just purchased said good or service directly. Mises clarifies the strict distinctions between classes and members of a class:

> We have a complete table of mortality for a definite period of the past in a definite area. If we assume that with regard to mortality no changes will occur, we may say that we know everything about the mortality of the whole population in question. But with regard to the life expectancy of the individuals we do not know anything but that they are members of this class of people.[88]

In addition to the characteristic of a particular event being highly predictable, another condition that renders a particular event "uninsurable" is whether or not its occurrence can be largely affected by the prospective client's individual actions. In other words, if one is able to affect the risk of an event transpiring through his deliberate behavior, then this event is not one for which insurance can be taken out. Hoppe elaborates:

> Every risk that may be influenced by one's actions is therefore uninsurable; only what is not controllable through individual actions is insurable, and only if there are long-run frequency distributions. And it also holds that if something that was initially not controllable becomes controllable then it would lose its insurability status. With respect to the risk of a natural disaster — floods, hurricanes, earthquakes, fires — insurance is obviously possible. These events are out of an individual's control, and I know nothing about my individual risk except whether or not I am a member of a group that is, *as a group*, exposed to a certain flood or earthquake or fire risk.[89]

Imagine a scenario involving Florida coast customers purchasing hurricane insurance. Obviously, their choice to live near coastal areas will be reflected in the premiums they pay. This is because the insurance company groups one with others who live in similar proximities to the coast and who

---

[88]   Mises, ibid, 107-108.
[89]   Hoppe, "The Economics of Risk and Insurance," 2001.

have had similar frequencies in the past of being hit by hurricanes (or grouped with others who have similar overall risks to be hit by hurricanes as determined by relevant meteorological or geographical criteria). Relative to the other members in the insurance pool, one's individual actions will not increase or decrease the chance of being hit by a hurricane. The insurance company will likely assess what measures one has taken to defend against such damage. For instance, they may offer lower premiums in exchange for the construction of twenty-foot walls around one's residence. Such actions will be what are used to determine pooling, and, in turn, what premiums one will be charged. Any additional risks taken by subsequent actions not considered in the risk appraisal will likely not be covered by the insurance agency. That is to say, individual behaviors or actions not expressed to the insurance agency when it appraises your risk fall into the realm of personal or individual responsibility, of which the insurance company has no part.

An example of something that is undeniably uninsurable is committing aggression. Any given person is fully in control of whether or not he/she decides to *initiate* uninvited physical force against another and, as such, no insurance can be taken out for this action. An insurance agency which attempted to insure clients against the risk they will commit aggression will soon go broke as clients will be incentivized to engage in aggression deliberately for the sake of receiving insurance payouts. This should make clear the financial untenability of offering insurance against those risks which are largely within one's control.

Any insurance company who refuses to pay out for covered claims would be considered fraudulent if they are truly in breach of contract. Should they be found in breach of contract, then the matter may be handled via private arbitration. The arbitration agency used and the process taken for any perceived breach in contract will likely be agreed upon by the client and insurance agency in their service contract. As most people are concerned with the threat of not being indemnified, they would likely prefer those insurance agencies which accounted for such contingencies as opposed to those who did not account for them. As a consequence, the former insurance agencies, all other things equal, would tend to drive the latter ones out of business, if not cause them to change their own policies accordingly. However, even absent any legal rulings, if a given insurance agency develops a reputation for not granting payouts to its clients, they will quickly lose business to eager competitors with more attractive offers. Of course, it would also be in their competitor's best interest to maintain watch over this type of foul play so as to absorb any disgruntled clients.

Unfortunately, in today's environment, the utility and cost of insurance is greatly skewed against the consumer's favor by State interference taking the form of regulations, taxes, minimum coverage requirements, and prohibitions against various types of discrimination – up to and including pre-existing conditions in the health insurance markets.

Regulations and licenses serve as aggressive barriers to entry into various industries, resulting in decreased competition, higher prices, and less availability. Mandated coverage requirements force many to buy more than what they need, neglecting what those resources could have serviced if they were tailored to one's personal situation.

The preceding analysis is simply meant to be an evaluation of what types of insurance practices will be financially viable in a free market and which ones will not. There is no question that any insurance company may offer coverage for anything it deems appropriate, to include insurance against suicide or self-inflicted arson; it's just likely that such practices will result in huge losses in revenue and business to their more sensible competitors. Thus, the true scope of that which may be covered efficiently and to what extent will ultimately be revealed by the market place in the varying degrees of profits and losses. Remember, profits earned without aggression or legal favoritism represent value added to society, as they require an entrepreneur to combine certain inputs in such a way that they are worth more together than they are separately. We may rely upon such businessmen to work in pursuit of providing value to society as a whole, for achieving this end results in their greatest personal gain. The market place reveals the illusion of the personal gain/social gain dichotomy and instead serves to align the two, the only assumption being that man acts towards his own interests. As for those who do not add such value, their command over resources will be diminished in the form of losses and be increasingly transferred to those who use them in such a way that values society the most (as measured by profits). This is the way in which markets perpetually equilibrate in light of the ever changing advancements in technology, consumer demand, and the supplies of various goods so as to allocate all scarce resources in a manner most favorable to both our long and short term interests.

Chapter Seven

HEALTH CARE

UNDOUBTEDLY, THE PRESERVATION and furtherance of one's life ranks as one of the most potent driving forces of man. Many individuals cite the paramount importance of health care as the reason that its provision should be generously supported or completely provided by the State. However, this reasoning seems peculiar, because the more fundamental human needs for food, water, and shelter are largely provided by free market forces.[90] As in all other industries, however, the free market provision of medical care is not only more ethical, but also more effective at providing more accessible and higher quality treatment than any state-regulated or provided health care service.

In contrast to today's environment, health insurance in freed markets will likely play a much smaller role. This is due to the economic considerations discussed in the previous chapter. Hoppe provides some relevant commentary:

> The first thing we can say is that sickness is insurable only insofar as the health risk for a particular group is purely accidental. Such is the case with certain forms of accident insurance, or even for events such as cancer. But for most health risks, we would have to say that they fall into the province of individual control, and very little in this field is actually insurable. Such risks must be assumed individually and must be paid for out of individual savings.[91]

In other words, insurance is most effective when it can group a class of individuals who all share common levels of risk and whose coverage extends to those events which are largely unforeseeable and random in their occurrence. Thus, health risks which are largely in one's

---

[90] Of course, there are subsidies, regulations, and taxes present in those fields as well, but by comparison the State's intervention is much smaller in these industries

[91] Hoppe, "The Economics of Risk and Insurance"

control are not "insurable" as they are neither unforeseeable nor random in occurrence. If the occurrence of a particular event may be systematically predicted, then any attempt to cover this would undermine the purpose of insurance. That is to say, insurance is intended to act as a sort of lottery in the sense that each of its individual clients are largely uncertain in advance regarding the degree to which they will have insurable damages to claim. However, they realize if such an insured event occurred, they may not have the funds available to pay for the resulting damage. Thus, they may choose to purchase coverage as a means to protect them from this risk.

In the case where a largely foreseeable health risk was covered, many of the predictably affected individuals would buy into the insurance just prior to the occurrence of the covered risk. Conversely, most of those who would predictably be unaffected by such an event would abstain from buying insurance. Any insurer of largely foreseeable events will attract those whom expect to profit and, at the same time, detract those whom expect to lose from the arrangement. Insurance operations cannot perform under such conditions. Their business is risk management; they act, not only as a shield against damages, but to exchange unpredictable and dangerous risks for predictable, monetary payments. Without virtually unforeseeable risks, insurance serves no viable purpose.

Finally, it seems plausible that to become eligible for high-quality health care coverage in a free market, one would likely be required to submit to certain behavioral standards. In the case of automobile insurance, rules for entry may require that seat belts are worn and that drivers travel under a certain speed if they are to receive reimbursements for the treatment of injuries caused by collision. Various rules of these organizations may be amenable to clients as their observance will result in smaller payments, due to lessened risks. Additionally, such insurance may require its clients to receive a certain number of health exams a year, so as to detect and treat health risks early, when they are comparatively cheaper to treat and serve to prevent future, more expensive procedures.[92] In this way, the insurance agency's profit interests are aligned with its client's interests to be secure from the overwhelming costs of future unforeseeable medical procedures. In other words, preventing covered medical risks from occurring at all will be the greatest contributing factor to the profitability of a given insurance agency's services.

In today's State managed environment, minimum mandated coverage requires many clients to pay for unwanted or unneeded coverage, thus driving up the cost of such insurance provision altogether. On top of

---

[92] The checkups or health exams will likely be paid for by the client out of pocket, but will *not* be covered under his insurance. It may be the case that the agency would offer the purchase of these services through its own channels, but again this *foreseeable* service will be offered as a separate item distinct from insurance coverage precisely because it is *foreseeable* and therefore not viably insurable.

this, much of this mandated coverage includes risks which should not be insurable such as alcoholism, drug addiction, and the subsidization of predictable, routine checkups. These ailments are often self-inflicted or, in the case of pre-existing conditions, are clearly foreseeable. The willpower to resist submission to alcoholism and drug addiction is fully within man's capability. However, only those risks which are both unpredictable and largely beyond the client's control may be viably insured. Moreover, laws prohibiting discrimination amongst clientèle regarding preexisting conditions cause insurance agencies to inevitably pool higher-risk clients with lower-risks ones, thereby perverting the function of premiums, and causing the lower-risk to subsidize the higher-risk clients. Finally, as firms are mandated to cover many otherwise uninsurable risks, the incentive for clients to shop around will be decreased, as the potential variance between each insurance agency's services will have been artificially curtailed (i.e. as more risks are mandated to be covered, health insurance will have a lesser capacity for customization). Without allowing out-of-pocket costs to serve as a deterrent to unnecessary medical care (e.g. trivial or at-home treatable ailments), the demand for medical services will be artificially inflated and, with it, a corresponding rise in insurance costs due to this distortion. Hoppe comments on these unintended consequences of government interference in the health care industry:

> This is a lesson in the logic of interventionism. The first interventionist act brought about a big mess — insurance premiums always go up because insurers are no longer allowed to discriminate correctly and are even forced to include uninsurable risks. So now the problem arises of more and more people dropping out. For those who remain insured, premiums have to be raised to adjust for the fact that so many are dropping out.
>
> The next step, which we in the United States are on the verge of taking, is to make health insurance compulsory. No More Dropping Out! If this step is taken — compulsory health insurance, with all the other mandates remaining in place — then of course premiums will skyrocket even more than they have in the past.[93]

---

[93]   Hoppe, ibid.

Does this mean consumers will generally pay for most of their healthcare directly in freed markets? Yes, though there would likely be alternative arrangements available. For instance, individuals may choose to outsource risk by means of group insurance. Group insurance has the unique advantage of members being able to apply potent social pressures on anyone who abuses their coverage by either making false claims or going to the hospital for trivial ailments. Such practices were the norm in the early 20th century with the advent of "lodge medicine." This was a practice typically provided by various fraternities comprised of impoverished and working class individuals. It proved to be advantageous financially and qualitatively as David Beito describes:

> The leading beneficiary of lodge practice was, of course, the patient of modest means. He or she was able to obtain a physician's care for about $2.00 a year, roughly equivalent to a day's wage for a laborer. For comparable amounts, some lodges extended coverage to family members. The remuneration the lodge doctor received was a far cry from the higher fee schedules favored by the profession. The local medical society in Meadville, Pennsylvania, was typical in setting the following minimum fees for its members: $1.00 per physical examination, surgical dressing, and daytime house call and $2.00 per nighttime house call. Such charges, at least for ongoing service, were beyond the reach of many lower-income Americans. Hence it was not coincidental, an editorial in the Medical Council pointed out, that lodge practice thrived in communities populated by the working poor.[94]

As communities evolve and grow, the need for group insurance will tend to fall as individuals over time become more wealthy and productive. Many healthcare services will be paid for directly like most other services. When services are directly purchased, the consumer is more strongly incentivized to shop around for the lowest-priced and/or highest-quality

---

[94]   David T. Beito, *From Mutual Aid to the Welfare State: Fraternal Societies and Social Services, 1890-1967* (Chapel Hill: University of North Carolina, 2000), 117.

services. This, in turn, will spark fiercer competition between medical providers on the grounds of quality and price. Because the consumer will be much more involved in the selection of his/her service provider, there will be a comparatively higher demand for the development of new technology, which improves various medical procedures, making them safer, more effective, and more affordable over time. Furthermore, the absence of costly regulations and taxes will translate into lower prices for the consumer, allowing them greater access to healthcare of their own choosing. Finally, the absence of licensure requirements, patents, and other forms of intellectual property will result in a far greater supply of health care providers and medicine. Consequently, the cost for these services and products will be far cheaper in comparison.

Of course, a skeptical person may be worried about the quality or shade of free market health care providers as they are not forced to submit to State-set minimum standards. These standards, however, may easily be supplanted by private accreditation firms or other third-party ratings agencies akin to Consumer Reports. In free markets, reputation is vital to the success of every firm in every industry. Without State oversight or monopolistic boards of approval, transparency will increasingly be demanded of medical providers. When reputation markets inform and determine massive consumer choice (imagine a vast and detailed Yelp), companies and associations that refuse to allow third-party evaluations will be pressured accordingly. What is more likely: any quality health care firms would be more than happy to submit themselves and their staff to third-party evaluations as a means of distinguishing themselves from the competition and to assure any prospective patrons that their services will be performed safely and efficiently. Firms which do not submit themselves to such independent, third-party evaluations would be seen as suspect when compared to their more transparent counterparts.

Some fear the propensity for such ratings agencies to be bribed. While bribery is inherent in all human institutions, this sort of foul play will be greatly tempered by the presence of competitive upstarts in the ratings industry. For a ratings agency to accept a bribe or engage in any foul play would be to put its reputation and, therefore, its future profitability at great risk. Their competitors would be eager to investigate any claims of foul play and to make public any damning evidence that may be discovered.

Of course, different health care firms may hold different standards, however, the various levels of standards of care will be reflected by higher or lower prices. For example, one may only be willing to pay twenty dollars for a physical and, as such, settle for patronizing a firm which provides a moderate quality of service or whose staff has little experience. Quality diversity is valuable, because most people who are unwilling or unable to afford the highest-quality healthcare prefer to purchase the quality of service they can afford. While there may be the "Motel 6" quality of healthcare closer to the bottom rungs, there will also be the "Four Seasons" quality healthcare closer towards the top. In markets freed from regulation and taxation, all levels of service increase in quality and decrease in price over time. For instance, modern Toyota cars are a much higher quality good than a Mercedes Benz from seventy-five years ago. It is understood that value is subjective, however, this manner of speaking is short hand for properties overwhelmingly desired by consumers such as greater safety, fuel efficiency, speed, acceleration, reliability, automation, etc.

Freed markets allow and incentivize consumers to discriminate between health care providers on the basis of many criteria ranging from where the practitioners studied, what private certifications they have, their years of experience, the number of successful and failed procedures, asking price, the friendliness of staff, the cleanliness of facilities, their bedside manner, and much more. Furthermore, the reputable third-party agencies may make up for the lack of expertise held by the average consumer required to make a credible evaluation of a given firm or medical practitioner. Just as many of us turn to Google or other sources of public information to research products, so too would references given by established and legitimate ratings agencies inform us on which medical provider to select.

The sight-corrective procedure LASIK exemplifies the incentives to which medical providers adjust in the face of unadulterated demand from consumers. This practice is unique in that it is not covered by most standard insurance, causing the majority of consumers to pay for it directly out of pocket. This incentivizes them to discriminate more thoroughly among the various levels of price and quality. Vijay Boyapati explains the results of this practice:

> With these incentives in place, the LASIK procedure has been reported to have fallen in cost by over 30 percent during the last decade. Even more importantly, the quality of the procedure has improved dramatically in that period as providers competed to deliver the most efficacious treatment. According to Erik Gross, an expert in the field of LASIK technology, 'Early procedures were not LASIK at all, but uncomfortable surface ablations with no astigmatism correction. Subsequent generations of the procedure increased the treatable range, added correction for astigmatism, correction for hyperopia, the lasikflap to increase stability and comfort,

accuracy and safety features, and finally
moved to true custom wavefront analysis
and correction.'[95]

   The same methods of quality assurance in the medical care industry
– competition, mercurial consumer choice, and influential third party
evaluations – may also be applied to the pharmaceutical industry. Some
theorists maintain that, without patents and the over-arching edifice of
intellectual property law, pharmaceutical companies will not have enough
incentive to perform expensive R&D, unless they can recoup it through
monopoly profits in the future.[96] What must be considered is that one of
the greatest expenses associated with ongoing research is the cost of
complying with mandated tests and trials conducted by the FDA, which can
last decades! Not only are these mandatory testing requirements incredibly
expensive, thereby creating huge barriers to entry in the industry, but they
also keep otherwise life-saving drugs off the market for long periods of
time. In the interim, many people suffer and die while they wait for the
FDA to grant approval for the drug. Patients in very dire circumstances
may prefer to take the risk of consuming experimental or untested drugs as
opposed to waiting for their deaths – which all too often occurs while
waiting for FDA testing to complete. Of course, this is not an argument
against testing and research per se. Rather, it is meant to show the
destructive and wasteful effects of giving quality assurance to a
monopolistic agency.
   Competing pharmaceutical firms will have to find the optimal
balance between testing and release times for their drugs. If they release
them with too little testing, their customers may suffer unduly from harmful
side effects. However, should they take too long to test, they may be losing
market share to competitors who are in a better position to release their
own, safe versions of the drugs sooner. One innovative option would be to
release their drugs throughout all testing stages and label them according to
their respective stages of testing, thus allowing the consumer to express
their own risk profiles individually. As there will be no one-size-fits-all
method for testing and release, such varying methods of production and
testing will be competing against one another creating a tendency towards
ever more safe and efficient practices. Not unlike medical care providers,
pharmaceutical companies may seek third-party-safety certification as a
means of assuring their customers. Different third-party-safety certifiers will
have different levels of reputability, which will affect the credibility of their

---

95   Vijay Boyapati, "What's Really Wrong with the Healthcare Industry." (editorial
     published at Ludwig Von Mises Institute, Auburn, Alabama, March 26, 2010. Web.
     <https://mises.org/library/whats-really-wrong-healthcare-industry>.
96   For more arguments against the validity and efficacy of Intellectual Property laws,
     see chapter 2.

respective certifications. This will, of course, just be one more factor for the pharmaceutical entrepreneur to consider.

Finally, there is the ethical consideration of a free market-based health care system. State interference in the health care industry taking the form of regulations, minimum-mandated coverage, occupational licensing, taxes, the enforcement of intellectual property laws, etc., are unique in that they are unilaterally imposed and enforced via aggressive means. That is to say, the ultimate consequence for not complying with them is imprisonment or potentially death, should one resist arrest. In sharp contrast, however, the consumer and entrepreneur are only held to standards upon which both parties agreed beforehand. Even the formation of tacit agreements – such as eating at a restaurant and being asked to pay the bill – are legitimate in free markets, because the restaurant, as a private institution, is legitimately owned by the person setting the rules of service. In contrast, the State dictates policies over property on which it has no legitimate claim.[97] Unlike the State, private entities must adhere to general norms and practices in society, and *persuade* others to trade with them on good terms. Health care providers competing in free markets would have to rely upon voluntary consumer patronage to maintain economic viability, and any such providers who offer poor quality or undesirable services will continually stumble and fall in light of more satisfying and more efficient products and techniques. This is the way in which markets are organically and perpetually regulated in accordance with the consumer's ever changing desires.

---

[97] Due to the fact that its agents neither acquired the land they are ruling via original appropriation nor voluntary exchange. For more on this see Chapter 1: Libertarianism.

Chapter Eight

LAW AND ORDER

NEARLY THE ENTIRE spectrum of political thought includes the implicit assumption that the State is the institution best suited for the production, interpretation, and enforcement of law and order. In fact, the variance in most political discourse is confined to which laws the State ought to produce and how they should be interpreted and enforced. The questions often left unasked, though begged by traditional political thought: "Is the State the institution best suited for these tasks? If not, what is the superior alternative?" will be examined. This chapter will focus on a systemic evaluation and critique of the State as a monopolistic producer of law and less on the content of present legal systems. As such, this analysis will remain pertinent to any State-administered legal system despite its ever changing law code and/or legal procedures.[98]

The Problem of Social Order

Because the demand for various resources exceeds their availability, norms must be established to promote their economic and just use. As men are neither saints nor angels, disputes over resource ownership abound. Thus, a legal system based on property norms serves as the mechanism by which various disputes may be settled in a predictable and just manner. Recall that violent interpersonal conflict is only possible insofar as scarcity exists. Whether it is two men fighting over a beer, a mugger and his victim, or a breach in contract, every violent dispute has ultimately to do with the allocation and/or control over some scarce good (whether of one's own body or external good). The solution to the problem of social order thus lays in the formulation of a rational set of property rights such that, if followed, would negate the emergence of any and all violent conflict.

---

[98] Before I begin I would like to attribute credit to the men whose works have largely influenced the formulation of this chapter: Hans Hermann Hoppe, Stephan Kinsella, Robert P. Murphy, and David Friedman.

The Solution to Social Order

The solution to social order may be summed up in two words: private property. Private property is a norm and, as such, works towards facilitating the avoidance of interpersonal conflict. The way in which we compare the efficacy of any given norms will be by examining whether or not, and to what extent, they generate or avoid conflict. Hoppe cogently sums up why the norm of private property, compared to other property norms, is best suited for conflict avoidance:

> Contrary to the frequently heard claim that the institution of private property is only a *convention*, it must be categorically stated: a convention serves a *purpose, and* it is something to which an *alternative* exists. The Latin alphabet, for instance, serves the purpose of written communication and there exists an alternative to it, the Cyrillic alphabet. That is why it is referred to as a convention.
>
> What, however, is the purpose of action norms? If no interpersonal conflict existed — that is: if, due to a prestabilized harmony of all interests, no situation ever arose in which two or more people want to use one and the same good in incompatible ways — then no norms would be needed. It is the purpose of norms to help avoid otherwise unavoidable conflict. A norm that generates conflict rather than helping to avoid it is *contrary to the very purpose of norms*. It is a dysfunctional norm or a perversion.
>
> With regard to the purpose of conflict avoidance, however, the institution of private property is definitely *not* just a convention, because no alternative to it exists. Only private (exclusive) property makes it possible that all otherwise

unavoidable conflicts can be avoided.
And only the principle of property
acquisition through acts of original
appropriation, performed by specific
individuals at a specific time and location,
makes it possible to avoid conflict *from the
beginning of mankind* onward, because only
the *first* appropriation of some previously
unappropriated good can be conflict-free
— simply, because — *per definitionem* —
no one else had any previous dealings
with the good.[99]

Before any talk of legal punishment, however, it should be made clear that a victim is not obliged to punish or press charges against his aggressor. However, the following discussion will examine the extent to which a given victim *may justifiably* punish his aggressor. In a free market or voluntary society, it is likely that many victims would prefer a monetary or some other material restitution from their aggressors, over inflicting physical harm on them. Such a society, being largely composed of voluntary and peaceful relations, will probably be more opposed to violence *as an end in itself* than our current environment (even when justified). Finally, monetary or material restitution permits someone a wider range of options to satisfy his desires, whereas using physical force against a perpetrator constitutes only one fleeting means of satisfaction.

There is an important distinction between *defense* and *punishment*. The former has to do with what is justified in the defense of one's person or property as it is being violated, while the latter has to do with applying punishment after the fact when the perpetrator is no longer actively violating property rights. One may justifiably use as much force as necessary to stop a person who is actively committing aggression, no matter how trivial the violation may seem. For instance, if someone were to trespass on another's property and refuse to leave despite the owner's requests, then the owner would be justified in using any level of force against this trespasser to defend his property. Though, technically, the owner would be justified in killing this trespasser, this does not mean that doing so would be without consequence. The consequences may include an increase in the owner's defense/insurance premiums, and he may face some degree of social ostracism for the perceived excessive use of force (if someone commits a justified act, this merely entails that a *violent* response to said act would be unjustified or criminal). Anyone may ostracize anyone else for whatever reason they deem appropriate, such as killing trespassers.

---

[99]   Hans-Hermann Hoppe, "State or Private Law Society?"

Thus, harsh behavior may be tempered by social/economic pressures.

Punishment

Defending oneself physically, however justifiable, is not sufficient for the attainment of justice. Prudence demands knowing what consequences may be justifiably imposed *ex post* on someone who commits an injustice and violates property rights. Violations of property rights are unique from any other activity in that they may justifiably be met with physical force or threats thereof. Stephan Kinsella provides what is known as the "Estoppel Justification for Punishment" as a proof for why such violent or physical recourse may be warranted. To clarify, the term estoppel refers to a "common-law principle that prevents or precludes someone from making a claim in a lawsuit that is inconsistent with his prior conduct…"[100] To show the relevance this principle has on a justification for punishment, Kinsella states:

> In short, we may punish one who has initiated force, in a manner proportionate to his initiation of force and to the consequences thereof, exactly because he cannot coherently object to such punishment. It makes no sense for him to object to punishment, because this requires that he maintain that the infliction of force is wrong, which is contradictory because he intentionally initiated force himself.[101]

He then uses this Estoppel approach to demonstrate why defensive force and punishment may be justifiably employed in response to threats made against one's body or property:

> This method of analyzing whether a proposed punishment is proper also makes it clear just why the threat of violence or assault is properly treated as an aggressive crime. Assault is defined as putting someone in fear of receiving a

---

[100]   Stephan Kinsella, "Punishment and Proportionality: The Estoppel Approach" in *Journal of Libertarian Studies* 1st ser. 12 (1996): 51-73.
[101]   Kinsella, "Punishment and Proportionality."

battery (physical beating). Suppose A assaults B, such as by pointing a gun at him or threatening to beat him. Clearly B is entitled to do to A what A has done to B---A is estopped from objecting to the propriety of being threatened, i.e. assaulted. But what does this mean? To assault is to manifest an intent to cause harm, and to apprise B of this, so that he believes A (otherwise it is something like a joke or acting, and B is not actually in apprehension of being coerced). A was able to put B in a state of fear by threatening B. But because of the nature of assault, the only way B can really make A fear a retaliatory act by B is if B really means it and is able to convince A of this fact. Thus B must actually be (capable of being) willing to carry out the threatened coercion of A, not just mouth the words, otherwise A will know B is merely engaged in idle threats, merely bluffing. Indeed, B can legitimately go forward with the threatened action if only to make A believe it, so that he is actually assaulted. Although A need not actually use force to assault B, there is simply no way for B to assault A in return without actually having the right to use force against A. Because the whole situation is caused by A's action, he is estopped from objecting to the necessity of B using force against him.[102]

One is only bound to respect the rights of another so long as this person reciprocates. The right of self-defense allows those under attack to respond with violence. As one is not required to suffer abuses to his body or property, but can justifiably defend himself from such abuses, it follows that he must regard an aggressor as having lost or relinquished some claim of peace and non-invasion. By his own conduct, such an attacker demonstrates a desire for aggression over agreement, and, as such, tarnishes his status as an innocent party. The concept of property rights itself entails

---

[102] Kinsella, ibid.

that physical force may be used against those who violate one's just possessory claims. This is the very characteristic that separates rights from non-rights.

If defensive violence is justified, perhaps violence for restitution or for retributive reasons is as well? If so, what would its limits be? A hallmark of justified punishment has long been meeting the criteria of proportionality. What is meant by proportionality? It would seem at first glance that what is truly proportional is purely subjective, and admittedly, there is significant grey area in this realm. However, there are some situations in which we may be able to objectively identify an excessive amount of force used as punishment for a particular property rights violation. For instance, if person B steals person A's pack of bubble gum, then executing person B as punishment for this crime would be clearly disproportionate. Other than an intuitive notion that this would be excessive, we may also be able to rationally defend this position. At the very least, person A would be justified in taking back the pack of gum from B, as well as some additional desired goods for the inconvenience and violation that person A was made to suffer. It is because person B *initiated* this force upon person A that person A would be justified in taking more from person B than the identical pack of gum he stole, for this would only restore person A to the position he was in before the incident, however, it would not compensate him for the subsequent inconvenience and violation he had to endure in the interim. Additionally, we may determine that executing person B for this petty theft would be excessive, because this would involve the *absolute* destruction of person B's rights (for life is a necessary prerequisite of rights) as punishment for an act which violated only a *portion* of person A's rights. This distinction is more than arbitrary sentimentality; it reveals the categorically scalar nature of rights. The unjustified ending of a life is a more egregious infraction of justice than is the pilfering of sugar-free Chiclets. B's minor rights violation only warrants minor force to be used against him, contrary to his victim's preference to impose capital punishment.

However, the degree to which stealing a pack of gum harms person A may differ from how much it harms person C, as they may each value the gum differently for whatever reason. As we cannot compare value interpersonally, it is impossible to assess the degree to which people gain and lose from actions.[103] As a result of such incongruities in valuation, the punishment person A may be justified in imposing on B may vary in regards to how person C may punish person B for the same act. (The level

---

[103] In every voluntary transaction, both parties gain *ex ante*. Neither would exchange anything if he believed he would be worse off after the exchange. They must each prefer what the other offers to what they offer. Yet, which party gained more? The buyer or the seller? As neither party's cardinal valuations are observable, it becomes impossible to answer. Thus, no such comparisons are warranted.

of psychological trauma A and C suffered from this encounter will also be relevant when determining to what extent they may justly apply punishment). Of course, as it is impossible to determine exactly how much one values a thing, determining a proper punishment for B will be difficult. If person A and person B cannot come to a mutually agreeable resolution on their own regarding compensation, they may solicit outside opinion for their case, in a process known as arbitration.

Decentralized Law Finding Systems vs. Centralized Legislation

For this section, we will compare and contrast the general characteristics of decentralized legal systems, such as common law and private law, with legislation. Legislation, or law by decree, is by its nature less predictable than decentralized legal systems whose development is limited to extrapolations from previously established legal principles. As a result of the comparatively less predictable nature of the legislative legal system, fewer contracts are made owing to the uncertainty of their enforcement. Stephan Kinsella discusses the implications of this decrease in predictability under a centralized legislative system:

> Another pernicious effect of the increased uncertainty in legislation-based systems is the increase of overall time preference. Individuals invariably demonstrate a preference for earlier goods over later goods, all things being equal. When time preferences are lower, individuals are more willing to forgo immediate benefits such as consumption, and invest their time and capital in more indirect (i.e., more roundabout, lengthier) production processes, which yield more or better goods for consumption or for further production. Any artificial raising of the general time-preference rate thus tends to impoverish society by pushing us away from production and long-term investments. Yet increased uncertainty, which is brought about by a legislation-based system, causes an increase in time-preference rates because if the future is less certain, it is relatively less valuable

compared to the present.[104]

With this relative increase in time preference and decrease in prosperity, there comes an associated increase in crime. This general increase in time preference makes crime more appealing as it serves to satisfy more immediate desires. Accordingly, the prospect of potential punishment will be less of a tempering factor for one with a higher-time preference – i.e., one who places a high premium on current consumption versus future consumption.

In addition to this, an arbitrary edict-based legislative system lacks access to a pricing mechanism, which would otherwise serve as an invaluable indicator of the effectiveness or desirability of a law relative to consumer or societal preference. With a pricing mechanism, one can judge such things by measuring their profitability. However, edict-based legislative systems are generally promoted by States which are funded in a compulsory manner (taxation). Thus, whether or not a certain law or set of laws is more or less desired by the public is comparatively more uncertain and difficult to determine. Without such institutionalized aggression, such things would be relatively easier to apprehend as one could check his balance sheet to verify customer satisfaction. Hence, the pricing mechanism enables such a decentralized free market legal system to continually refine and reinterpret various legal codes more rationally relative to consumer preference. Not only does the pricing mechanism serve as an indicator for *what type* of law is favored, but also *how much* it is favored over alternative attempts to produce law. Moreover, in edict-based legislative environments there is bound to be an over/under production of law in various fields as there is no rational feedback that provides data comparable to a profit and loss system.

Legislative law systems also tend to be inferior as the legal system is comprised of many disparate laws unrelated to any rationally justified principles, and as such, are less credible compared to decentralized legal systems which tend to extrapolate from organically established legal principles. Furthermore, the unbridled scope of what legislative law systems may cover tends to result in an over-expansion of legal codes. One consequence of this ever-expanding legal code is that it creates more *de jure* criminals. By definition, as the law expands to constrict greater amounts of human conduct, more people will be rendered and prosecuted as criminals. As more and more people are said to be engaging in criminal behavior, credibility will continue to be lost by the legal system, especially if such outlawed behavior does not constitute aggression against other people or their property. Worse yet, such a system makes virtually everyone vulnerable to prosecution by the State whenever its agents deem fit. Of course, this threat of impending punishment serves as an effective tool of

---

[104]   Stephan Kinsella, "Legislation and the Discovery of Law in a Free Society" in *Journal of Libertarian Studies* 11.2 (1995): 132-81.

intimidation used for ensuring obedience to State rule. Kinsella summarizes the advantages of a *decentralized* legal system:

> … [T]he position of common-law or decentralized judges is fundamentally different from that of legislators in three respects. First, judges can only make decisions when asked to do so by the parties concerned. Second, the judge's decision is less far-reaching than legislation because it primarily affects the parties to the dispute, and only occasionally affects third parties or others with no connection to the parties involved. Third, a judge's discretion is limited by the necessity of referring to similar precedents. Legal certainty is thus more attainable in a relatively decentralized law-finding system like the common law, Roman law, or customary law, than in centralized law-making systems where legislation is the primary source of law.[105]

The State as Provider of Law and Order

Before discussing the State's role in the provision of law and social order, a proper definition of the State is required:

> The State, according to the standard definition, is not a regular, specialized firm. Rather, it is defined as an agency characterized by two unique, logically connected features. First, the state is an agency that exercises a territorial monopoly of ultimate decision making. That is, the state is the ultimate arbiter in every case of conflict, including conflicts involving itself. It allows no appeal above and beyond itself. Second, the state is an

---

[105] Kinsella, "Legislation and the Discovery of Law in a Free Society."

agency that exercises a territorial monopoly of taxation. That is, it is an agency that unilaterally fixes the price that private citizens must pay for the state's service as ultimate judge and enforcer of law and order.[106]

Put more simply, the State is that institution which enjoys a monopoly over the production, interpretation, and enforcement of law. In addition to this, the State also has the sole right to force its citizens to pay for its services, the price and scope of which are also dictated by the State and are subject to change at its discretion. The resulting conflict of interest and moral hazard from a single institution being equipped with these exclusive legal privileges should be readily apparent. Hoppe brilliantly summarizes the logical incoherence of holding both the belief that monopolies are bad for the consumer, and that law and order must be exclusively provided by the State:

First of all, among economists and philosophers two near-universally accepted propositions exist:

1. Every "monopoly" is "bad" from the viewpoint of consumers. Monopoly is here understood in its classic meaning as an exclusive privilege granted to a single producer of a commodity or service, or as the absence of "free entry" into a particular line of production. Only one agency, A, may produce a given good or service, X. Such a monopoly is "bad" for consumers, because, shielded from potential new entrants into a given area of production, the price of the product will be higher and its quality lower than otherwise, under free competition.
2. The production of law and order, i.e., of security, is the primary function of the state (as just defined). Security is here understood in the wide sense adopted in the American Declaration of Independence: as the protection of life,

---

property, and the pursuit of happiness from domestic violence (crime) as well as external (foreign) aggression (war).

Both propositions are apparently incompatible with each other. This has rarely caused concern among philosophers and economists, however, and in so far as it has, the typical reaction has been one of taking exception to the first proposition rather than the second. Yet there exist fundamental theoretical reasons (and mountains of empirical evidence) that it is indeed the second proposition that is in error.[107]

Hoppe demonstrates that the State is *not* immune from the principles of economics. The exercise of a State monopoly over the provision of any service will lead to the same inefficiencies and destruction of wealth as any other monopolistic operation. The second major disadvantage of State provided law and order is the lack of contract:

If one wanted to summarize in one word the decisive difference and advantage of a competitive security industry as compared to the current statist practice, it would be this: contract. The state, as ultimate decision maker and judge, operates in a contract-less legal vacuum. There exists no contract between the state and its citizens. It is not contractually fixed, what is actually owned by whom, and what, accordingly, is to be protected. It is not fixed, what service the state is to provide, what is to happen if the state fails in its duty, nor what the price is that the "customer" of such "service" must pay. Rather, the state unilaterally fixes the rules of the game and can change them, per legislation, during the game. Obviously, such behavior is inconceivable for freely financed security providers. Just imagine a

---

[107] Hoppe, ibid.

security provider, whether police, insurer, or arbitrator, whose offer consisted of something like this:

'I will not contractually guarantee you anything. I will not tell you what specific things I will regard as your to-be-protected property, nor will I tell you what I oblige myself to do if, according to your opinion, I do not fulfill my service to you — but in any case, I reserve the right to unilaterally determine the price that you must pay me for such undefined service.'[108]

Finally, under a Statist legal system, citizens are much less incentivized to take an active role in shaping the rules which govern them. The reason for this is simple: one's vote has relatively little impact on determining the laws that will govern him, and the cost of maintaining an informed vote is high. To vote according to one's interests, one must determine what policies are actually in line with his interests and who represents these policies.

The relatively high cost of conducting the research and introspection required to achieve this tends to be greater than the impact a person's single vote will have in an election. Thus, he chooses to remain in a state of rational ignorance, as the costs of alleviating his ignorance are not worth the benefits of him doing so.[109] Furthermore, any representative may change his stance at any time with little to no recourse, despite his campaign promises. This representative is not bound by any contract to exercise or manifest his promised course of action. To further compound the issue one may only like polices 1, 3, 5, and 7 of representative A and policies 2, 4, 6, and 8 of representative B. In such a situation, one is put in a position where he has to accept an unfamiliar and diverse basket of policies depending on the unique opinions of the representative he chooses. This is converse to the situation in which one is permitted to choose between a variety of law providers and insurers under free competition. In the latter scenario, his choices will have a far greater impact on the "laws" that rule him than they would under a State system.

---

[108] Hoppe, ibid.

[109] Bryan D. Caplan, "Rational Irrationality" in *The Myth of the Rational Voter: Why Democracies Choose Bad Policies* (Princeton: Princeton University Press, 2007), 132. Caplan writes: "Since delusional political beliefs are free, the voter consumes until he reaches his "satiation point," believing whatever makes him feel best. When a person puts on his voting hat, he does not have to give up practical efficacy in exchange for self-image, *because he has no practical efficacy to give up in the first place.*"

Speculations on Free Market Law and Order

> Specifically regarding the problem at
> hand: in a private-law society the
> production of security — of law and
> order — will be undertaken by freely
> financed individuals and agencies
> competing for a voluntarily paying (or
> not-paying) clientèle, just as the
> production of all other goods and
> services.[110]

In a free market society, the functions of security, auditing, media, consumer evaluations, insurance, investigation, arbitration, and law enforcement will be provided in tandem in order to maintain the protection of the consumers that finance them. Highly contingent and specific details cannot be determined beforehand, however. The particular configuration of agencies and their functions, to what degree competition will exist, and how many agencies there may be in a given geographic area cannot be known in advance. Though the possibilities are endless, a few remarks may be made regarding how economic incentives would structure organizations within this industry. Given the obvious concerns of bribery, moral hazard, and various conflicts of interest, it behooves the reader to scrutinize every proposal offered.

Emerging from the accumulation of billions of minds' worth of creativity is a spontaneously-ordered legal system that adjusts to fulfill the ever changing desires of families, communities, businesses, and individuals: its customers. As organic legal systems emerge to replace State-sanctioned legislatures and courts, there will be a strong diversity of practices in different regions. Over time, improvements in technology and organization will further develop the success of private-law structures empowering everyone to command and act in accordance with justice. The following scenario will be used to illustrate some of the general characteristics of such a system.

Bob desires two things: security and, in the cases where his liberty is violated, restitution. He wants to employ human and material goods to defend himself from attempts on his liberty/property, and he also wants a mechanism that restores him to his natural state before the violation. To accommodate this demand, competing defense insurance agencies (DIAs) offer Bob their services of protection and indemnification in exchange for

---

[110] Hoppe, ibid.

monthly premiums commensurate with his security risk. Bob has several firms from which to choose and makes his decision according to which DIA has a reputation and plan that suits his individual needs. Bob chooses Shield, a DIA renowned for its low prices, harm prevention, and excellent history of providing solid restitution for its clients. He chooses the basic plan which covers acts of mugging, assault, and murder in most areas of his hometown. Shield offers Bob the option of carrying a tracking and panic device with him at all times, in order to more effectively offer its assistance during emergencies. In exchange for Bob's willingness to carry such a device, Shield agrees to lower his monthly premium for its services.

One day, while riding his bike to work, Bob is confronted by a man demanding his bicycle at knife-point, who then rides away with it. Using the device, Bob immediately alerts Shield, but, unfortunately, by the time they arrive, the mugger is long out of sight. Per Bob's contract, Shield covers the cost of Bob's bike as well as additional compensation for his troubles and trauma resulting from the incident. As a means to mitigate harm to its reputation and to recover the funds that it had given out to Bob, Shield commences an investigation. After some detective work, Shield gathers enough evidence to confidently name Terry as the mugger. Shield agents then approach Terry instructing him to pay the amount they had given to Bob, along with the expenses of the investigation. Terry refuses, claiming he is innocent. Because Shield competes on reputation as well as price, it hears Terry's case and cross references his testimony with the evidence it gathered earlier. However, despite Terry's testimony, Shield still believes Terry to be guilty.

In the case that Terry has no DIA coverage, Shield may contract with a third party arbiter to review the evidence and testimony of each party and come to its own verdict. Contrary to a legislative system, there is no *single* law pertaining to Terry's conduct. Anyone is free to enter the judiciary business and offer verdicts. The type of standards such arbitrators and judges use are tempered by consumer preference. If they are seen as out of touch with justice, then this will have a negative impact on this particular arbitration agency's desirability and reputation.

Terry would be encouraged to participate in such arbitration, to make his voice publicly and explicitly heard, so as to make the ruling more legitimate. If Terry refuses to participate, Shield may offer alternative arbitration agencies to handle the case in the hopes that Terry would reconsider. In the case that Terry adamantly refuses to go to any arbitration, Shield may proceed with arbitration without him and he would be tried *in absentia*. Shield is willing to go through all this trouble to encourage Terry's participation, because it would bolster the legitimacy of any subsequent ruling on the case. Shield will also be incentivized to offer Terry arbitration through agencies which have a reputation for impartiality, fairness, and expertise in the matter concerned for similar legitimacy considerations. In the event the trusted arbitrator concludes that Terry is not guilty, Shield will compensate him for his troubles associated with these false allegations. It is this prospect of reputational damage and financial loss which incentivizes the DIAs not to accuse people of crimes without substantial corroborating evidence.

In the case that the arbiter rules that Terry is guilty, Shield will proceed on insisting that Terry pay up. If Terry is able, but refuses, then Shield – with its large established name and influence – may contract with his employer to garnish his future wages with interest until Terry's debt is satisfied. If Terry is able to pay, but earns no outside income, then Shield may confiscate his property and auction it off as a means to satisfy his debts and the costs of the auction. If Terry is unable to pay, then Shield may have him work at a securitized camp until his restitution is paid off. To avoid reputational damages and accusations of inhumane conduct, Shield will have the incentive to ensure that such camps meet certain safety standards. If Shield neglects to ensure that Terry is sent to a safe camp, then its competitors, humanitarian organizations, or other third party evaluators would be happy to expose Shield as a cruel or negligent DIA. This would then result in a loss of legitimacy and therefore business for Shield. Thus, it is the prospect of these consequences that will compel Shield to ensure Terry is indeed sent to a humane and safe work camp. Of course, at any time throughout this process, Terry may have a third party pay off his debts to Shield in whole and relieve him of his work camp duty.

In addition, it needn't be Shield that runs the work camp; they may delegate it to subcontractors. The work camp selected by Shield will also be tempered by the reputational/economic considerations listed above. These same considerations would equally apply to the firms which manage the work camps, deterring them from employing draconian measures or refusing to maintain a safe environment. To demonstrate the safety of the environment and the humane treatment of its inhabitants, the work camps would likely welcome regular and random third party audits of their facilities and practices. If the work camp passes the inspection, it may then be certified by this third party auditor as a humane and safe environment. This certification is only valuable insofar as the agency granting it withstands bribery or other forms of foul play, thus any attempts for the work camp agents to pay off the auditors will likely be futile. In fact, any act intended to bribe the auditors would probably earn the camp an automatic failing grade. Finally, regardless of whether or not Terry pays off his debt, Shield will pass his information along to a criminal records bureau which will document his criminal actions on an archived record.

This sort of practice occurs in Las Vegas between different casinos. They may black list a person caught cheating and spread word to other casinos so as to create a reciprocal relationship wherein the other casinos will act in kind to continue this profitable and cooperative relationship. So, too, and for the same reasons, the various DIAs will want to share with each other information regarding risky individuals, so that they may be able to more effectively gauge security risks and require commensurate payment for their insurance. The criminal records bureaus will distinguish themselves from one another on their ability to verify the validity of criminal verdicts against individuals in an impartial manner. The less scrutiny such a records bureau would use against such verdicts, the less credible its records would become. Thus, such bureaus will likely review the investigative and judicial proceedings used on a particular person against their own standards prior to making the requested changes to this person's record.[111] An additional benefit of this process is that it grants credibility to both the DIAs and the arbitration agencies as passing such an audit further legitimizes these institutions and their practices. The criminal records also serve the purposes of enabling the DIAs to more accurately determine premiums for new clients and whether they should even provide a prospective client with coverage at all.

People who are prone to criminal activity are more likely to be engaged in violent disputes with others, costing the DIA more resources to insure than peaceful people. Moreover, many residential or commercial areas may choose to not allow a person with a violent criminal past on their premises at all. If applied generally or universally, it would leave this person limited to roaming more dangerous or undeveloped areas, causing his DIA coverage to become ever more expensive.

Of course, such areas would not want to be overly discriminatory (namely commercial areas), for these people are, after all, potential customers, suppliers, or supporters. For economic reasons perhaps, they may invite, hire, or trade with former criminals to the extent they demonstrate value and/or have participated in some form of reputable rehabilitation. Participating in such voluntary rehabilitation may also prompt other DIAs to offer recovering criminals lower premiums as well. The preceding scenario is an example of social and economic pressure, each of which serves as powerful deterrents to criminal and unsavory behavior.

Back to our scenario with Bob and Terry: assume that Terry *does* have DIA coverage. In this case, Terry may notify his DIA (Hammer Defense) that Shield is demanding restitution for a falsely-accused crime: mugging Bob. At this point, Hammer Defense may confer with Shield and its findings as well as conduct an investigation of its own into the matter. If, upon reviewing the evidence of its own investigation and cross referencing it with evidence gathered by Shield, it determines that Terry is indeed guilty, then Hammer Defense will compel its client to pay or drop his coverage.

---

[111] Though this may entail differences in the contents of records from one agency to another, the market process will tend toward deeming one or a select few bureaus as the industry standard(s) much like the "Non-GMO Project verified" seal serves as today's standard for identifying GMO free food.

Should Terry refuse and subsequently lose coverage, then his protection would be limited to what he can physically provide himself and what his resources can directly purchase. If, however, Hammer Defense comes to the conclusion that Terry is not guilty, – or that there is insufficient evidence to prove his guilt – it will likely share its findings with Shield. After reviewing contrary evidence, if Shield remains unconvinced, what is needed is arbitration: both parties will each agree upon a third party and be bound to its decision. As inter-agency disputes may occur frequently, there will tend to emerge a habit of multiple DIAs agreeing in advance, by contract, who will mediate or arbitrate which disputes. Suppose, however, that the arbitration agency used decides Terry is guilty, and, despite industry arrangements, years of goodwill, and most importantly, contractual obligations, Hammer Defense reneges on its agreement and refuses to abide by the arbitration ruling. What then? Will violence be used? No, most likely not. Instead, Shield along with the arbitration agency will threaten to publicize Hammer Defense's welching nature if it continues to be non-compliant. If Hammer Defense refuses to abide by the ruling even still, Shield and the arbitration agency could execute their threat, causing Hammer Defense to lose credibility and, by extension, business and power.

The simpler situation to observe would be if Bob and Terry were each clients of the same DIA. Prior to gaining coverage, each client would likely agree to abide by the ruling(s) of a given arbitration agency(s) to be used in the case a criminal dispute arises between himself and another person covered by the same agency. Alternatively, for the sake of saving costs for itself and the consumer, the DIA may offer its clients the option of allowing it to make the ruling itself as opposed to outsourcing to a third party arbitrator. In their coverage agreements, the clients may also sign off on which arbitration agencies will be used should one enter into a dispute with a client of a separate DIA. In a society populated by competing insurance and arbitration agencies, the "laws" to which any given person is subject will essentially be the standards used by the reviewing arbitration agency when rendering a verdict. For this reason, it is in the DIA's best interest to choose agencies whose standards are desirable to its clients. Some people, for instance, may never want to be subject to capital punishment. Of course, such individuals may not be able to live under the *exact* set of laws he would like because DIAs would still have to come to agreeable terms with each other in order to remain viable. However, the customer would undoubtedly have a much larger influence on choosing the governing principles he prefers than under a legislative system.

A client of DIA "X" may be under a different set of laws than a client of DIA "Y" due to the different preferences for law desired by customers of DIA "X" and DIA "Y" respectively. It is the preferences which guide the various DIAs to contract with those arbitration agencies that, in turn, produce the law that is most aligned with their customers' preferences. Perhaps customers of DIA X would be willing to pay more for their coverage if DIA X can ensure them they will never face the death penalty by only contracting with those arbitration agencies that refuse to impose it. Supposing this "no-death" stipulation is DIA X's largest concern, it will be willing to expend many resources to assure its customers they will never face the death penalty when negotiating with other DIAs regarding the arbitration agencies to be used in resolving disputes between their respective clients. An alternative to expending resources to secure favorable arbitration agencies may be for DIA X to compromise on other legal areas that are less significant to its interests, but are more significant to DIA Y or DIA Z. The reason different people may live under different laws is that their respective DIAs will be bargaining with one another on behalf of different sets of consumer preferences. The arbitration agency used to settle the disputes between customers of DIA Y and DIA Z may differ from the arbitration agency used to settle such disputes between customers of DIA Y and DIA X. Once more, this would be due to the fact that differences in their respective customer preferences for law will have caused them to ordain different arbitration agencies to settle disputes between their own clientèle and others.

Additionally, the DIAs will want to adopt policies which are most economically able to prevent conflict to ensure the greatest amount of profit. Thus, promoting the principles of peace and respect for private property will be very important. A society flourishing in peace and productivity will encourage two profitable effects: 1) Higher productivity implies there is simply more value for insurance and defense agencies to defend, growing their coverage, and; 2) Peace and prosperity implies fewer people are resorting to criminal and aggressive behavior. As such, any arbitration agency which frequently rules counter to the norm of private property would likely run out of business. There would be no legitimate defense agency willing to abide by terms contrary to respect for private property. Those norms which contradict that of private property only serve to generate conflict. *Thus, the market's pursuit for an efficient and equitable legal system will likely produce one which is consistent with private property and the non-aggression principle.* It is no coincidence, then, that the most efficient legal system will be the one that is most just.

Advantages of the Private Provision of Law and Order

In contemporary society, people are instructed and trained not to attempt to defend themselves, but to rely on State-provided monopoly defense agencies. Conversely, in freed markets, self-defense practices will

164

not only be permitted, but encouraged. After all, the better one may defend himself, the less risk he bears. As such, clients who can demonstrate that they have the means and ability to defend themselves – perhaps through some form of certification process – will likely be able to secure lower premiums from their DIAs. Furthermore, in a comparatively better armed society, there would be far less crime as the cost of engaging in criminal behavior would be relatively higher than in our current environment where weapon ownership is significantly abridged. Competition is another obvious benefit of such a system:

> First, competition among police, insurers, and arbitrators for paying clients would bring about a tendency toward a continuous fall in the price of protection (per insured value), thus rendering protection increasingly more affordable, whereas under monopolistic (statist) conditions the price of protection will steadily rise and become increasingly unaffordable.[112]

A multiplicity of private defense firms is beneficial as they will compete not only on price, but also on the basis of the quality of their services. What constitutes quality may be comprised of some of the following factors:

- Emergency response times
- Rigor of third party auditing
- Diplomatic acumen
- Crime prevention
- Investigative and executive prowess
- Contractual relations with reputable and desirable judicial (arbitration) agencies, etc.

Through competition, an efficient division of labor would abound and tend to weed out inefficient security firms and arbitration agencies, freeing up land, labor, and capital to be used by more efficient agencies of this industry or any other. It is this process which allows these services to evolve according to the ever changing desires of the consumer and development of technology. This economization produces a sort of spontaneous order that no central planner could ever hope to emulate.

Because these services will be privately provided on the marketplace, a pricing mechanism will manifest that enables entrepreneurs

---

[112]   Hoppe, ibid.

to rationally calculate ever-more optimal allocations of resources. Losses imply that resources are being combined in value-destroying ways, and vice versa with profits. The advantage of having access to such a pricing mechanism is that it yields a much more productive output of service and quality:

> ... [I]n a system of freely competing protection agencies, all arbitrariness of allocation (all over- and underproduction) would disappear. Protection would be accorded the relative importance that is has in the eyes of voluntarily paying consumers, and no person, group, or region would receive protection at the expense of any other one. Each and every one would receive protection in accordance with his own payments.[113]

The incentive structure of DIAs is also quite different from State agents, in that the members of a reputable insurance firm have a vested financial interest in preventing crime, apprehending criminals, and recovering stolen loot. If a DIA is unable to prevent a crime, or to apprehend the criminal responsible for a given crime, then it will have to bear the total cost of restitution to its affected client, resulting in financial loss and reputational damage.

Such a private law system would have a larger peace promoting effect than its State-administered counterpart. This is largely due to the fact that private institutions are not able to externalize the high costs of aggression onto its customers in the same way the State can. Private businesses are typical economic actors; they and consumers alike are governed by the law of demand. Higher prices for security services – to finance increased aggression – translates into fewer sales as consumers begin to purchase said services elsewhere. In contrast, no matter how high the cost of law and security becomes under State rule, its corner on the marketplace is largely unaffected since it has the legal authority to force its citizens to pay, while at the same time artificially suppressing competition with threats of brutality and imprisonment. Conversely, a private institution would have to worry about the loss of business resulting from the increased expenditures and reputational damage associated with its aggressive conduct, along with legal liability.

An alternative concern for DIAs would be the prospect of their clients engaging in provocative behavior or vigilantism. Such behavior

---

[113] Hoppe, ibid.

would likely be discouraged as it tends to be messy, costly, and more out of line with justice than other more civilized means:

> … [E]very insurer must restrict the
> actions of his clients so as to exclude all
> aggression and provocation on their part.
> That is, any insurance against social
> disasters such as crime must be
> contingent on the insured submitting
> themselves to specified norms of
> civilized, nonaggressive conduct. Further,
> due to the same reasons and financial
> concerns, insurers will tend to require that
> their clients abstain from all forms of
> vigilante justice (except perhaps under
> quite extraordinary circumstances), for
> vigilante justice, even if justified,
> invariably causes uncertainty and
> provokes possible third-party
> intervention. By obliging their clients
> instead to submit to regular publicized
> procedures whenever they think they have
> been victimized, these disturbances and
> associated costs can be largely avoided.[114]

Additionally, in some cases, DIAs may only be able to cover aggression in certain pre-approved geographical areas. For similar reasons, the premiums offered may also be largely affected by the geographical area in which the client may wish to be covered. If this client is violated outside of these covered areas, then the insurance company would not be obligated to reimburse him for his injuries. Thus many commercial or residential areas will attempt to meet DIA approved standards of safety and civility, so as to encourage tourism and the immigration of high-net worth individuals.

Should one lose his DIA coverage due to his engagement in aggressive behavior, then his social status will be greatly damaged. Criminal record bureaus may track the conduct of such individuals and provide their information upon request to interested parties such as credit agencies or prospective employers. These interested individuals may also include property owners in residential or commercial areas, to whom such information will likely have a substantial effect on the decision of whether or not to let a person enter their property. Of course, these employers or property owners may overlook past criminal behavior if the individual in

---

[114] Hoppe, ibid.

question can demonstrate the completion of some form of rehabilitation as previously mentioned.

A common concern with a private law system lies with the idea that the rich will end up purchasing unjust legal favor by bribing arbitration agencies or DIAs. This practice is certainly common today. It is clear that wealthier individuals convicted of the same crime tend to be dealt less severe punishments than their less wealthy counterparts in contemporary State-run legal systems. Worse yet, the State holds a monopoly on the provision of law and order. It has no competitors and does not fear extinction. The otherwise tempering prospects of losing market share to one's competitors is absent. Unsurprisingly, the State also claims the authority to arbitrate any and all conflicts involving its own agents or agencies which yields a clear conflict of interest that would never pass in a private law system. It is a lawless institution as it ultimately never submits itself to the decision of a neutral, third party.

However, it is still worth addressing the possibility of foul play occurring in a private law system. It is the preservation of reputation and legal status that deters DIA agents from acquiescing to bribes or any other form of foul play in the execution of their services. For as soon as it is discovered that a DIA's agents committed a serious injustice, the DIA as a whole will be vulnerable to losing significant credibility and business. In the event that said agents commit an injustice, the slighted individual could publicize the transgression, perhaps to various watch dog agencies or even criminal records bureaus that perform regular audits on such firms. Next, if foul play has been indicated by the investigation of these disinterested third parties, then the competitors of this dubious firm would see to it that such behavior was widely marketed along with whatever publications the watch dog agencies produce. If a given DIA refuses a request to undergo an audit by a credible watchdog agency or criminal records bureau, then such evasive behavior would also likely be publicized in a similar manner resulting in the denigration of this dubious firm's reputation and business. A firm's credibility in the private law industry is paramount to its viability in a truly free market. The same such considerations will likewise deter foul play on the part of arbitration agencies.

With alternative, competitive markets in defense and judicial services, prohibitions on all types of "victimless crimes" will disappear. Today, many billions of dollars are spent on the drug war, which is responsible for untold levels of violence. However, the ownership, production, distribution, or consumption of drugs does not entail a violation against property or persons – likewise for gambling and prostitution. As such, very few people would likely be interested in paying for protection against such activities:

Lastly, it is worthwhile pointing out that

> while states as tax-funded agencies can —
> and do — engage in the large-scale
> prosecution of victimless crimes such as
> "illegal-drug" use, prostitution, or
> gambling, these "crimes" would tend to
> be of little or no concern within a system
> of freely funded protection agencies.
> "Protection" against such "crimes" would
> require higher insurance premiums, but
> since these "crimes" — unlike genuine
> crimes against persons and property —
> do not create victims, very few people
> would be willing to spend money on such
> "protection."[115]

The legalization of such activities would also render a crippling blow to violent organized crime syndicates as they tend to be the greatest source of revenue for these institutions. This loss in revenue will result in a corresponding loss of power and influence previously enjoyed by these criminal organizations.

In a freed market, no single protection agency holds all the cards. Power is decentralized amongst those who provide protection. It is unlikely that any single agency will succeed in submitting his competitors and customers to its arbitrary will. Customers, for instance, can demand ample assurances and checks on their power. This could include having the DIA subject itself to third party auditing and the like. Robert Murphy adds some relevant commentary:

> … [T]he private companies providing
> legal services would have far less power
> under free market anarchy than the
> government currently possesses. Most
> obvious, there would be no power to tax
> or to monopolize "service." If a particular
> insurance company were reluctant to pay
> legitimate claims, this would become
> quickly known, and people would take
> this into account when dealing with
> clients of this disreputable firm. The fear
> that (under free market anarchy) private
> individuals would replace politicians
> overlooks the true causes of state

---

[115] Hoppe, ibid.

mischief. Unlike feudal monarchs, democratic rulers don't actually own the resources (including human) that they control. Furthermore, the duration of their rule (and hence control of these resources) is very uncertain. For these reasons, politicians and other government employees do not exercise much care in maintaining the (market) value of the property in their jurisdiction. Shareholders of a private company, however, have every interest in choosing personnel and policies to maximize the profitability of the firm. All the horrors of the state — onerous taxation, police brutality, total war — are not only monstrous, but they're also grossly inefficient. It would never be profitable for anarchist insurance and legal firms to mimic the policies set by governments.[116]

As third-party protection and arbitration agencies gain popularity relative to State agencies, there will be noticeable civilizing effects. As the price of protection collapses, criminals will find honorable work as more rewarding to their ends than committing aggression. Time preferences will lower as individuals hire competent security and resolution agencies and abandon brutal and petty municipal police departments. Hoppe elaborates:

As a result of the constant cooperation of various insurers and arbitrators, then, a tendency toward the unification of property and contract law and the harmonization of the rules of procedure, evidence, and conflict resolution would be set in motion. Thus, in buying protection insurance, every insurer and insured becomes a participant in an integrated system of conflict avoidance and peacekeeping. Every single conflict and damage claim, regardless of where and by or against whom, would fall under the jurisdiction of one or more specific

---

116 Robert P. Murphy, *Chaos Theory: Two Essays on Market Anarchy* (New York: RJ Communications LLC, 2002).

> insurance agencies and would be handled
> either by an individual insurer's
> "domestic" law or by the "international"
> or "universal" law provisions and
> procedures agreed upon by everyone in
> advance. Hence, instead of permanent
> conflict, injustice, and legal insecurity —
> as under the present statist conditions —
> in a private-law society, peace, justice, and
> legal security would hold sway.[117]

Crime, unfortunately, will always exist, and it is not the purpose of this argument to prove that implementing a private law system will convert all men to saints and angels. Rather, it is intended to demonstrate that such a system is preferable to State-provided "justice." This argument for a private law system only takes for granted that mankind is inherently self-interested. That people prefer to get the most amount of gain for the least amount of effort, and it takes these seemingly negative characteristics and aligns them with the welfare of society. This, of course, does not mean one must not have charitable inclinations for free market anarchy to function properly or even that the profits sought must be of a monetary nature. It simply means this: given that human beings purposively use means to achieve ends, a free and open market in law will be the most conducive in satisfying the greatest number of desires to the greatest degree. The beauty of the free market is that this practical end is achieved *precisely by adhering to the libertarian principles of justice.*

---

[117] Hoppe, ibid.

Chapter Nine

DEFENSE AND SECURITY

FOR CENTURIES, LAW and political economy held sacred the notion that a sovereign must hold power over the masses. This notion, to the extent it is philosophical, has Hobbesian roots. Hobbes argues that a state of nature is a dangerous and wild place, where life is "nasty, brutish, and short."[118] The argument continues: Therefore, to install peace among the disparate peoples, they should submit their will and freedoms to a single sovereign, who, as a neutral, third party, will impartially administer justice and thwart crime for the commonwealth. The implication is that the people, without such a centralized institution, would spend too little on their own defense, making for a situation of near perpetual conflict. For this reason, many contend that security must be provided unilaterally by the State, and that its cost should be imposed on everyone irrespective of any individual's willingness or unwillingness to pay. This notion must be challenged. Contrary to Hobbes' arguments, defense and security are goods that can be sufficiently produced privately and exchanged on markets to willing buyers. Gustave de Molinari, in the 19th century, made the economic case for competitive governments:

> If there is one well-established truth in political economy, it is this: That in all cases, for all commodities that serve to provide for the tangible or intangible needs of the consumer, it is in the consumer's best interest that labor and trade remain free, because the freedom of labor and of trade have as their necessary and permanent result the maximum reduction of price.
>
> And this: That the interests of the consumer of any commodity whatsoever

---

[118] Thomas Hobbes, *Leviathan: Or the Matter, Forme, and Power of a Common-Wealth Ecclesiasticall and Civill.* edit. Ian Shapiro (New Haven: Yale University Press, 2010).

should always prevail over the interests of
the producer.
Now in pursuing these principles, one
arrives at this rigorous conclusion: That
the production of security should, in the
interests of the consumers of this
intangible commodity, remain subject to
the law of free competition.

Whence it follows: That no government
should have the right to prevent another
government from going into competition
with it, or to require consumers of
security to come exclusively to it for this
commodity.[119]

It is important not to confuse the term "government" with the
State. The State is a type of government; however, it is a coercive or
aggressive variant. Free markets also wield governing forces, however, such
forces are not artificially imposed by decree. They include the laws of
supply and demand, consumer sovereignty, reputation, competition, the
prospect of profits/losses, etc. As Molinari insinuates, security, just as any
other service, is most efficiently produced in freed markets.

The State Problem

The Immediate Contradiction

The State claims its role is to defend persons and their property.
Prior to the provision of such service, however, it must first steal from
people the very property it claims to protect via taxation. The State
essentially says "We are going to take your property under the threat of
violent reprimand, so that we may protect your property and your person."
Hoppe summarizes this ridiculous and self-refuting notion by referring to
States as expropriating property protectors. The State must first violate
property rights before being able to defend them.

---

[119] Gustave de Molinari, "Competition in Security" in *The Production of Security* (New
York: Center for Libertarian Studies, 1977).

The "Necessary Evil" Argument

A monopoly on the legal right to initiate force does not decrease the danger peaceful people face from aggressive people; in fact, an institution such as this serves to attract those who desire power and coercive control over others to its own positions of authority. This has only exacerbated the very premise for which State advocacy is based: that we require a State to protect the innocent from the criminal. Even the phrase "necessary evil" itself is self-refuting. Evil, by its very nature, is destructive and thus completely unnecessary to achieving the ends of life, liberty, and prosperity. Moreover, something that is truly necessary cannot be given the title of evil.

The State as a Monopoly Enterprise

Monopoly here is defined as an exclusive legal privilege to provide a given good or service enforced at the threat or application of violence. Fitting within the scope of this definition is the State's role as security provider. The State assumes and enforces the exclusive right to provide general security against aggressors both domestic and foreign. Despite the intentions of its agents, however, the State's provision of security must perpetually increase in cost and decrease in quality. Moreover, the State may modify the price and scope of this service on a whim. However, in order for the State to raise the price of this or any other services, some degree of public support is needed. Thus, the State will tend to provoke or allow crime or the threat of foreign aggression to increase, so that it may cite these security threats when expanding its own budget for defense. Take, for example, the destruction of the twin World Trade Center towers. Subsequent to the terror attacks on 9/11, the Department of Defense budget was massively increased, federal agents took over the role of providing airport security, and the Department of Homeland Security was born.

The Economic Calculation Problem

The State has no access to an accurate pricing mechanism with which to evaluate the profitability of its operations, so waste will necessarily abound. This is because its revenue is derived from taxes as opposed to voluntary contributions. Consequently, this perverts the feedback mechanism used to convey to producers how best to fulfill the desires of the consumer. The State does not operate in a profit or loss system, so it has neither the proper incentive nor the capacity to be economically efficient. However, the State is not lacking of incentives altogether. The prospect for re-election and, thus, campaign funding from various special interest groups and lobbyists will have a profound influence on the policy decisions of any given representative. Perhaps more funding is provided to county A as a political favor while county B enjoys little to no public works investments at all. Likewise, it is not difficult to imagine the prospects of military conflict increasing due to political favor garnered from elements in the military industrial complex.

The State as Ultimate Representative

Because the State acts as a unit, all the actions executed by its representatives are reflected on the people, for they must be funding these acts via taxes. Due to this financial connection, all of a given State's citizens become potential targets of retaliation for disgruntled foreign actors. If all property in a given geographic area is seen as generating revenue for the State, then it naturally represents a potential enemy target. It is this very set up that has brought about the modern form of total warfare.

Self Defense

The State has a tendency to disarm the populace so that it may be able to more effectively assert its dominion. However, this act of disarmament only increases vulnerability to foreign invasion as a potential invader would otherwise have to worry about State forces *and* heavily armed civilians. A heavily armed civilian populace constitutes a dangerous and unpredictable wild card that serves as an effective deterrent against invasion.

The Moral Hazard

The State's ability to externalize the costs of aggression onto taxpayers creates a moral hazard that enables it to implement more aggressive and costly policies than it otherwise could. Without centralized tax structures to bilk the people, the costs for such policies would be prohibitive, as they would have to be translated into higher premiums that drive customers away to more peaceful and affordable competitors. Lastly, if private security agencies employed aggressive measures, then they would suffer reputational damage, financial losses, and be held legally liable for property violations by competing security and arbitration agencies.

In addition to the State's comparatively increased propensity for engaging in aggressive activities, it provides no clear standards or measurements of effectiveness for its defensive services, and thus is much less accountable for any shortcomings. This is no mere accident. A *democratic* State has less deference still for long term defense or foreign policy impacts, as its ruling agents are only given temporary access to positions of authority. These temporary office holders are incentivized to exploit their positions of power and the resources they command as much as possible with no regard to maintaining their capital value. This is because the costs their policies generate may be deferred to their successors, the tax payers, and future generations through debt financing and inflation. Moreover, as politicians are merely stewards of the public domain, any advantage they do not press while in office will disappear forever. They may utilize, but cannot directly sell State assets and pocket the receipts. Once their official terms expire, they are unable to tap the State's resources in such a manner.

The Free Market Solution

Properly Aligning Incentives

Humans are rationally self-interested creatures. Due to the conflicts represented in the tragedy of the commons, public ownership of property will usually be less preferable when compared to the incentives associated with private property. When all property is privately owned, the personal interests of the individual to accrue wealth will be harmonized with the incentive to maintain the value or integrity of his property. Of course, some people will take better care of their property than others. However, on the whole, people are comparatively more inclined to take care of their own property than they are to take care of common or public property.

Who will Provide Defense?

Various types of insurance agencies (DIAs) will likely take over the role of security provision for the following reasons: They have a large amount of capital required to cover any claims made immediately after their provision of coverage. Hoppe explains:

> [Insurance agencies] operate on a nation-wide and even international scale, and they own large property holdings dispersed over wide territories and beyond single state boundaries. Accordingly, they have a manifest self-interest in effective protection, and are big and economically powerful. Furthermore, all insurance companies are connected through a network of contractual agreements of mutual assistance and arbitration as well as a system of international reinsurance agencies, representing a combined economic power which dwarfs that of most if not all existing governments.[120]

They have the financial incentive to *prevent* vandalism, violence, and intrusion by any party (whether it be a foreign nation-state or domestic criminal) for this is the outcome that yields them the greatest amount of profit. Finally, an infrastructure for reciprocity and cooperation between insurance agencies already exists.

The Mechanics of Free Market Security Provision

Defense Insurances Agencies (DIAs) will incentivize people to live in safe and easily defendable areas by offering them lower premiums. DIAs will also offer lower prices to those with long, peaceful records; conversely, they will penalize aggressive behavior or misconduct by increasing premiums, along with perhaps imposing scrutinizing monitoring requirements if coverage is to be maintained. DIAs may also offer lower

---

[120]   Hans-Hermann Hoppe, "The Case for Private Security" in *The Private Production of Defense* (Auburn: Ludwig Von Mises Institute, 2009), 22.

premiums for those who can provide them with proof of personal defensive capabilities. In this way, DIAs are able to incentivize good behavior and self-defense whilst simultaneously discouraging misconduct. Furthermore, it is in the DIA's financial interest to investigate, detect, and apprehend aggressors to hold them accountable for their crimes, as opposed to having to cover damages out of its own pocket. Contrast this with the agents of State-provided security who will laugh if asked to track down a stolen radio, or to compensate one for it.

As insurance revolves so much around the collecting of valuable information – namely, risk and financial assessments – it seems likely that DIAs would keep tabs on aggressors and share them with other insurance agencies, much like banks share information between themselves regarding bad credit risks. Banks, insurance agencies, law firms, and others could share this data so that they may be able to enjoy reciprocal relationships, allowing them to better determine the security risks in various environments. This "discipline of constant dealings" is what also incentivizes these various agencies to honor their agreements with one another. That is to say, many of them will realize that the long run benefits of their cooperative relations in this capacity will likely outweigh the short term benefits of reneging on a current undesired arrangement (such as an unfavorable arbitration ruling). The sharing of this information on various aggressors will have the mutually beneficial effect of allowing each of these agencies to set premiums which correspond more closely with actual risks.

The "Free Rider" Problem

Before anything, it is important to note that millions of people already act as free riders with respect to current State systems, despite the State having the legal right to demand payment. With that said, some suggestions for how to mitigate free riders and fraud:

- The DIAs may provide their clients with identifiable signs or medallions to carry on their persons to indicate coverage. DIA agents may also have, in addition to a database of covered persons, programs to provide their clients with tracking devices as a means to monitor and locate them when endangered. The client may be incentivized to carry such a device by the prospect of reduced premiums.
- They may publicly post maps of their covered and uncovered households. This will have a two-fold effect: First, it is likely that many aggressors would take into consideration the level of security around a household or person before deciding to commence

his/her act of aggression. Therefore, having access to such a map may deter him/her from targeting covered homes. Second, the people who do not patronize this service may realize their lack of coverage encourages and consolidates aggressors as they begin to specifically target homes without the resources of DIAs to defend them. It is this prospect of aggression that will further incentivize their adoption of DIA coverage.

- Various businesses may decide to restrict business to individuals who can provide proof that they contribute to a DIA. This restriction may be set with the intention of gaining PR for promoting the defensive strength of these free territories. Custom and culture play strong roles in circumventing the traditional issues associated with collective action problems. Due to reputational considerations and our adopted social mores, most of us leave tips at restaurants even if we plan on never returning to them. Likewise, in such a free society, people would likely encourage others to contribute to protection agencies as doing so benefits everyone with additional security.

- Many residential or commercial areas may implement exclusionary policies prohibiting the entrance of uncovered persons. A lack of DIA coverage may indicate two things: they are either unable to afford or are ineligible for coverage owing to a history of recurring aggressive behavior. These areas would be disinclined to invite persons lacking coverage as they would be unable to prove civilized behavior.

Of Secret Armies

It would be catastrophic to realize the agency to which one delegated his security and protection was actually his greatest threat. This is, in fact, true with regard to the State today (but of this we have no choice). When individuals have the option to browse and purchase protection, they will doubtlessly take into consideration the trustworthiness of the organization in question. Just as no one invests in a safe before being assured of the integrity of the lock, so too will scrutiny be placed upon the capacity of these organizations to effectively neuter and bind their own use of force. The threat of an agency using its resources to hire mercenary soldiers against its own customers will be felt by all, and that consideration will play a serious role in one's patronage. As this will be one of the primary concerns shared by most customers, the onus will be on the DIAs to set up their service in such a way that its prospective clients are assured that no such secret army bent on conquest will ever manifest, let alone turn against them. The DIA may be able to qualm these concerns by subjecting itself to random third-party arms inspections, and by obliging itself to pay X amount of money to its clients if it is found to be operating outside of contractual guidelines, and in still other ways. This money may be kept in an escrow account. In this way, the client may be assured that the DIA will not be able to renege on this agreement without serious financial recourse.

Additionally, it would be very difficult for such an army to be assembled, as the costs of amassing such a force would necessarily cause a rise in premiums for this DIA's customers. However, such a rise in premiums would drive them away to competitors and cause a major disruption in revenue. Finally, it will be difficult for this DIA to find suppliers willing to fulfill massive orders for materials relating to such an endeavor, as they too are concerned with their reputation, and do not wish to abet murderers and robbers.

Preventing the Manifestation of a State

A voluntary society, replete with competitive upstarts, would be a decentralized and dynamic society. Protection could take the form of martial arts, shooting practice, a gang or clique, professional security agencies, and any number of as-of-yet undiscovered means. In order for a State to (re)assert itself onto a public, it would need to defeat every competitor that could defend itself among any number of these lines. If a powerful army bent on domination did somehow manifest, most, if not all, of the remaining DIAs would be compelled to band together to counter the State's aim of conquest in the interest of their own personal and financial survival, along with the increased attention from having acted heroically. Competitors to the State may utilize any number of attack vectors to neutralize the threat posed by a State, including physical impediments, cyber-warfare, espionage, assassinations of key figures, ending/establishing commercial agreements and treaties, influencing social opinion, inciting riots, and other ways. However, even granting the risk that a State may manifest in a stateless society, it must continue to be fought for the same reasons many choose to fight cancer despite the possibility of recurrence.

Foreign Nations and Free Territories

The relationship between organizations of free peoples and established nation-states has been varied over the course of history. Many kings, presidents and parliaments have waged cruel war on "natives" who,

180

lacking Eurocentric conceptions of hierarchical legal systems, have appeared to Western invaders as idiots or savages, without government, justice, law, civility, without nuance or subtlety at all. In some instances, where the similarity between peoples was great, nation-states have recognized the sovereignty of free territories. For instance, between the Revolutionary War and the ratification of the Constitution, each American colony became a sovereign, an independent political autonomy. Relations with foreign nations would depend on much, including comparative religion, trade, ethnicity, language, wealth, and the character the people demonstrate abroad.

There are a number of reasons, however, to regard the *institutional structure of the defense organizations in society* as a crucial matter in determining foreign relations. As in other aspects of life, the incentives matter. In an anarchist society, there are many defenders, each armed with their own skills. Potential invaders would recognize a very different structure than they are used to seeing. Instead of a single organization acting to defend a complex society, they would see a plurality of firms offering various levels of coverage and physical protection, big and small, for the individual, family, or business. Furthermore, the goal for the invader is itself not clear. As there is no State to defeat, there is no existing tax machine to acquire. There is no easily-accessible mechanism with which to rob one's recently-conquered subjects. The terrain of an anarchist society further implies guerrilla tactics and insurgency, counter-economies, encryption tools, large-scale gun ownership, and further barriers to State encroachment.

Indeed, beyond this, the prospective invader would have a very difficult time garnering the support for such an invasion, as there would be no grounds or justification for such an act. If a foreign State had a legitimate issue with a particular person or group of people, then the DIAs would happily offer to mediate and resolve the issue, either dissolving or covering the claim as trials determined. As individuals in such a society are not "citizens" of any nation, but are free and independent people, the only potential for retaliation or calls for retribution would be against specific individuals. Without a particular government to blame, foreign aggressors have a more difficult time with the act of dehumanization. Consequently, potential invaders would have to consider the risks of losing legitimacy at home and abroad for attacking free territories. One unique consideration would be the uncertain military and civilian defensive abilities of the occupants one is invading. In such a society, there would be no universal or mandated arms regulations in distinct contrast to its State counterparts. The arsenal of some of these DIAs could include nuclear or biological weapons, which may serve to deter otherwise aggressive nations from invading. Historically, the leaders of other nations are hesitant to invade countries armed with nuclear weapons as their own personal survival will be directly threatened in pursuit of such an endeavor.

Trusting Private Actors With Nuclear Arms

Nuclear warheads and other weapons of mass destruction are designed specifically to indiscriminately annihilate groups of people. There cannot be a targeted use of a hydrogen bomb or a vial of plague; by their nature, they are intended to spread and cause damage to any human, guilty of an injustice or not, and cause terrifying pain and death.[121] That said, these weapons currently exist, and until the day they are abandoned and disarmed, they will be held by some parties. It would be more advantageous for DIAs to acquire nuclear weapons as opposed to the heads of state of various nations. Of course, the onus will be on the DIAs to discover the right configuration of checks and balances within its operational procedures to assure its prospective clients that such weapons will not be used without just cause. Moreover, they will have the burden of coming up with a way to demonstrate that such weapons will not be used against innocent people. The obvious reason is purely financial: if such agencies incur any form of collateral damage, they would be subject to the same legal and financial liability as any other individual. Another reason is marketing, branding, and how the agency wants to be seen – as a paladin on a hill, ready to protect, not a marauding berserker, ready to plunder.

There are no reasons why a State should demonstrate an advantage over protecting and safeguarding the use of such weapons over similar attempts made by a DIA. It is individuals that handle nuclear weapons under State control just as it is individuals who would handle them under the auspices of a DIA. One chief difference, however, is the incentive structure: the survival of a DIA is predicated upon the proper handling of these dangerous weapons, whereas the State may easily fail in such a duty, and yet demand more funding for the sake of accomplishing the task more effectively in the future. In business, failure is met with losses or liquidation; in government, failure is met with larger budgets. One may see how the prospect for an increased budget may make the State a poorer candidate for handling such dangerous materials than a private defense agency.

---

[121]   Rothbard, "War, Peace, and the State" in *Egalitarianism*, 115-32. "These weapons are *ipso facto* engines of indiscriminate mass destruction. (The only exception would be the extremely rare case where a mass of people who were all criminals inhabited a vast geographical area.) We must, therefore, conclude that the use of nuclear or similar weapons, or the threat thereof, is a sin and a crime against humanity for which there can be no justification."

DEFENSE AND SECURITY

Worst Case Realized

In the event a foreign belligerent attempts to conquer or kill groups of free people, they would first encounter the civil resistance of their own people, and then the physical resistance of their victims. Without a State to provide defense, protection of property will be ensured by mutually coordinating defense firms. Most of the defensive agencies would likely band together to ward off any foreign aggressor for the sake of retaining the capital value of their overlapping covered territories. Furthermore, these free territories may have the technological advantage over any opposing outside force since free markets tend to produce more advanced technology and attract stronger talent, all other things being equal.

In defense, guerrilla and/or asymmetric tactics would likely be implemented as they have proven to be highly effective against much stronger foes. Take, for example, Vietnam, the Soviet/Mujahedeen conflict, and today's prolonged War on Terrorism. It would be far more expensive for the invader to take offensive actions than it would be for the defender to take defensive actions through unconventional means. The resultant financial drain and loss of lives suffered through attrition will serve to dampen the invading country's support, which is requisite for its sustained involvement. Moreover, because there will be competing defense agencies, there will not be any system-wide vulnerabilities in which the invading force can exploit. The defense will be decentralized and have many independent sources of power, communication, and weaponry. One must also consider the inherent advantage afforded to those with previously set up defensive fortifications. Unlike in other State realms, the general populace will be much better armed due to the lack of gun prohibitions and the presence of financial incentives provided by DIAs for people to develop their own defensive capabilities. Finally, people from these free territories would likely have valuable trade relations with the citizens of foreign countries; thus any threat to these prosperous trading ties may prompt these foreigners to request their own governments to join in the defensive efforts against such an invading nation.

Conclusion

The incredible benefits of security offered in freed markets are not confined to a more "economical" use of resources with fewer incidents of crime. In the wake of a safer environment, human cooperation is truly able to abound and flourish. This will increase the rate of technological progress by orders of magnitude. With such increases in technology and human cooperation, the time and resources previously spent towards securing basic human needs (food, shelter, clothing, etc.) would then be freed up for use towards higher pursuits and leisure. Self-actualization would take over as life's primary objective for most, displacing mere sustenance as a focal point.

Chapter Ten

TRANSPORTATION NETWORKS

Economics of Public Roads

IN DISCUSSING THE operations and economics of an anarchist society, specific attention must be paid to understanding transportation networks, including their infrastructure, their environment, their management, and more. Because networks that connect people are so valuable, many people consider parts of such a network public. They regard everyone as having "share" in the network, and that, therefore, the State, being "impartial," should be its steward. This is the popular opinion regarding the maintenance and upkeep of roadways, highways, waterways, and even the airspace.

Today, the vast majority of roads and other such networks are funded through means of expropriation: taxation. Taxation is simply the confiscation of the property of others enforced through the threat or application of initiatory violence against dissenters. Predictably, this constitutes a clear violation of libertarian non-aggression. Many believe that only by such shakedowns are roads and such able to be financed. Unlike all other goods, narrow strips of painted land are supposedly unable to be produced in sufficient quantity or quality by market interactions emerging from freely consenting adults.

In reality, roads may be sufficiently financed through voluntary means. These funds may come from any number of sources: the businesses they connect, individual drivers themselves, and others. Various charitable organizations may offer travel credits to rehabilitated or impoverished members of society. In any case, payment would fall only on those who assume it – never on uninvolved third-parties – and use of the road would be subject to the discretion of its legitimate owner(s). This is in contradistinction to State provision where taxpayers are mandated to fund all roads, including those some will never use. It should be clear that this arrangement does not require one's prior consent; it is an imposition, not a purchase. In addition to the injustice of their provision, State roads are economically wasteful and dangerous.[122]

The collectivization of roads carries many economic disadvantages. Often times, advocates of the State will make critiques of free markets, which inevitably apply to the State as well. Such folly will be avoided here. In the first place, as roads provided by States are treated as "public goods," typical consequences related to the tragedy of the commons emerge. Because nobody can exercise ownership claims over public roads there is a comparatively lesser incentive to maintain their quality. As no individual can reap the capital value of the resource in question, the incentive emerges for each individual to consume as much and as quickly as possible. Public roads will be regarded as "free for all" and massive over-consumption in the forms of traffic jams and rush hours will be the result. Similarly, one may see that an individual is more likely to keep his own yard landscaped than he is to take over the landscaping duties of a public park. It is a fact of economics that people are more willing to take care of their own property than they are to take care of common property.

In the second place, by monopolizing the road network, the State ensures there is no authority higher than itself through which to hold its own agents accountable. Naturally, this creates a moral hazard in the State's provision of any service. Moreover, the State offers itself no quantitative standard by which others may hold it accountable, such as levels of traffic congestion, road serviceability, or the number of road fatalities. Additionally, State agencies lack a profit/loss incentive due to their power to externalize costs onto the general public through taxation. There is no relation between improved road infrastructure and State revenue. As the State lacks a profit incentive, to improve its services, it is left to take by force whatever amount it deems necessary in order to maintain and grow the service. The State is actually incentivized to provide lower quality service and charge greater prices. This is a result of the disutility of labor, which simply states that leisure is preferred to labor, and that people prefer to exert the least amount of energy required to achieve a particular end. The influence of the disutility of labor on State agents is evidenced by the

---

[122] A study conducted by Infrastructure Report Card.org in 2008 showed that "Americans spend 4.2 billion hours a year stuck in traffic (about 40 hours a year per motorist) at a cost of $78.2 billion a year – $710 per motorist. Roadway conditions are a significant factor in about one-third of traffic fatalities. Poor road conditions cost U.S. motorists $67 billion a year in repairs and operating costs – $333 per motorist; 33% of America's major roads are in poor or mediocre condition and 36% of the nation's major urban highways are congested." http://www.infrastructurereportcard.org/fact-sheet/roads. According to statistics provided by the National Highway Traffic Safety Administration, between 1995 and 2010, there was an average of 37,000 fatal crashes on highways per year. http://www-fars.nhtsa.dot.gov/Main/index.aspx The renowned Austrian Economist Walter Block projects that under a completely privatized road system one may expect closer to 8,000 casualties per year as opposed to the State's 37,000. Walter Block, "Road Privatization: Rejoinder to Mohring" in *The Privatization of Roads and Highways: Human and Economic Factors* (Lewiston: Edwin Mellen, 2006).

increased expenditures on roads and highways every year by the State: an increase in cost which is borne by the taxpayer. Because State agents do not bear the cost for public services, they will generally favor and promote increased expenditures in various bureaus and departments as a means to secure their own livelihoods.

In the third place, the State lacks a pricing mechanism. Even supposing that the State has every intention to provide the most desired road service to the greatest number of people, without a resource-allocation mechanism like the price system, it cannot possibly hope to discover the most economical manner in which to do so. This sort of optimization is only possible when dealing with numbers derived from voluntary transactions. The demand for a good or service is represented by how much, and at what price, people as a whole are willing to purchase it. Thus, the price system takes into account to what degree consumers desire a given good or service. It is superior to pure voting, which cannot capture the relative intensities of the desires of each individual for a given plan. Perhaps some prefer roads to be managed one way as opposed to another, but many may prefer more for those resources used to be employed for an entirely different end. The pricing mechanism, untainted by government interference, guides entrepreneurs into making those economic decisions which yield the lowest opportunity costs, and encourages them to concentrate their energies on tasks for which they are well-suited. For the entrepreneur to optimize the allocation of his resources, he must offer them at the market clearing price. This is the price at which consumers are willing to purchase the same number of units of a given product or service as those being offered. Generally, this clearing price will yield the entrepreneur the greatest amount of profit as, by definition, there are no mutually-agreeable exchanges left to complete. Efficiency in economics refers to the number of people whose desires are being satisfied with a scarce amount of resources, and to what degree, in relation to the available set of alternatives. In order for one to get an accurate picture of what people want, where they want it, and how much of it they want, he must first have access to profit and loss figures – accounting – generated on the market through voluntary transactions. In contrast with entrepreneurs on the market, the revenue the State accrues is through involuntary means. Thus, it must necessarily have an inaccurate picture regarding how best to economize the resources it commands. Consequently, there will be an over production of roads in some areas and an underproduction in others.

It may be the case that many politicians are motivated and influenced by the aim of providing safer and less congested roads and highways, but it would be naive for one to assume that is their only motivation or influence. Political factors and special interests have a considerable effect on decisions regarding where to allocate resources for the production or maintenance of various roads. Unfortunately, these outside influences are seldom in line with consumer interest.

Some critics may object that private roads are perfectly legal, yet rather uncommon. Though this statement may be true, it fails to identify a few key considerations. In order to be a patron of a private road service, one is not simply purchasing it instead of supporting public roads. He is paying twice – once for a private subscription and again when he bears the taxes for public roads. The fact that one's payment for the usage of public roads is legally required of him and therefore a sunk cost greatly deters him from choosing to purchase additional road services. Moreover, the State has usurped much of the prime real estate for road building through the use of eminent domain. This is land theft through legal privilege, which its private counterparts are not able to commit with impunity. Private roads are not as prevalent as one might expect today because the State grants itself illegitimate legal privileges over this industry via its exclusive powers to coercively assert its will over others.

In the fourth place, the costs of building and maintaining roads are externalized to the taxpayers. This serves to artificially increase the demand for those industries affected by road travel, namely the oil, automobile, and rubber industries. This is why many of the special interests beckoning for the expansion of the highway system tend to come from one of the three aforementioned business sectors. The result of such an expansion is a greater amount of profits and resources directed towards these industries than there otherwise would be in a free market system. These industries are often times criticized for being exploitative and monopolistic – rightfully so. However, this has little to do with their greed and much more to do with having access to the coercively empowered institution known as the State. Just as mafia families have connections in various industries relevant to their power, so too does the State. It cultivates and distorts firms in many industries: banking, entertainment, mass media, education, etc. Naturally, those industries related to movement of persons and materials become captured by States. This relationship is absolutely not representative or consistent with freed markets, as they are inherently absent such an aggressive State apparatus.

Privatization and Desocialization

Many interpretations exist regarding the concept of privatization. Some see privatization as government agencies doing business with their own market-like imitations[123], while others see it as a pure gift to any "private" actor whatsoever.[124] In reality, privatization simply refers to the

---

[123]   Examples of this include Fannie Mae and Sallie Mae.
[124]   Privileged contracts given to specific construction companies come to mind.

change in management from a public entity to a private one, whether in charitable or commercial pursuits. As in many things to do with State administration, the Devil is in the details. After all, it would be a violation of libertarian norms if the federal government were to one day claim the Jones family owns the entire state of New York. Jones' family management of the lives, land, and property in the state of New York would not necessarily constitute a substantial improvement over State management – and may perhaps be more injurious. The government should not, then, "privatize" in this manner. A preferable solution is desocialization; return the land and property to those who provided the funds for their purchase/production: the taxpayers.[125] The free transfer of equity from previously State-managed industries would quickly create markets and entrepreneurs eager to earn business.

Private road providers have a vested interest in the flourishing of the businesses, cities, and residential communities they connect as their abounding value will increase the demand for the roads which connect them. Naturally, the self-interest of the road provider is aligned with those of his customers. As road providers realize that their customers desire assurances regarding safety and liability, the road providers may require all their patrons obtain insurance. The premiums the insurance agencies charge will serve to regulate their clients' driving habits. These agencies will be permitted to take into account all factors or demographics that indicate one's actuarial risks in the determination of his premiums. Discriminating practices, however, will be tempered by public relations considerations. A bigoted reputation may be followed by a loss of profits and business. A list of some factors that may be used when determining the premiums for various clients include:

- Driver safety courses taken
- Frequency of driving
- Time of day typically driven
- Driving history
- Installation of safety features (e.g., automatic braking, etc.)

The auto insurance agency may verify some of this data by offering their clients GPS devices, which track driving habits, in exchange for lower monthly premiums. These insurance agencies may also encourage or insist clients wear seat belts, drive soberly, and practice other risk mitigating behavior as a condition for maintaining coverage. Alternatively, the road providers themselves may require their prospective patrons to adhere to such safe driving behavior as a precondition to using their roads. Insurance

---

[125] Murray N. Rothbard, "How and How Not to Desocialize" in *The Review of Austrian Economics* 6.1 (1992): 65-77.

agencies do not expect their customers to take all of these steps simply out of the kindness of their hearts. Rather, it is in the best financial interest of both the auto insurance agency and road provider alike to ensure that neither you nor your car are harmed during your trip.

Another valuable benefit of complete road privatization is the presence of uninhibited competition. Such competition need not necessarily be between two roads going to the same destination. Rather, it could be between various road provider companies. In order to secure future contracts or venture capital from investors, these companies will have to demonstrate a reputable and competent ability to manage roads that are safe, open, and profitable. It is this reputation which will influence any potential investor or patron to choose provider X as opposed to provider Y. From the consumer's perspective, many more factors than price alone may be considered in his decision. For instance, he may value the speed and responsiveness of a given road company's towing and ambulatory services. Moreover, this prospective patron may evaluate the quantitative standards by which various road companies hold themselves accountable (e.g., the speed of rush hour traffic). Such promised standards could be supported by the road providers' contractual obligations to compensate any individuals affected by conditions that fall outside of said standards. For example, if someone misses a flight due to excessive road congestion, the road provider may offer to pay for the customer's next plane ticket or simply compensate him for his troubles.

In contrast to the State provision of road services, a privatized system would yield a greater level of diversity in road planning amongst the competing road companies. The allure of larger profits will incentivize these road companies to continually refine the efficiency and safety of their road systems. It is, however, unlikely that this competition would result in a severe mismatching of road rules, as each road provider would understand that such awkward and tedious transitions would serve to deter and discourage customers from using their roads. Compatibility is important in protocols, principles, and rules. Take, for example, the private railroad companies of the 1800's and the cell phone companies today. Each implemented a high degree of interoperability in their services so as to maximize their respective customer's satisfaction, which ultimately translates into profits. Imagine owning a Sprint phone and being unable to call someone with Verizon. Finally, entrepreneurs have access to an unadulterated pricing mechanism which allows them the ability to make rational economic calculations – i.e., whether or not one aspect of their current service should be altered, retained or scrapped.

Environmental Considerations

190

A completely privatized road system may also be better for the environment in that it would encourage people to use lighter and more fuel efficient cars. Cars that contribute less wear and tear on the road will cost their drivers less in subscriptions, since such factors will likely be factored into the price of using a given road service. Likewise, people may be more incentivized to car pool or travel via bus or some other form of mass transit. This, of course, would result in less harmful pollutants emanated per traveler. Furthermore, because people have a choice of whether or not to contribute funds toward road services, cheaper and more efficient alternatives may arise such as maglev trains or flying vehicles. A privatized road system would be more judicious in its distribution of costs as road providers strive to charge each customer in proportion to the degree of services used. Private road providers may also charge higher rates during peak hours as a means to increase road safety by decreasing traffic congestion. In other words, with peak pricing, the timing of transportation can be staggered and road consumption can be smoothed out over the course of a day. Due to this, one's employer may take into account the additional costs of using the road during certain peak hours when creating his employees' work schedule. Scheduling employees around peak hours would save them money and/or prevent the employer from having to increase their wages as a means to compensate for additional transportation fees.

Security Considerations

The desire for safety is a universal trait. Few people desire to shop at a store where they are likely to be robbed, or to travel through a neighborhood where their car may be stolen, or to drive on a road where dangerous road racing, daredevils, and drunkards abound. This is an obvious concern, and as such will be addressed by the owners. The owner(s) of a given road will have a great financial incentive to provide reliable measures of security, as this will directly impact the value of their services and property. The means by which they can address these issues can include video surveillance, hired police services, speed detecting sensors, etc. A rule might be stipulated that drunk drivers involved with any collision automatically assume the liability. Other conditions and terms of use will exist on other roads, and the constant desire to attract customers will incentivize a continual exploration and experimentation into various rules aimed at discovering their optimal configuration. Perhaps speed limits may be rejected and individual sets of rules for each lane of traffic will emerge. These road providers, as legitimate business owners, can set the terms of use for their property just as any restaurant, shopping mall, or amusement park owner(s) can specify accepted behaviors and demand adherence to regular norms. Customers unwilling or unable to abide by such specified rules will be prevented from using this particular road service, and must arrange for alternative transport. This is in contrast with the State, who is not the legitimate owner of the roads and, therefore, may not justly apply or enforce any policies regarding how they are to be utilized.

Possible Payment Methods

Entrepreneurial road providers would realize that frequent stops to throw change in a bucket would congest their roads and deter future customers from using them. The installation of digital readers on customer cars may be a possible payment alternative as they can communicate with sensors on the road that track how far a person has traveled and the weight of his vehicle. With this information, the road provider may send the customer a bill in the mail, directly charge his bank account, or send invoices to a digital currency wallet. Some road providers may offer fixed rates for those who do not want to be tracked in such ways. These rates will likely be higher than those determined by actual usage, but may be seen as a worthy value to consumers who place a high degree of importance on maintaining anonymity.

Capital Considerations

As road networks need to interface and connect with networks of competitive providers, constructing the foundations of such a network can quickly become cost prohibitive. To finance early stages of construction, road providers may seek out venture capital. Alternatively, some expanding businesses or residential developers may offer to help finance such an operation as they have interests in areas not currently serviced by roads. Finally, there is nothing written in stone demanding that one company has to own a road as extensive as a cross country interstate. Different sections of a conjoined road could be managed and owned by different road companies. In this way, the costs of starting up or maintaining a vast highway can be spread out amongst many companies.

Price Gouging

As the real estate and physical road improvements are goods owned by road providers, they are free to charge any amount for their services. The GoodSmith road network is reliable and often uncongested, and it charges a penny per mile. ShippingWay, however, allows 18-wheel trucks and maintains elaborate safety mechanisms to protect drivers, and it charge three pennies per mile. Any individual road provider who dramatically increased his rates would be met with desertion. A price hike encourages his customers to patronize competing road services. Additionally, such a hike in prices would encourage his customers to increase their level of carpooling, thereby cutting into his profits. Such carpooling, once embraced on a mass scale, may not revert back to its original levels even if the road prices return to their original rates. This is because many customers may have become accustomed to their new arrangements, or would simply not trust the company not to raise rates so drastically again in the future. Additionally, such capricious price swings would damage the road provider's future business prospects with other businesses or customers. Such actions may also incite economic ostracizing as a means to pressure this road provider to reduce rates or suffer major losses of lucrative business relations with other members of the community.

If none of these aforementioned consequences hold sway, the businesses which are currently serviced by his highway may campaign to raise funds in order to bring in an alternative road provider. This sequence of events will be the market's way of weeding out such disruptive price hikes, and leaving behind, in its wake, entrepreneurs whose primary aims are to satisfy their customers. One's ability to satisfy his customer base is what ultimately determines the prosperity or failure of his business.

Resolving Difficult Situations

In the event critical geographic regions are already owned, road companies may implement any number of solutions including: offering to pay the owner of the obstructing property for passage through his property; building, over, under and around the individual's property; organizing public campaigns to encourage road construction, and more.

Moreover, hypothetical consumer fears – like a single encompassing road holding a residential community hostage – are often unfounded. It is in the road provider's economic best interest to not breach contract or capriciously raise prices to exorbitant levels as doing so would only cause ostracism and losses in future business. For instance, future

193

prospective residents may be deterred from moving into this community due to the high travel rates. With fewer residents, there would be fewer paying customers for the road provider. Additionally, the issue may be circumvented by building an alternate road above or below the road which surrounds the community. Moreover, people would likely acquire contractual assurances regarding access to their homes prior to sale. The terms of this road access may be discussed as a precondition to purchasing a home. For instance, one may only offer to buy a given house if the road provider servicing it agrees to certain fixed payment, service, or quality conditions. Finally, this issue would most likely be addressed by a residential developer prior to construction. Either the real estate agency or the building developer may understand that people want assurances that there are dependable and predictable means to travel from their houses on a reliable pricing schedule. Accordingly, the developer may require such concerns to be addressed in his contract with the corresponding road service provider prior to starting construction of the residential community.

The *exact* shape and nature of transportation networks in a free market system cannot, of course, be predicted. However, considering the more closely aligned economic incentives, one may conclude with confidence that whatever form they take will correspond far more closely with ever changing consumer preferences.

Chapter Eleven

EDUCATION

EDUCATION IS, WITHOUT a doubt, an essential component of life. In fact, by the mere act of living consciously, one cannot help but observe the nature and behavior of the world and its inhabitants. Every day is filled with experiences which may either affirm to a greater degree one's currently held beliefs or reveal something new and previously unobserved, which may cause his beliefs to be altered accordingly. Life involves the process of refining one's understanding of himself, others, and the environment surrounding his existence until he is no longer. Hence, education is held in high regard and rightly so. However, the value of education by society in general has, as many other noble concepts, been manipulated into justifying a strict regulation of the minds of the youth. Language, arithmetic, and basic literacy seem to be indispensable building blocks for future learning. Many have cited the importance of such skills when advocating public schooling, compulsory attendance, and the regulation of curriculum taught in both the public and private spheres. Tragically, such mandates and regulations impede the flowering and proliferation of these essential skills as well as innumerable other avenues of knowledge relative to the education and growth of children in free societies. Competition and economic calculation inherent in freed markets incentivizes and enables entrepreneurs to provide many methods of teaching tailored to an individual's mental acuity and personal interests. As with knowledge itself, such teaching methods will never be perfected, but they *will* be most efficiently and perpetually refined under a paradigm of freedom from administrative coercion.

It is indeed *because* proper education is so integral that we cannot afford to allow it to be regulated, restricted, and usurped by State functionaries. The use of aggression to ensure the provision of any product or service precipitates and manifests the very fears for which its use was originally demanded. This is no different in the provision of education. The only tool wielded by the State to which market participants are not privy is that of aggression. Markets are defined by their absence of systemic aggression, because it may only be used to destroy, diminish, and pervert. Aggression does not satisfy the inherent demands of existence, i.e., the demand for acquiring food, shelter, water, education, love, etc. On the contrary, it exacerbates such needs and creates a zero-sum game between the members of society, where one may only gain at the direct expense of others. Aggression thus promotes chaos, not cooperation. Only when individuals choose to deal with each other voluntarily and respect private property rights may their dealings result in mutual benefit and a net increase in their wealth. Ludwig von Mises describes the economic purpose of cooperation:

> The fundamental social phenomenon is the division of labor and its counterpart human cooperation. Experience teaches man that cooperative action is more efficient and productive than isolated action of self-sufficient individuals.[126]

Only this paradigm of voluntary cooperation and peace may truly mitigate the risks we encounter as organic beings which require certain resources to survive, multiply, and thrive. Finally, through the promotion of diversity and specialization of tasks inherent in the division of labor, we may be able to optimally enhance our wealth in the material, mental, and psychological realms. Peaceful markets are the key to promoting such ends. Rothbard explains the role of diversity in creating a flourishing society:

> But human individuals, despite similarities in ends and values, despite mutual influences, tend to express the unique imprint of the individual's own personality. The development of individual variety tends to be both the cause and the effect of the progress of civilization. As civilization progresses, there is more opportunity for the development of a person's reasoning and tastes in a growing variety of fields. And from such opportunities come the advancement of knowledge and progress which in turn add to the society's civilization. Furthermore, it is the variety of individual interests and talents that permits the growth of specialization and division of labor, on which civilized economies depend.[127]

---

[126] Mises, "Action Within the Framework of Society," in *Human Action*, 157.

[127] Murray N. Rothbard, "The Individual's Education" in *Education, Free & Compulsory* (Auburn: Ludwig Von Mises Institute, 1999), 5.

EDUCATION

Positive Rights vs. Negative Rights

Many people believe everyone has a right to education; others contend that we have rights against such impositions. For the purpose of disentangling this philosophical mess, a review of positive and negative rights is in order. Positive rights essentially entail that one is entitled to a certain product, service, or environmental arrangement, i.e., that some other person must *perform* some activity in order to fulfill such rights. Conversely, negative rights refer to rights which an individual holds that entitle him to be free from certain actions. Put differently, negative rights entail that individuals may *not* justifiably engage in certain activities against others. In other words, positive rights require others to *commit* certain acts whereas negative rights require them to *refrain* from particular behavior. Examples of positive rights may include a right to healthcare, education, or food; a prime example of a negative right is the right to free speech.

Philosophical libertarians believe that positive rights are morally illegitimate as they require others to commit or perform certain actions regardless of their consent to do so. Having a right entails that its violation implies the use of violence would be justified in attaining a remedy or restitution. Thus, positive rights entail that one may use violence against another if he does not receive a particular product or service to which he is supposedly entitled. *The only rights people have, according to free market anarchists (libertarians), are property rights.* The Non-Aggression Principle itself is simply a derivative of one's ownership of his own body and property. Owning something, after all, entails the *exclusive* right to employ said something so long as such employment does not entail aggressive interference with the persons or property of others.

Free market anarchists thus believe that to enforce any positive right is to necessarily violate the negative rights of others. Those who espouse positive rights, such as a right to education, believe if one is not receiving the education to which he is entitled, he may coerce another into either providing education or in surrendering a portion of his property for its funding. Property rights, non-aggression, and self-ownership are all logically incompatible with any inherent positive right. An additional complication of positive rights is the ambiguity of the level of service to which one is entitled. Is he entitled to merely being taught the alphabet and simple arithmetic? Or is he entitled to be educated in advanced literature, calculus, and quantum physics? Perhaps something in between? Any such determination is highly arbitrary. If a theory of rights includes such arbitrary and unclear boundaries, it becomes counter-productive to its purpose of mitigating interpersonal conflict.

State Management vs. Free Market

One of the most pernicious aspects of the public schooling system is its compulsory attendance laws. Such laws have the effect of sending children to school against their will. The effects on a child's creativity and psyche from being compelled by threat of force to go to such sterile institutions are incalculable. Such institutions are not tailored to his individual preferences or capacities to any substantial degree. Some children may withdraw into depression and other anti-social behavior; other children may act out and rebel, which is not only an indication that such a situation is unhealthy for them, but also renders the educational environment for their peers less suitable for growth. An environment of child-selected education would eliminate the majority of anti-social behavior.

Institutions that were voluntarily chosen by parent and child alike would yield greater and more direct incentives to please parents and children. Such institutions would provide the methods and content of education that is most highly desired and/or under-serviced relative to what they observe to be the market demand. In contrast, compulsory attendance laws coupled with taxation create an environment filled with moral hazard for these schools. If school funding is guaranteed by the State, then the focus will be geared much more towards satisfying government bureaucrats than catering to the desires of parents and, least of all, to the desires of children. Public schools are only marginally concerned with parental satisfaction as they cannot, under threat of force, withdraw their financial support from them. Aaron Smith offers a few remarks on compulsory attendance laws:

> Current laws vary by state in details, but they are quite homogeneous in spirit. All require a minimum amount of instructional time (ranging from 160 to 186 days annually) at approved institutions. The majority of Americans between the ages of 5 and 18 are compelled to meet this requirement, with several states enforcing slightly more lenient laws. Although parents are free to pursue private education for their children, such options are almost always regulated by state governments.[128]

---

[128] Aaron Smith, "The Costs of Compulsory Education." (editorial published at Ludwig Von Mises Institute, Auburn, Alabama, June 22, 2011.)

In essence, compulsory attendance laws and the regulation of curriculum effectively subject children to imprisonment and mass indoctrination. When a single institution may dictate the length of formal schooling as well as regulate to a large degree the content which must be taught, such power will ultimately be used to benefit itself irrespective of its purported goals or intended beneficiaries. A population which at its youth is taught to obey authority for its own sake and that is, to a large degree, reared by State functionaries (public teachers) will be far easier to control and manage once it transitions into adulthood. Though this end may not be consciously acknowledged or pursued overtly by public teachers, it is nonetheless a prominent result. Even if various politicians truly believe that it is in the best interest of all children to be in school for a set period of days or to receive a certain type of education, these intentions do not alter the fact that different children have different interests, aptitudes, and preferences that must be sacrificed to the central plan. Fully in agreement with Hayek, Mises remarks that "The alternative is not plan or no plan. The question is: whose planning? Should each member of society plan for himself or should the paternal government alone plan for all?"[129]

The degree to which education is uniform and involuntarily imposed upon children is the degree to which they will suffer *now* in the form of boredom, intimidation, and despair and in the *future* in the form of untapped potential, a dulled mind, and a greater susceptibility to the whims of arbitrary authority. The many hours spent at school enduring tedious and vacuous instruction could have instead been used for more engaging and stimulating learning activities tailored more closely to the capacities and desires of the individual child. Though a voluntary or free market education system will not always be *perfectly* tailored, its incentive structure would be much more appropriately aligned with achieving the ends of edification, growth, and maturity than its Statist counterpart equipped with the exclusive powers to aggressively demand payment for its services and to unilaterally dictate the scope thereof. Even those parents who send their children to private schools or who decide to homeschool are still subject to compulsory attendance laws and curriculum requirements. In essence, they and their children remain subject to the same aggressive and monopolistic oversight perpetrated by the State. Aaron Smith comments on the State's destructive role in squashing private educational alternatives:

> Private schools and homeschools are rarely truly free-market alternatives to government-regulated education. By mandating attendance, states have a

---

[129] Ludwig Von Mises, "Planning for Freedom" (speech presented at the American Academy of Political and Social Science, Philadelphia, Pennsylvania, 1945).

virtual stranglehold on the nature of private education. After all, in order to become a state-approved program of study at which "official" attendance is recognized, private actors are forced to satisfy some combination of curricular, reporting, and testing requirements... The state's monopoly on what defines "education" inevitably suppresses alternative views, thereby eliminating the complexity and diversity that should be prevalent in the market. Instead, a homogeneous system is used to serve heterogeneous students — yet another cost of compulsory education... The natures of schools should be as diverse as the population itself. Curriculum, delivery method, and instructional time are but a few of the myriad variables that must be customized if the individual needs of a child are to be met. Rothbard noted the advantage of unfettered development of private schools in that "there will tend to be developed on the free market a different type of school for each type of demand."[130]

This analysis of the State managed education system may be perceived as hyperbolic to some. However, this has much to do with the doublethink inculcated in the youth during public instruction. Simply replace the term "State" with "Corporation" and try to imagine how people would react in horror to the idea of this institution exerting monopolistic control over the education industry, dictating what must be taught and how many days out of the year children will have to endure instruction. In addition to this, imagine that this corporation is granted the power to force everyone to pay for this service at the threat of violence, to include even those who have no children at all! Consider the outrage and slew of criticisms which would shower down upon such an idea: "monopolies result in ever increasing prices," "such a monopoly would suppress innovation and diversity!" Virtually nothing separates the State from this hypothetical corporation. The same criticisms which apply to this monstrous monopolist apply equally to the State! The State is akin to a mega corporation that owes

---

[130] Smith, "The Costs of Compulsory Education."

its size and largesse to its exclusive legal rights to violently impose its will upon others and to force its subjects to pay for the costs of the enforcement of its edicts through taxes. The State is comprised of human beings, just as a corporation, just as a club, just as any other organization is comprised and as such is subject to the same temptations, corruptions, and perversions associated with arbitrary power. Isabel Paterson describes the mental constriction such an organization employs:

> Political control is… by its nature, bound to legislate against statements of both facts and opinion, in prescribing a school curriculum, in the long run. The most exact and demonstrable scientific knowledge will certainly be objectionable to political authority at some point, because it will expose the folly of such authority, and its vicious effects. Nobody would be permitted to show the nonsensical absurdity of "dialectical materialism" in Russia, by logical examination… and if the political authority is deemed competent to control education, that must be the outcome in any country.

> Educational texts are necessarily selective, in subject matter, language, and point of view. Where teaching is conducted by private schools, there will be a considerable variation in different schools; the parents must judge what they want their children taught, by the curriculum offered. Then each must strive for objective truth… Nowhere will there be any inducement to teach the "supremacy of the state" as a compulsory philosophy. But every politically controlled educational system will inculcate the doctrine of state supremacy sooner or later, whether as the divine right of kings, or the "will of the people" in "democracy." Once that doctrine has been accepted, it becomes an almost superhuman task to break the

stranglehold of the political power over
the life of the citizen. It has had his body,
property, and mind in its clutches from
infancy. An octopus would sooner release
its prey...

A tax-supported, compulsory educational
system is the complete model of the
totalitarian state.[131]

The Economics of State vs. Free Market Education Systems

For a minute, assume away all of the corruption that comes with
arbitrary power. Suppose, instead, that every State agent is benevolent and
has the best intentions for its citizens. The question now is: how do they
know the most efficient allocation of resources so as to minimize costs?
How do those employed by the State know what size a given school should
be? How many teachers ought it to employ? What type of food it should
serve? What method and content of education should it deliver? What
assortment of supplies, software programs, and disciplinary techniques
should it utilize? They may hold democratic votes on these questions, but
scarcely anyone voting would have any idea of the opportunity costs
involved in their decisions. The parents would, of course, want the "best"
computers, teachers, supplies, food, etc. for their children yet they will not
desire the high taxes that may be associated with the provision of such
goods. Perhaps the capabilities of super computers exceed the demands of
the students; perhaps a teacher with a Ph. D would be more optimally
employed in a college setting as opposed to a kindergarten class. The most
obvious hurdle is that every scarce resource used for one end is a resource
that cannot be used for another mutually exclusive end simultaneously.

These calculation issues do not stop merely at the use to which
these educational resources are put, but expand into the general economy.
More resources used for the educational system result in fewer resources
being available for other ends, which may include healthcare, food
production, provision of security, etc. Because the service of education is
largely subsidized and regulated by the State apparatus, any sort of pricing
mechanism which may have otherwise served as an invaluable guide for
such resource considerations is now rendered defective. Prices are only
effective at guiding economic decisions and determining opportunity costs
to the extent they are voluntarily and organically developed. In the case of

---

[131]   Isabel Paterson, *The God of the Machine* (New York: G.P. Putnam's Sons, 1943),
       271-72.

public schooling, consumers do not voluntarily pay for this service. Their property is taxed at a rate totally unrelated to what they may have otherwise been willing to pay. Because their payment is coerced, the quantitative indicator (price) representing the relative supply of educational resources and the demand for these resources is rendered hopelessly muddled.

In contrast, when such services are patronized on an exclusively voluntary basis, the price system provides an accurate and objective reflection of the collective value of all resources. These market generated prices would then serve as an invaluable guide for making economic decisions as they reflect with greater precision the opportunity costs associated with hiring one teacher over another or purchasing one computer over another. Furthermore, such prices allow entrepreneurs to compare the profitability or efficacy of their business models with others. Of course, due to one's subjective preferences, maximizing monetary profits may not be the ultimate goal, however, the level of one's profits or losses would still provide the entrepreneur with valuable feedback regarding which services are satisfying customers and to what degree they enjoy them. This will be a crucial factor in most business decisions as ignoring consumer preferences – as public schools are in the habit of doing - would in the long run lead to bankruptcy or business failure.

Without grants of State protection or legal favoritism, those decisions which make the most economic uses of resources will also be the ones that yield the greatest amount of profits for entrepreneurs, aligning their self-interests with the interests of the consumer. Unlike the public schooling system, there will not be widespread misallocation of various supplies and services. There will be objective indicators, noted in terms of profits and losses, which reveal whether or not the employment of a particular teaching method or the content taught is desired or if the supplies used are lacking, necessary, or excessive in the process. The unsuppressed competition will continue to drive entrepreneurs to seek more innovative, economic, and tailored ways to satisfy a growing share of the market for childhood growth and edification. This is a realistic system for achieving these goals as it takes into account scarcity, opportunity costs, subjective preference, consumer heterogeneity, and the self-interests of educational entrepreneurs. The organic market system of freely consenting individuals harmonizes all of these factors absent central direction. The resulting satisfaction from such a spontaneous order is something that cannot be paralleled by aggressive control or political management, no matter how competent those in power may be. Certain popular standards will undoubtedly emerge from this kaleidoscopic mixing, however, such standards and the successful enterprises that utilize them will only remain so long as they continue to provide a desired service in a more economic manner than the competition.

A SPONTANEOUS ORDER

The State's Effect on Post-Secondary Education

University tuition is prohibitively expensive, yet attendance rates remain as strong as ever. What accounts for this? Once again, government meddling has produced an artificially high demand for post-secondary education, which is creating price hikes at an increasing rate. This artificial demand is fueled by subsidized student loans, grants, and the moral hazards generated by the State guaranteeing privately provided student loans. B.T. Donleavy comments on the extent to which university students lean on the State for assistance:

> The Department of Education reports having a $63.7 billion budget in appropriations for 2010. It has also received $96.8 billion from the American Recovery and Reinvestment Act of 2009. The department's website states that "department programs also provide grant, loan, and work-study assistance to more than 14 million post-secondary students." That is roughly 4 million short of every college student in the country. Does this mean that only 22% of students in the United States have adequate means to pay for college? Based on America's economic model, this statistic should theoretically be impossible. This means that over 3/4 of Americans attending higher-education institutions are "in need."[132]

Former president of the Mises Institute, Douglas French, has this to say about the effects of State credit subsidization on post-secondary education:

> Like all booms, higher education has been fueled by credit. In June of last year, total student-loan debt exceeded total credit-card debt outstanding for the first time, totaling more than $900 billion... All of this credit has pushed the average cost of tuition up 440 percent in the last 25 years,

---

[132] B. T. Donleavy, "The Education Bubble" (editorial published at Ludwig Von Mises Institute, Auburn, Alabama, May 12, 2010).

204

more than four times the rate of inflation. But while the factors of production on campus have been bid up, just as they are in any other asset boom, the return on investment is a bust. In 1992, there were 5.1 million mal-employed college graduates. By 2008, the number was 17 million.

Not only are the returns poor, but the quality of the product is poor (as in the case of new-construction quality in the housing boom). According to the authors of Academically Adrift: Limited Learning on College Campuses, 45 percent of students make no gains in their critical reasoning and thinking skills, as well as writing ability, after two years in college. More than one out of three college seniors were no better at writing and thinking than they were when they first arrived at their campuses.

Many projects contemplated and started during the real-estate boom are never completed, as prices are bid up, and owners run out of capital. Such is the case for many attending college, as over 45 percent of those who enroll as freshmen ultimately give up, realizing they lack the disciplinary and mental capital, and do not graduate.[133]

Once again, unintended consequences pervade the actions of the State, despite the good intentions of its subsidized and managed services. It is important to remember that prices serve a critical function for the economic rationing and allocation of scarce resources relative to their demand. Price manipulation by involuntary redistributions of wealth undermines the ability for prices to spread information of economic realities. In this case, student loans are subsidized with tax dollars involuntarily confiscated from taxpayers and redistributed either to the schools directly or to the students via grants and guaranteed loans. It is no

---

[133] Douglas French, "The Higher-Education Bubble Has Popped" (editorial published at Ludwig Von Mises Institute, Auburn, Alabama, August 10, 2011).

surprise, then, to witness how such interventions have inflated the prices and degraded the quality of the higher education services being offered today.

In distinct contrast, a privatized education system without enormous takings from Peter given to Paul would not be subject to such folly. Entrepreneurs who provided poor services or charged excessive prices would lose business to their more apt competitors who more astutely recognized what students wanted and were able to provide it to them. Prospective students would be confronted with the true costs of schooling when deciding which schools to attend or whether they should even attend formal post-secondary schooling at all. Perhaps they would be happier learning a vocation or participating in an apprenticeship outside of the academic rigmarole of university life. In a free market system, it is the consumer that ultimately determines the configuration of their services, and the providers of those services only benefit insofar as their voluntary subscribers benefit.

What About The Poor?

Perhaps the most common objection to a non-State education system is the possibility of the poor having access only to lesser education, if any at all. However, what can be readily discerned is that the costs of education in such a system would be significantly lower than what private education costs today, as such schools would not have to abide by mandated regulations, occupational licensing requirements, curriculum mandates, et al. Schools would therefore have much more flexibility in the provision of their services. In addition, rabid competition in this industry would tend to drive entrepreneurs providing education to continually decrease costs and increase the quality of their services.

Moreover, educational institutions in free markets would not have to unfairly compete with the State which is able to demand payment from all persons under its jurisdiction, whether or not they take advantage of its services. Private entrepreneurs, on the other hand, cannot resort to such jackboot tactics; they would have to persuade potential clients to pay through the art of sales and influence. In addition, the option of online classes may become prevalent as they are highly effective and relatively inexpensive, if not completely free. Bountiful, free, online educational resources already exist such as Wikipedia, Code Academy, and the Mises Institute. With the advent of the Internet and digital learning, even the most esoteric topics may be accessible to virtually everyone in the world. In 2014, one may enroll in a Bachelor degree's worth of courses entirely for free from MIT, Stanford, and numerous other prestigious institutions which host their lectures online absolutely free. Arcane topics such as cryptography, technology entrepreneurialism, environmental protection, statistical mechanics, and many others are offered on monthly or quarterly bases – no payment is asked, and students may enroll or cancel at any time they choose without obligation. This paradigm of free and open courseware is utterly revolutionizing; the gates of knowledge and information are being torn down and free entry is offered to any student, child or adult, enterprising enough to take part in the course material. This has the capacity to educate whole swathes of underclass, marginalized, and disenfranchised populations who were prevented, directly or indirectly, from participating in the great adventure of higher education.

Currently, under the State-managed education system, anyone who wishes to send their children to a private school is also required to fund public schools through taxes. In a free market, however, those who purchase education services for themselves or their children would not be paying twice – once for a lean, efficient operation and twice for a bloated, indoctrination facility. With boundless freedom, a student may take courses which pertain to his interests as opposed to being compelled by curriculum standards to take courses for which he cares nothing, saving valuable time and money.

Naturally, in such a free environment, there would be disparities in the quality of services just as sunglasses from Wal-Mart are of considerably lower quality than those offered by Versace. The difference, however, is that those devices, products, and services which are currently only accessible to the rich would, over time, tend to become accessible to the middle class and eventually the poor. When the middle class and the poor witness the luxuries enjoyed by the rich, they begin to yearn for them. With this new demand comes an impetus for entrepreneurs to discover a way to provide these luxuries to the lesser socio-economic classes at prices they can afford.[134] In other words, the envy of the middle class and the poor represents a business opportunity for entrepreneurs that drives the market to find cheaper and more efficient ways to make these goods more accessible. This has been the case with automobiles, computers, colored televisions, cell phones, and every other type of consumer electronic. Though there may be a disparity in services present in the market, the tendency will be for all levels of services to increase in quality and to decrease in price. This is the beauty of unhampered markets; they transform

---

[134] "The classical factory of the early days of the Industrial Revolution was the cotton mill. Now, the cotton goods it turned out were not something the rich were asking for. These wealthy people clung to silk, linen, and cambric. Whenever the factory with its methods of mass production by means of power-driven machines invaded a new branch of production, it started with the production of cheap goods for the broad masses." Mises, "Work and Wages," in *Human Action*, 616. See also, Deirdre N. McCloskey, *The Bourgeois Virtues: Ethics for an Age of Commerce* (Chicago: University of Chicago, 2006).

goods only the wealthy can afford today into goods owned by virtually everyone tomorrow.

Finally, various educational institutions may be more than happy to recruit bright students that are financially lacking. Schools operating in a marketplace have the incentive to acquire as many bright students as possible so as to appear more attractive to a slew of financially-able parents and guardians. The poor, yet bright, student would benefit by gaining access to high-quality facilities and teaching faculty and the school would profit by being able to more effectively solicit its services as a training ground for inquisitive minds. Naturally, schools of every variety face this incentive. Art schools want talented art students, vocational schools want technically gifted individuals, etc. Smith highlights how the restriction of private education hurts precisely those for whom public education was intended to benefit:

> The poor and middle class are most injured by the lack of innovation that results from government monopoly on education, as they are without the means to pursue the artificially limited supply of private education available. Instead, their children are forced to attend under-performing public schools that often have little regard for the unique faculties of individual students. It is likely that the generalized education imposed on them will do nothing but retard their development, suppress their talent, and instill in them a permanent disdain for learning.[135]

On Standards

Standards in any industry are important, as standards allow for the comparison of performance and the evaluation of service. It is precisely because some form of standards would be desired that the market will produce them. For example, entrepreneurs may want to advertise the average test scores of their school and how they compare to the competition as a selling point. Any educational institution which did not offer a reference point by which to compare its services with others would

---

[135] Smith, ibid.

lose market share to those firms which displayed prominently their fitness on standardized grounds. In addition, third party organizations which specialize in evaluating and comparing different schooling institutions, companies, textbook providers, lesson plans, and projects would flourish. Without the State enforcing its own arbitrary metrics, watch-dog organizations would arise to take over the role instantly. In higher education, the process of accreditation has been a largely private function for hundreds of years (though this too is being swallowed by the vanity of State oversight). Judith Eaton outlines the history and nature of accreditation:

> Accreditation is a creation of colleges and universities that dates back more than a century. Its fundamental purposes are quality assurance and quality improvement in higher education. A process of self-regulation through peer and professional review, it is the oldest such system in the world. Today more than seven thousand colleges and universities and more than twenty thousand programs serving some twenty-four million students willingly undergo periodic accreditation review by nineteen institutional accreditors and sixty-one programmatic accreditors. Accreditation is nongovernmental by design and relies on funding from colleges, universities, and programs (some $92 million in 2007, according to the Council for Higher Education Accreditation, of which I am president). Accreditation depends heavily on volunteers from higher education who participate in self-studies, serve as peer and professional reviewers, and serve on accrediting organizations' decision-making bodies.[136]

As in anything else, there will be competition in the field of providing standards and other metrics for these institutions. Particular third party evaluation companies will gain reputation over time based on how

---

[136] Judith S. Eaton, "Accreditation and the Federal Future of Higher Education" (editorial published at American Association of University Professors, September-October, 2010).

effective they can measure aptitude and quality. If employers tend to, on the whole, favor metrics from company A to company B, then more educational institutions will be compelled to subject themselves to the standards set by company A. Of course, different metrics may be offered for different types of schooling, however, the process of market selection will remain the same. Those standards which never garner popularity will fade away and the practices of the more successful metrics will be copied and improved upon by others. The resulting metrics will have been driven by individuals in the market, and not by the arbitrary caprice of politicians and bureaucrats. Such standards, being products of the market, would be perpetually and accurately modified in accordance with the vicissitudes of consumer preference.

Though the tool of education is largely under State control, it is also the key to our salvation. Instilling in our children and in our peers the virtues of peace, critical thought, logic, and empathy will enable them to break free from the mental shackles of the State. State power is, in the end, rooted in the sanction of its subjects. Free minds who question their training will ultimately reject the conditioning of their State handlers. As in other industries, freed markets in education are defined by the capacity to privately own or employ all scarce goods – including capital, land, buildings, materials – and to organize them on consensual grounds. This paradigm substantially and sustainably promotes innovation, peace, cooperation, wealth, and an overall greater standard of living. It accomplishes this by enabling participants to measure and compare their business ventures through market prices, and by aligning their personal interests in accruing wealth and influence with the interests of greater society. The State is simply the inverse; through its commands and dictates, it destroys the capacity for critical thinking and free expression. It seeks to create identical subjects, like goods on a mass production line, obedient to established authority, deferential to "the rules," controlled by bells and punch clocks, and ultimately unable to discover the barbaric nature of their master.

Chapter Twelve

POVERTY

IT IS OFTEN asserted that, in a free market, the rich get richer at the expense of the poor growing ever poorer. It is true that most decent human beings believe everyone should have access to basic education, healthcare, food, and shelter. However, the overwhelming majority remains convinced that it is only through the State that such complex social issues may be sufficiently remedied. It is widely believed that without the State compelling its subjects to contribute to the "common good," there would be insufficient aid available for those in need. In addition to providing for the common good, many believe the State is necessary for protection against the predation of the wealthy and elite.

Contrary to this picture, however, Statist measures used to "fight poverty" tend to result in its exacerbation. What separates the State from its market counterpart is its power to limit freedom of contract, coercively redistribute wealth, and to impose rules on how its subjects may employ their property regardless of their consent: That is, the State imposes rules above and beyond restricting us from using aggression against the persons or property of others. Unfortunately, exercising such powers deters others from trading, producing, and maintaining the value and integrity of their property. This deterrence manifests as a decrease in overall wealth and standard of living. Logically, this may be confirmed by reflecting on the nature of human action within the context of economic relationships. For one to contract, trade, or deliberately do anything is to indicate that he believes this action will transform his current state of affairs into one more desired. Consequently, insofar as one's non-aggressive behavior is artificially restricted, the potential value of his actions will be diminished. One need only extrapolate this fact to a market wide scale to realize State regulations prevent millions of valuable trades from coming into existence.

Unlike agents of the State, private actors are not subject to such economic folly with the management of their own property, because they have the ability and greater incentive to maintain its value and to produce desired goods/services. The ability stems from having direct access to market prices which themselves are generated through the voluntary exchange of goods/services, and the incentive from the fact that it is only through their production that they may accrue wealth. The beauty of the free market is that every transaction results in mutual benefit, increasing the wealth of each person involved. Unfortunately, reality is far removed from the standard narrative depicted above.

In the absence of clear and consistent property norms, significant obstacles to economic planning or investing would arise due to the lack of criteria for rationally arbitrating between mutually exclusive desires on how to employ scarce resources. Interpersonal conflict would abound in such an environment at the expense of time, energy, and resources, which may have otherwise been employed for economic production and cooperation. The question then becomes "what rules or norms are best suited for mitigating such interpersonal conflict?" It is the contention of this work that the private property norm, whereby economic goods may only be acquired via original appropriation or voluntary exchange, is the one best suited for this end. Consequently, adhering to this norm leads to the greatest production of wealth.[137] Hoppe expands on this:

> The reason this institution [the Libertarian/Private Property Ethic] leads to the greatest possible production of wealth is straightforward. Any deviation from this set of rules implies, by definition, a redistribution of property titles (and hence of income) away from user-producers and contractors of goods and onto non-user-producers and non-contractors. As a consequence, any such deviation implies that there will be relatively less original appropriation of resources whose scarcity is realized, there will be less production of new goods, less maintenance of existing goods, and less mutually beneficial contracting and trading. This naturally implies a lower standard of living in terms of exchangeable goods and services. Further, the provision that only the physical integrity of property (not property values) be protected guarantees that every owner will undertake the greatest possible value-productive efforts, i.e., efforts to promote favorable changes in property values and to prevent or counter any unfavorable changes in property values (as they might

---

[137]   For an elaborated proof, see Chapter 1: Libertarianism

result from another person's actions
regarding his property). Thus, any
deviation from these rules also implies
reduced levels of value productive efforts
at all times.[138]

Thus, the true obstacles to wealth generation are the entities which attempt to artificially regulate the use of economic goods for which they themselves have *no just claim*. The State is a prime example of just that: an institution which asserts control over economic goods that its agents never acquired through original appropriation or voluntary exchange.

With such an institution in place, the *alleged* atrocities of the free market are now able to come to fruition under a Statist framework. The rich are now able to become richer *at the expense* of everyone else. They may accomplish this by persuading the State's agents to erect artificial barriers to entry into various industries in the form of taxes, intellectual property laws, minimum wage laws, occupational licensures, etc. These barriers are then sold to the public as protections for the consumer and the employee. Tragically, this could not be further from the truth. Such barriers only benefit the State and the businessmen who beckon for them while limiting the temperance provided by market competition. This perversion undermines the market's ability to sustainably generate wealth and a destructive cycle ensues:

1) State intervention destroys and/or hinders the production of wealth
2) The resulting economic woes are attributed to an "under-regulated" market
3) The State increases the scope and degree of its interventions
4) Steps one through three are repeated until the economy falls to ruin

Fortunately, this cycle is not inevitable; it merely reflects past tendencies. With all this in mind, the best solution to poverty becomes quite clear: allow the market to operate unimpeded. This entails the widespread recognition and respect for private property rights. Thus, to reach the point where this solution may be feasible, we will first demonstrate how the free market is in fact the *cure* for destitution, and not its cause. Before examining how things can go wrong, let us, as Hayek suggests, examine how things should ever go right.

In a truly free market, resources flow to their most value-productive ends. This occurs in a decentralized process with each individual

---

[138]   Hoppe, "The Justice of Economic Efficiency," in *Private Property*, 332.

simply doing that which he believes will yield him the greatest satisfaction. This pursuit of satisfaction/profit will motivate actors to minimize their costs and maximize their benefits. They are also able to evaluate the costs of various actions by comparing market prices which themselves are byproducts of voluntary exchange. The advent of money enables this process to be even more efficient by providing the actor with quantitative figures by which he may be able to compare the costs of heterogeneous or different types of goods/services directly. The use of money allows for a common denominator by which an actor can compare his opportunity costs more easily than he can in barter. He then compares the costs of his chosen endeavor with the gain in satisfaction he projects he will receive in its execution. If his projected gain exceeds the costs of his project, then he may conclude it to be a profitable one. However, being merely profitable is not sufficient in itself; the task must be profitable *enough* to warrant the time and energy he puts into it versus any other action he could have taken. Our actor determines this by evaluating other courses of action he may take, and how profitable he thinks *they* will be. For instance, if he makes one thousand shoes and only receives five dollars in monetary profit, he may see this as an ultimate loss as he may value the time it took to make the shoes more than he values five dollars. (Important to keep in mind is that profit or satisfaction may be of a psychic nature, instead of purely a monetary one. Subjective desires are the ultimate cause of man's actions, and it would be incorrect to presume man is guided solely by money.)

This process is then repeated by himself and all other market participants until large, sustainable trading networks and markets form. As these market participants bid for various resources, their prices begin to reflect their demand in relation to their supply. The resulting prices of goods in turn influence the individuals' evaluations of these goods and the profitability of their projects, which in turn causes them to modify their behavior accordingly. Through this fluid and organic cycle, an incredibly efficient economy emerges through the mere acts of individual actors peacefully pursuing their own self-interest. Market prices serve as their guides; potential value opportunities and desire for profit serve as their motivation.

Taxation

Perhaps the most notorious tool of the State is its ability to lay taxes. Do not be fooled by the seemingly innocuous wording of "laying taxes," this phrasing simply serves as a belittling euphemism for theft on a mass scale. If taxes were voluntary, they would instead be considered "donations" or payments. It is important to consider that before the State is able to do *anything*, it must first violate the property rights of its citizens through the collecting of taxes. Despite this fact, however, the State is still predominately held as the single institution capable of competently protecting private property rights. This blatant paradox may only be perpetuated through incessant propaganda. For the few who do reflect upon this clear contradiction, they generally respond by appealing to the equally paradoxical "necessary evil" argument. Partiality to tradition has indeed stunted reason for the time being, however it is the mission of truth seekers to confidently beat the drums of reason until they may no longer be ignored.

In addition to its purely criminal nature, taxation also hinders the production of wealth. The funds taken by taxes do not reflect consumer demand for a given good or service, but rather are the result of violent confiscation. This mass expropriation of wealth nonetheless affects market prices as the purchasing decisions of market participants will be altered due to smaller money balances. Moreover, the State will spend these expropriated funds in a manner wholly divergent from their unfettered market allocation. As such, and insofar as this State interference extends, the capacity for prices to reflect genuine consumer demand for various economic goods will be undermined. These price distortions then result in less efficient economic activity as the information-guiding role prices once conveyed has been tainted by violent redistributions of wealth on a mass scale. This destructive process culminates in an underproduction of some goods/services and overproduction of others relative to an otherwise free market yield. Hoppe brilliantly sums up the economic effects of taxation:

> One last remark on the economic effects of taxation: Every tax *is* a redistribution of wealth and income. Wealth and income is forcibly taken from their owners and producers and transferred to people who did *not* own this wealth and did *not* produce this income. The future accumulation of wealth and the production of income are thus *dis*couraged and the confiscation and consumption of existing wealth and income is *en*couraged. As a result, society will be poorer. And as for the effect of the eternally popular, egalitarian proposal of taxing the "rich" to give to the "poor" in particular: Such a scheme does not reduce or alleviate poverty but, quite to the contrary, it *increases* poverty. It reduces

the incentive to stay or become rich and
be productive, and it increases the
incentive to stay or become poor and be
unproductive.[139]

Working Conditions

Like all other services in the free market economy, the price of
labor is determined by the subjective valuations of those looking to hire
labor along with its corresponding availability. Thus, contrary to the
popular narrative that people are slaves to the terms on which a given
employer may be willing to hire them, the employers themselves are subject
to concrete economic incentives not to short change employees either on
the basis of wages or working conditions. Such incentives are due to
competition between employers for labor, just as there is competition
between prospective employees for jobs. If employer A offers wages or
working conditions that are substantially less appealing than what employer
B offers, then the most productive labor will tend to be allocated to
employer B whilst employer A is left with the less productive leftovers.
Because employer B's labor would be more productive, he would be able to
afford to pay his employees more, provide them with better working
conditions, and/or sell his goods at lower prices than the miserly employer
A. Such a situation will eventually lead to employer A's bankruptcy if he
does not offer better working conditions or higher wage rates. A common
response to this explanation is to say, "There are too few options available
for this competitive mechanism to work!" First of all, what constitutes
successful "working" in this context is completely subjective. Someone
choosing to work at company A is an indication that he would rather work
there than work somewhere else or not at all. Thus, this is still a mutually
beneficial relationship, and in fact from the perspective of the employee
and the employer, it's the *most* beneficial arrangement relative to the
available known alternatives. Mainstream economics promotes the fallacy
that the number of firms is what demonstrates "monopoly," but so long as
entry into the field is permitted, this can create competitive results.
Potential competition can act as real competition. The free market is one in
which competition is able to most abundantly thrive as it is defined as the
lack of aggressive barriers to entry into any given industry.
The tendency of the free market economy is to develop technology

---

[139] Hans-Hermann Hoppe, "Interview on Taxation" (interview by Nicolas Cori of
Philosophe Magazine, March 10, 2011)
<http://www.hanshoppe.com/2011/03/philosophie-magazine-interview-on-
taxation/>.

and machinery which enables each individual to produce more output with the same or similar levels of input. As workers are able to produce more with the same level of input, the employer is both able and incentivized to pay them higher wages or to provide more satisfactory working conditions, lest his competitor draw away his labor by implementing said measures at his place of business.

Conversely, an employer cannot be reasonably expected to pay his employees more than he projects their labor will produce, for to do so would be to deliberately generate losses. Thus, even if a noble intentioned employer decided to pay his employees a "living wage" of $20/hour despite the fact that their labor only brings in $15/hour of revenue, he would eventually go bankrupt and his resources freed up to be used more efficiently by those who did not engage in such wasteful practices.

Industrial Revolution

One may concede that the preceding analysis sounds good in theory, but in practice has yet to be the case! The industrial revolution and the infamous working conditions associated with it are generally cited as damning evidence against the capitalism-as-free-trade theory. However, this assessment is generally marred by mistakenly comparing those working conditions with the ones enjoyed today, as opposed to comparing them with *previously existing alternatives*. The fact that workers in the industrial revolution *chose* to work at the factories logically indicates that such conditions were preferable to the available alternatives.

The free market is not claimed to be a Utopian environment where everything is always cheap and abundant and where work is always pleasant and enjoyable. Rather it is only claimed that instituting a free market will perpetually *improve* upon current economic conditions. So, if working conditions start off as terrible and improve to "bad," then this is an improvement despite it not being ideal. Working conditions today are much improved not due to legislation, but rather to the increase of the marginal productivity of labor brought on by the accumulation of capital and the development of more productive technology. It is true that the passing of "pro labor" legislation coincided with improvements in working conditions, however so too did the accumulation of capital and development of technology, which allowed workers to be more productive. Hence, the State conveniently took credit for improved working conditions while it was indeed the Capitalist who was responsible for making such improvements sustainable and permanent. Mises cogently remarks:

The history of capitalism in Great Britain
as well as in all other capitalist countries is
a record of an unceasing tendency toward
the improvement in the wage earners'
standard of living. This evolution
coincided with the development of
prolabor legislation and the spread of labor
unionism on the one hand and with the
increase in the marginal productivity of
labor on the other hand. The economists
assert that the improvement in the
workers' material conditions is due to the
increase in the per capita quota of capital
invested and the technological
achievements that the employment of this
additional capital brought about. As far as
labor legislation and union pressure did
not exceed the limits of what the workers
would have got without them as a
necessary consequence of the acceleration
of capital accumulation as compared with
population, they were superfluous. As far
as they exceeded these limits, they were
harmful to the interests of the masses.
They delayed the accumulation of capital
thus slowing down the tendency toward a
rise in the marginal productivity of labor
and in wage rates. They conferred
privileges on some groups of wage earners
at the expense of other groups. They
created mass unemployment and decreased
the amount of products available for the
workers in their capacity as consumers.[140]

In reference to the horrid working conditions that existed during the
Industrial Revolution, Mises stated:

In the first decades of the Industrial
Revolution, the standard of living of the
factory workers was shockingly bad when
compared with the contemporary

---

[140]   Mises, "Work and Wages," in *Human Action*, 622.

conditions of the upper classes and with the present conditions of the industrial masses. Hours of work were long, the sanitary conditions in the workshops deplorable. The individual's capacity to work was used up rapidly. But the fact remains that for the surplus population, which the enclosure movement had reduced to dire wretchedness and for which there was literally no room left in the frame of the prevailing system of production, work in the factories was salvation. These people thronged into the plants for no reason other than the urge to improve their standard of living.[141]

Mises then concludes his argument by comparing the conditions that existed prior to the Industrial Revolution with those that existed after its inception:

The factory owners did not have the power to compel anybody to take a factory job. They could only hire people who were ready to work for the wages offered to them. Low as these wage rates were, they were nonetheless much more than these paupers could earn in any other field open to them. It is a distortion of facts to say that the factories carried off the housewives from the nurseries and the kitchens and the children from their play. These women had nothing to cook with and to feed their children. These children were destitute and starving. Their only refuge was the factory. It saved them, in the strict sense of the term, from death by starvation.

It is deplorable that such conditions existed. But if one wants to blame those responsible, one must not blame the factory owners who — driven by

---

[141] Mises, ibid, 620.

selfishness, of course, and not by
"altruism" — did all they could to
eradicate the evils. What had caused these
evils was the economic order of the pre-
capitalistic era, the order of the 'good old
days.'[142]

Child Labor

    The next common concern is that of child labor. "Do we as a
society really want to allow children to be taken from their studies to work a
tedious job at a factory?" The answer is simply no. However, most people
want even less to starve. Virtually all parents, if given the practical choice,
would not have their children work. This is evidenced by the relationship
between family income and child labor as depicted by Benjamin Powell:

> Take child labor for example. Anti-
> sweatshop groups universally condemn
> child labor and call for laws banning
> products made with it. But the process of
> development is the best cure for child
> labor. In countries with average incomes
> above $12,000, there is virtually no child
> labor. But for countries whose incomes
> are below $2,000, more than 30 percent
> of children work.
>
> ... It's no accident that the United States
> didn't pass meaningful national child
> labor legislation prohibitions until 1938.
> At that time, average per capita income
> was more than $10,000 (in 2010 dollars).
> It was simply codifying what the market
> process had already achieved. The same is
> true of other workplace health, safety, and
> maximum hour legislation in countries
> with sweatshops today.[143]

---

[142] Mises, ibid.
[143] Benjamin Powell, "Sweatshops: A Way Out of Poverty" (interview by Ludwig Von
Mises Institute, March 2014). <https://mises.org/daily/6696/Sweatshops-A-Way-
Out-of-Poverty>.

Once more, we reach the conclusion that State intervention has either a neutral or negative impact on the economy. The negative consequences of passing such legislation prior to economic conditions organically improving include unemployment and the diversion of labor to less desirable ends. Prohibiting an activity does not necessarily stop everyone from performing it; it simply increases the costs of doing so. This increases the risks and harm undergone by people in situations desperate enough to persist despite a formal legal ban. The unintended consequences of prohibiting child labor are briefly outlined by Thomas Dilorenzo:

> Capitalistic competition is also why 'child labor' has all but disappeared, despite unionist claims to the contrary. Young people originally left the farms to work in harsh factory conditions because it was a matter of survival for them and their families. But as workers became better paid – thanks to capital investment and subsequent productivity improvements – more and more people could afford to keep their children at home and in school. Union-backed legislation prohibiting child labor came *after* the decline in child labor had already begun. Moreover, child labor laws have always been protectionist and aimed at depriving young people of the opportunity to work. Since child labor sometimes competes with unionized labor, unions have long sought to use the power of the state to deprive young people of the right to work. In the Third World today, the alternative to "child labor" is all too often begging, prostitution, crime, or starvation. Unions absurdly proclaim to be taking the moral high road by advocating protectionist policies that inevitably lead to these consequences.[144]

---

[144] Thomas J. DiLorenzo, "Markets, Not Unions, Gave Us Leisure" (editorial published at Ludwig Von Mises Institute. Ludwig Von Mises Institute, Auburn, Alabama, August 23, 2004). <https://mises.org/daily/1590>

Sweat Shops

The economic analysis of sweatshops is the same of any other voluntary labor arrangement. Insofar as the conditions for labor are artificially regulated, the level of available attractive work will decrease. The fact that people choose to work for these institutions demonstrate they value working at them more than not working at all. Competition between all industries in which one can be employed, will create a lower limit to the level of wages and working conditions he will accept for his labor. The existence of sweatshops merely indicates that the surrounding market is relatively undeveloped. Benjamin Powell comments on the developmental advantages provided by sweatshops:

> In fact, sweatshop earnings even compared favorably to the average incomes in the countries where they were located. In six of the 17 countries, the average reported sweatshop wage exceeded the average income in the country — in Haiti, Honduras, and Nicaragua it was more than twice the national average. In another six countries, the average reported sweatshop wages were around the national average. In four of the five countries where sweatshop wages were 50 percent below the national average, the workers were immigrants (sometimes illegal) from other countries and their sweatshop wages exceeded the average wage in their native country.
>
> In short, sweatshops provide the least-bad option for the workers who work in them. But sweatshops are better than just the least-bad option. Sweatshops bring with them the proximate causes of economic development — capital, technology, and the opportunity to build human capital. If countries respect private property rights and economic freedoms, these proximate causes of development lead to higher productivity, which

eventually leads to higher pay and better working conditions.[145]

Wage Labor

A common Marxist critique of the employer-employee arrangement is that wage laborers are exploited by being paid less than what they produce. Such critics claim the leftover surplus is then used to line the pockets of the evil capitalist in the form of profits. However, this criticism fails to recognize the existence of choice in the matter! The employee does not *have* to work for the employer. If he wants, he may start his own business. If he does not have the capital or the will to do this, then he can choose to work for a cooperative. Any voluntary alternative is compatible with the free market. Thus, when someone chooses to work for an hourly wage in the free market, nothing inherently exploitative is occurring.

This analysis may seem simple and obvious, but it eludes even the more renowned economists. Employees who decide to work for a wage are demonstrating that they prefer the security a fixed wage brings as well as the immediacy of its payout to the comparatively lesser degree of certainty associated with entrepreneurship and variable payout. The business owner's salary is completely contingent upon the whims of his customers, and he has no guarantee whatsoever that they will purchase the goods and services he offers. It is true that if a business goes under, then the employee will go unpaid as well. The difference here, however is the employer is contractually obliged to pay the employee while customers have no such contractual obligation to patronize the services offered by an entrepreneur. Thus, all other things being equal, there is more certainty regarding ones' pay in his capacity as an employee than there is in his capacity as an entrepreneur. The role of the entrepreneur is to bear uncertainty, and profits are the income he earns for executing that role. Therefore, the reaping of the "surplus profit" of the employee's labor for the entrepreneur is justified by his willingness to incur greater risks and forego consumption for a date later than what his employees are willing. The employer and employee have reverse time preference orderings, thus their dealings with one another results in mutual benefit.[146]

The entrepreneur is essentially being rewarded for his ability to make profitable projections and to efficiently manage the capital at his disposal. He is a coordinator and a pioneer, whose livelihood is to create goods which are valued more highly than the sum of their individual parts. The role entrepreneurship plays in the free market is perhaps the most

---

[145] Powell, "Sweatshops: A Way Out of Poverty."
[146] Hoppe, "Marxist and Austrian Class Analysis," in *Private Property*, 121-123.

critical. It is the entrepreneur that decides to acquire or not acquire more capital goods, it is the entrepreneur that introduces and makes accessible previously unheard of products and services, and it is the entrepreneur who lives closest to the mercy of the consumer.

Entrepreneurship is carried out for personal gain, but those who succeed at it should nonetheless be touted as heroes of mankind. The notion that one may best serve society only by depriving himself is vanquished by understanding that the greatest humanitarian contributions have come from the foresight of entrepreneurs seeking to help themselves *by helping others*. Without aggression, self-interest is channeled into socially beneficial, profit-earning enterprises. Self-interest and profits are therefore nothing to be ashamed of; they should instead be embraced as an integral motivating characteristic of human nature. Technically, one is precluded from even being *able* to conduct a truly altruistic act. If one does not intend to receive monetary gain from some form of action, then he is seeking psychic gain in its stead. Actions are always undertaken with the goal of alleviating the actor's uneasiness. In fact, the claim that all action is self-interested is a tautology.

Being subject to aggression strongly increases the likelihood that one may fail to profit from an action or exchange. Thus, any attempt to vanquish wage labor or any other voluntary contractual relationship must necessarily displace otherwise profitable behavior. Hoppe responds to the Marxist critique of wage labor:

> What is wrong with this [Marxist] analysis? The answer becomes obvious, once it is asked why the laborer would possibly agree to such a deal! He agrees because his wage payment represents present goods-while his own labor services represent only future goods-and he values present goods more highly. After all, he could also decide not to sell his labor services to the capitalist and then map the full value of his output himself. But this would of course imply that he would have to wait longer for any consumption goods to become available to him. In selling his labor services he demonstrates that he prefers a smaller amount of consumption goods now over a possibly larger one at some future date. On the other hand, why would the

capitalist want to strike a deal with the laborer? Why would he want to advance present goods (money) to the laborer in exchange for services that bear fruit only later? Obviously, he would not want to pay out, for instance, $100 now if he were to receive the same amount in one year's time. In that case, why not simply hold on to it for one year and receive the extra benefit of having actual command over it during the entire time? Instead, he must expect to receive a larger sum than $100 in the future in order to give up $100 now in the form of wages paid to the laborer. He must expect to be able to earn a profit, or more correctly an interest return. He is also constrained by time preference, i.e., the fact that an actor invariably prefers earlier over later goods, in yet another way. For if one can obtain a larger sum in the future by sacrificing a smaller one in the present, why then is the capitalist not engaged in more saving than he actually is? Why does he not hire more laborers than he does, if each one of them promises an additional interest return? The answer again should be obvious: because the capitalist is a consumer, as well, and cannot help being one. The amount of his savings and investing is restricted by the necessity that he, too, like the laborer, requires a supply of present goods large enough to secure the satisfaction of all those wants whose current enjoyment is considered more urgent than the advantages which a still greater lengthening of the period of production would provide."[147]

---

[147]   Hoppe, ibid.

Minimum Wage

The argument against the minimum wage is fairly simple and straightforward, so this analysis will be brief. Minimum wage laws do not alter the fact that employers cannot sustainably pay their employees more than they produce. The existence of competitive pressures, as mentioned earlier, will have already created a tendency where laborers earn nearly what they produce. Thus, a minimum wage law will tend to create unemployment in fields whose market wages are lower than what is mandated by the new law. Minimum wage laws thus amount to removing the bottom rungs of the economic ladder. One unintended consequence of minimum wage laws is that the resulting unemployment is mostly shouldered by the young, unskilled persons, and ethnic minorities.[148] Tragically, the consequence of this policy tends to most negatively impact the very people it was "supposed" to help. The industries under the burden of this law will then face choices: they either have to lay off workers, increase all the "illegal" wages to be in compliance at their own expense, or raise the prices of the goods and services they offer. Any choice or combination among these negatively impacts, not only the standard of living for the patrons of these services, but the economy as a whole. As goods are made more expensive, consumers and their trading networks will have comparatively less money left over for other things.

Critics who argue from the basis of statistics which reveal no increase in unemployment after such minimum wage laws were passed are making a logically deficient argument. They are simply not accounting for other factors such as: a corresponding decrease in the overall tax/regulatory burden, an increase in the marginal productivity of labor due to accumulation of capital, which makes labor more valuable, the fact that the rate of decline in the unemployment rate may have been lessened or stagnated due to this law, etc. These critics fail to understand "ceteris paribus" (i.e. other things equal) – that existence of economic law is prior to interpretation of data. In other words, that minimum wage laws must either have either a negative or neutral impact on the economy must logically follow from the nature of price floors. If one were to analyze two cases, identical in all respects save for one enacting a compulsory minimum wage law, the one where such a law is present will almost certainly generate greater unemployment than the one without (it *could* be the same level, though this is unlikely as wages will already nearly match the productivity of laborers for reasons outlined above). As the productivity of workers increases, so too will their wages lest their employers lose valuable

---

[148]   Walter E. Williams, *The State Against Blacks* (New York: New Press, 1982).

226

employees to competitors. Thus, minimum wage laws destroy jobs which can only be feasibly compensated at a rate below the minimum wage. Murray Rothbard sums this up:

> In truth, there is only one way to regard a minimum wage law: it is compulsory unemployment, period. The law says: it is illegal, and therefore criminal, for anyone to hire anyone else below the level of X dollars an hour. This means, plainly and simply, that a large number of free and voluntary wage contracts are now outlawed and hence that there will be a large amount of unemployment. Remember that the minimum wage law provides no jobs; it only outlaws them; and outlawed jobs are the inevitable result.

> … If the minimum wage is, in short, raised from \$3.35 to \$4.55 an hour, the consequence is to disemploy, permanently, those who would have been hired at rates in between these two rates. Since the demand curve for any sort of labor (as for any factor of production) is set by the perceived marginal productivity of that labor, this means that the people who will be disemployed and devastated by this prohibition will be precisely the "marginal" (lowest wage) workers, e.g. blacks and teenagers, the very workers whom the advocates of the minimum wage are claiming to foster and protect.

> The advocates of the minimum wage and its periodic boosting reply that all this is scare talk and that minimum wage rates do not and never have caused any unemployment. The proper riposte is to raise them one better; all right, if the minimum wage is such a wonderful anti-poverty measure, and can have no unemployment-raising effects, why are you such pikers? Why you are helping the

working poor by such piddling amounts?
Why stop at $4.55 an hour? Why not $10
an hour? $100? $1,000?[149]

Labor Unions

      In a free market, there is absolutely no reason why voluntary labor unions could not form. In fact, they may even serve as an effective incentive for various employers to maintain satisfactory wages and working conditions for their employees. Organized strikes and collective bargaining does not entail any activity which is inherently at odds with the principles of private property or maintaining free markets. Issues arise when unions embrace the utilization of State power to further their agenda. One way this is done is by funding the political campaigns of various congressional or presidential candidates on the condition that, when in office, they pass legislation which furthers the given unions' cause, at the expense and against the wishes of their respective employers. *This* is antithetical to free markets, as such legislation constitutes aggression against business owners and their property. As explained above, such aggressive intervention only serves to destroy wealth on the net to the benefit of a select, privileged few. Aggressive labor intervention can be seen when unions require prospective employees to join their ranks as a precondition of their employment. If an employee wants to work for an employer and the employer is willing to hire the prospective employee, then no outside individual or organization should have the right to forcibly impose any further stipulations on this arrangement. It becomes clear that mandating union membership and payments of dues conflicts with the rights of both parties to voluntarily contract with one another. Like all other rights violations, the source of such unjustified behavior may be traced back to aggression against one's person or property. Christopher Westley comments on the destructive Labor Union-State relationship:

> In the same way, labor unionism, when
> state supported, removes workers from
> the normal coordinating mechanisms
> found in labor markets. These markets
> operate like any other market for scarce
> resources. Firms demand labor and pay
> wages for it, demanding more at lower
> wages and less at higher wages. Workers

---

[149]   Murray N. Rothbard. "Outlawing Jobs, the Minimum Wage, Once More" in *Making Economic Sense* (Auburn: Ludwig Von Mises Institute, 1995), 133-35.

sell their labor to these firms, selling less for low wages and more for high wages. Through the interaction of buyers and sellers of labor, labor markets tend to clear, coordinating the movement of labor inputs in the production process.

The rise of unionism, on its own, would normally pose no threat to labor markets' coordinating tendencies. Any group of workers would be free to organize and demand higher wages in exchange for labor. Firms would be free to pay those wages—or not. If some workers held monopoly power in the supply of their labor—which could be the case if they had unique skills that were especially valued by firms—then firms may very well choose to pay higher wages. In a competitive labor market, these workers' success at earning higher wages would also sow the seeds for their eventual reduction, as the higher wages would signal other workers to obtain the skills necessary for their lines of work too. This benign case of unionism becomes destructive, however, when these workers receive protection from the government. This introduces violence into what otherwise would have been peaceful, voluntary exchanges of labor between buyers and sellers. Make no mistake: absent the state, any success that organized labor might have in obtaining higher wages, and thus increasing the costs of production, would be short-lived. With government comes the introduction of force in the relationship between labor producers and consumers, either directly (such as when authorities jail unanointed nonunion laborers for working in unionized industries) or indirectly (such as when union violence occurs, as allowed by the Norris-La Guardia Act of 1932).[150]

Private Relief

The working class has been discussed, but what about the truly indigent? What about the unemployed and homeless? The first point worth mentioning is that in a truly free society, one's reputation is intimately linked with his livelihood. For instance, if a given person is habitually belligerent, rude, violent, and obnoxious, then he may find himself relatively alone and with few friends or family to help him in times of need. The prospect of solitude and personal autarky serves as a peaceful incentive for someone to develop himself as an asset to others whether in a social or an economic capacity. There would also exist substantially more wealth in a free market society than in a society governed by a State. Thus, for an individual to get to the point where he would have no access to help, jobs, friends, family, churches, or other charitable organizations would likely mean that he had conducted himself in an extremely notorious and/or anti-social manner. In any case, concern for the poor is a prevailing one, and therefore in a society where there is more wealth being generated, one may conclude that there would also be a greater willingness to give towards charitable causes. In addition to becoming wealthier, people have a stronger incentive to give because they would be spared from the delusion that the government is, to some extent, already taking care of the poor. The truth is State agencies crowd out private charity and mutual aid. Tragically, the State rarely "helps" the poor; it merely subsidizes them, thereby increasing their number.

Having a poor, dependent class is, in fact, beneficial to the security of State power. Insofar as people believe they cannot live without the State, its longevity will be increased. Additionally, whenever the poorer classes grow under the regime of a State, the culprit is all too often thought to be a lack of funding for welfare programs. In consequence, public support and spending for the welfare State grows in concordance with the growing parasitic class that organizes, regulates, and administers the benefits. Its growth necessarily comes at the expense of taxpayers, which means there will be crowding out of private alternatives. By requiring payment into a State program, individuals are discouraged from supporting private counterparts. The very presence of the welfare State, then, undermines and displaces private charities which generally seek to empower the poor, so that they may escape poverty and become productive members of society. Even today, many private charities compete with one another on terms of the degree of impact on their target demographics as well as what

---

150   Christopher Westley, "The End of Unions," in *The Free Market* 26: 9 (Sept. 2005): 9.

percentage of contributions actually reach their intended recipients. Statistics are available which compare CEO salary, percentage of donations used effectively, etc. Competition between these various metrics drives charities to find ways to increase their impact per dollar and incentivizes them to discover new ways to minimize administrative costs so that a growing portion of their received contributions reach those in need. The incentives of the State are starkly contrasted with this, as the funds it uses for such programs are generated through compulsion, i.e., taxes. Because income for these State welfare programs is not generated by consumers enjoying their service and voluntarily patronizing the anti-poverty measures, they are funded regardless of their efficacy. Thus, the State's only incentive is to make token efforts towards helping the poor, while actually minimizing their productive output.[151] For the State, it is a win-win situation if its efforts coincide with a shrinking of the impoverished, it will usurp more revenue for this end as it has "proven" to be a successful program!" The State will capture more tax revenue from an increasingly wealthier society. If, on the other hand, the poor class expands, it will yet again seek to increase its expenditures on the grounds that the programs in place are "clearly under-funded." The resulting moral hazard renders State welfare programs much less efficient than their private counterparts. For example, in his essay "The Costs of Public Income Redistribution and Private Charity," James Edwards reveals that only about 30% of government aid reaches its intended destination, whereas the remaining 70% lines the pockets of government bureaucrats. In contrast, the inverse is true for private charities, where on average only about 30% of funds get absorbed for administrative costs, and 70% reach the people in need.[152]

Prior to the growth of the Welfare State, voluntary and private mutual aid societies served as a social safety net for those in need. As opposed to relying on direct charity, they would operate under conditions of reciprocity, where all the members would contribute membership dues to collectively insure everyone while they were healthy and employed in the event that they may need assistance themselves should they ever become sick or unemployed. Social pressures and auditing mechanisms developed to ensure that mutual aid societies were not being defrauded or exploited. Unfortunately, the State effectively legislated them out of existence and ultimately displaced them with its own compulsory welfare system. Joshua Fulton briefly describes mutual aid societies:

> Mutual aid, also known as fraternalism,
> refers to social organizations that

---

[151] Hoppe, "Rothbardian Ethics," in *Private* Property, 391.
[152] James Rolph Edwards, "The Cost of Public Income Redistribution and Private Charity," in *Journal of Libertarian Studies* Summer 21.2 (2007): 3-20. <https://mises.org/journals/jls/21_2/21_2_1.pdf>.

gathered dues and paid benefits to members facing hardship. According to David Beito in *From Mutual Aid to the Welfare State*, there was a "great stigma" attached to accepting government aid or private charity during the late 18th and early 19th centuries. Mutual aid, on the other hand, did not carry the same stigma. It was based on reciprocity: today's mutual-aid recipient could be tomorrow's donor, and vice versa.

… By the 1920s, at least one out of every three males was a member of a mutual-aid society. Members of societies carried over $9 billion worth of life insurance by 1920. During the same period, lodges dominated the field of health insurance. Numerous lodges offered unemployment benefits. Some black fraternal lodges, taking note of the sporadic nature of African-American employment at the time, allowed members to receive unemployment benefits even if they were up to six months behind in dues.

… Mutual-aid societies also founded 71 orphanages between 1890 and 1922, almost all without government subsidy. Perhaps the largest of these was Mooseheart, founded by the Loyal Order of Moose in 1913. Hundreds of children lived there at a time. It had a student newspaper, two debate teams, three theatrical organizations, and a small radio station. The success of Mooseheart alumni was remarkable. Alumni were four times more likely than the general population to have attended institutions of higher learning. Male alumni earned 71 percent more than the national average, and female alumni earned 63 percent more.[153]

232

A free market society is one that is absent of any institutionalized aggression or legal privilege. This society allows all possible mutually beneficial exchanges between parties, and it therefore produces the greatest amount of wealth. There are no artificial barriers to entry into any industry, and one's income is completely contingent upon how competently he provides desired goods/services to others. This system harmonizes self-interest with the interests and welfare of greater society. Every transaction that takes place is of mutual benefit, and every loss that occurs frees up resources to be used for more efficient ends elsewhere. This system is organic and humanitarian. It grants each person involved the greatest opportunity to transfer the contents of their imagination to the physical realm. No voluntary association is prohibited nor is any idea patented or monopolized. This paradigm serves as a breeding ground for ingenuity, prosperity, cooperation, and peace. As time progresses, the whole of society becomes more wealthy, despite the fact that some individuals may be more so than others. The lack of regularized crime creates greater stability and motivation for everyone to save, allowing them to experience rapidly improving living standards. The absence of the State is not a lacking of governance or a social safety net, but rather the presence of a beautiful spontaneous order whose efficacy and humanitarian output could never be paralleled by central fiat.

> The very principle of capitalist entrepreneurship is to provide for the common man. In his capacity as consumer the common man is the sovereign whose buying or abstention from buying decides the fate of entrepreneurial activities. There is in the market economy no other means of acquiring and preserving wealth than by supplying the masses in the best and cheapest way with all the goods they ask for.[154]

---

[153] Joshua Fulton, "Welfare before the Welfare State" (editorial published at Ludwig Von Mises Institute, Auburn, Alabama, June 21, 2011). <https://mises.org/daily/5388>. See also, Beito, *Mutual Aid to the Welfare State*, 2000.

[154] Mises, ibid, 621.

Chapter Thirteen

ENVIRONMENTALISM

IT IS OFTEN thought that free enterprise is somehow at odds with environmental preservation. That is to say, there is an argument that one may only be able to profit financially through the consumption, depletion, and exhaustion of the Earth and its precious resources. This philosophy is applied to the whole spectrum of environmental concerns ranging from atmospheric integrity to the preservation of the myriad of species in the animal kingdom. The primary suspects for such poor stewardship of the earth go by many names, but supposedly involve the same concepts: capitalism, money, profits, greed, industry, and private property itself. The consensus tends to be a beckoning for the State to regulate and temper such environmentally-destructive free enterprise behavior through the imposition of taxes, regulations, fees, licensure, and downright prohibitions. It is thought only by superseding the property rights of others can the Earth and its species be protected from the pursuit of our myopic and petty self-interests.

Contrariwise, free enterprise and market activity are *not* the primary culprits of environmental waste and degradation. In fact, it is through these mechanisms that men may best coexist with the Earth in harmony.

The Tragedy of The Commons

One of the more salient concepts to understand when discussing environmental trauma is the tragedy of the commons – a situation in which untrammeled public use of a resource reduces its value to each user. To illustrate this, suppose a teacher throws a pizza party for her class and buys each of her students a personal pan pizza and a can of soda. Presumably, the children would proceed to consume the soda and pizza at a leisurely rate based primarily on hunger. In another case, instead of the teacher offering each of her students their own cans of soda and personal pans, she purchases three large pizzas and six liters of soda and places no restrictions on how much they may each eat or drink. Are the children more inclined to consume the pizza more slowly, at the same rate, or more quickly? One does not need to be an economist to answer this question; the children,

234

other things being equal, will tend to consume these goods more quickly. Sally knows that for every slice of pizza and ounce of soda the rest of her peers consume, there will be less pizza and soda for herself. Sally is not alone in this understanding, however. Most of her peers are also aware of the opportunity costs of eating pizza and drinking soda at a leisurely rate. The resulting effect is a classroom of kids who are now consuming their treats at a much faster pace than they otherwise would have with regards to their own individual servings. Tragically, this may also preclude many of them from being able to enjoy the pizza and soda as much as they otherwise would have. Ludwig Von Mises describes the tragedy of the commons by using the examples of publicly owned land and waters:

> If land is not owned by anybody, although legal formalism may call it public property, it is utilized without any regard to the disadvantages resulting. Those who are in a position to appropriate to themselves the returns — lumber and game of the forests, fish of the water areas, and mineral deposits of the subsoil — do not bother about the later effects of their mode of exploitation. For them the erosion of the soil, the depletion of the exhaustible resources and other impairments of the future utilization are external costs not entering into their calculation of input and output. They cut down the trees without any regard for fresh shoots or reforestation. In hunting and fishing they do not shrink from methods preventing the re-population of the hunting and fishing grounds.[155]

Private owners of goods have a direct incentive to maintain and improve their capital value as they stand to personally and directly benefit from the value the goods retain. For instance, it is often in one's best interest to maintain his home in good quality in the event he desires to sell it or pass it down to his children. The home itself may be more beneficial if its integrity is maintained. Conversely, a politician who has temporary control over a given set of resources – but has neither the right to sell the resources for personal gain nor does he suffer substantial consequences for their abuse – will be more inclined to exploit those resources as much as possible for

---

[155] Mises, ibid, 652.

political gain with relatively less care for their future capital value.

Easements

When one homesteads unowned land, he is not merely conferring to himself exclusive right to occupy a certain space, but also, in his use of said good, he is acquiring rights to do with it as he wishes given that the activities performed do not involve uninvited physical interference with the property of others. To illustrate this, suppose John homesteads or purchases a plot of land and decides to start a rock band which, at the time, does not cause uninvited physical interference with the property of others. He is, say, too remote to have any effect on his neighbors. By doing so, he earns the right to produce the level of noise associated with his band on his property, despite the fact that the noise may traverse beyond the physical boundaries of the property itself. Such a right is commonly referred to as an easement. Now, suppose Sue purchases property adjacent to John's and complains about the excessive noise. Of course, Sue is free to request that John keep the noise down or that he only perform at certain times, but from a libertarian standpoint, she would have no legal grounds to forcibly stop John from producing the noise his band generates. As John was within his rights to play music when he had no neighbors, he develops an easement where he has already acquired the right to produce such noise by operating his rock band prior to Sue's moving in. The same methodology may be applied with air, water, or any other form of pollution. If a factory was polluting the air of a surrounding area prior to a residential community being established in its vicinity, then the residents of said community would have no just legal grounds to force the factory owner to halt the practices of his factory.

However, in the case of John and Sue or of the factory owner and the residential community, if John begins to produce *more* noise than he was prior to Sue moving in next door or if the factory produces *more* pollution after the residential community was established, then both Sue and the residential community would have solid legal grounds to acquire an injunction against John and the factory respectively for the amount of noise and air pollution that is being generated in excess of their easements. Hoppe iterates the concept in a slightly different way:

> Another, equally common
> misunderstanding of the idea of private
> property concerns the classification of
> actions as permissible or impermissible
> based *exclusively* on their physical effects,

i.e., without taking into account that every property right has a *history* (temporal genesis).

If A currently physically damages the property of B (for example by air pollution or noise), the situation must be judged differently depending on whose property right was established *earlier*. If A's property was founded first, and if he had performed the questionable activities before the neighboring property of B was founded, then A may continue with his activities. A has established an easement. From the outset, B had acquired dirty or loud property, and if B wants to have his property clean and quiet he must pay A for this advantage. Conversely, if B's property was founded first, then A must stop his activities; and if he does not want to do this, he must pay B for this advantage. Any other ruling is impossible and indefensible because as long as a person is alive and awake, he cannot *not* act. An early-comer cannot, even if he wished otherwise, wait for a late-comer and his agreement before he begins acting. He must be permitted to act immediately. And if no other property besides one's own exists (because a late-comer has not yet arrived), then one's range of action can be deemed limited only by laws of nature.[156]

Trespass and Nuisance

Unbeknownst to many self-identifying environmentalists today, much of the pollution that occurs would be prohibited in a free market society as such pollutants would be considered a violation of property rights on the grounds of trespass or nuisance. William Prosser identifies the

---

[156]   Hoppe, ibid, 8.

distinction:

> Trespass is an invasion of the plaintiff's
> interest in the exclusive possession of his
> land, while nuisance is an interference
> with his use and enjoyment of it. The
> difference is that between... felling a tree
> across his boundary line and keeping him
> awake at night with the noise of a rolling
> mill.[157]

Indeed, both nuisance and trespass cause uninvited physical interference with the property rights of others. The simple upholding of private property rights is the legal defense against much of the pollution decried by modern day environmentalists. It is indeed the State's monopolization of the legal system and its refusal to uphold private property rights that is the cause of most the environmental destruction witnessed today. A commonly cited reason for such deviations from private property protection against third parties is to favor the "greater public good which may be diminished if such private property rights were upheld absolutely" – i.e., in the case of eminent domain.

Murray Rothbard explains *why* trespass and nuisance are indeed violations of property rights, and conversely why certain other invasions of ones property by particles or energy, which are undetectable by the senses and produce no harm, do not constitute such violations:

> First, a direct trespass: A rolls his car onto
> B's lawn or places a heavy object on B's
> grounds. Why is this an invasion and
> illegal *per se?* Partly because, in the words
> of an old English case, 'the law infers
> some damage; if nothing more, the
> treading down of grass or herbage.' But it
> is not just treading down; a tangible
> invasion of B's property interferes with
> his exclusive use of the property, if only
> by taking up tangible square feet (or cubic
> feet). If A walks on or puts an object on
> B's land, then B cannot use the space A
> or his object has taken up. An invasion by
> a tangible mass is a *per se* interference with
> someone else's property and therefore

---

[157] William Prosser and Werdner Keeton, *Prosser and Keeton on the Law of Torts* (St. Paul: West Publishing Company, 1984), 595.

illegal.

In contrast, consider the case of radio waves, which is a crossing of other people's boundaries that is invisible and insensible in every way to the property owner. We are all bombarded by radio waves that cross our properties without our knowledge or consent. Are they invasive and should they therefore be illegal, now that we have scientific devices to detect such waves? Are we then to outlaw all radio transmission? And if not, why not?

The reason why not is that these boundary crossings do not interfere with anyone's exclusive possession, use or enjoyment of their property. They are invisible, cannot be detected by man's senses, and do no harm. They are therefore not really invasions of property, for we must refine our concept of invasion to mean not just boundary crossing, but boundary crossings that in some way interfere with the owner's use or enjoyment of this property. What counts is whether the senses of the property owner are interfered with.

But suppose it is later discovered that radio waves are harmful, that they cause cancer or some other illness? Then they *would* be interfering with the use of the property in one's person and should be illegal and enjoined, provided of course that this proof of harm and the causal connection between the specific invaders and specific victims are established beyond a reasonable doubt.[158]

This explanation provides a more refined insight to the boundaries of

---

[158] Murray N. Rothbard, "Law, Property Rights, and Air Pollution," *Cato Journal* 2, No. 1 Spring (1982): 55-99.

property rights and how individuals may be able to internalize some common externalities.

Strict Liability

Strict Liability is the legal concept whereby the owner of some property is held legally liable for damages suffered by others from this property that is due neither to the negligence nor fault of the owner. Attorney and libertarian legal theorist Stephan Kinsella provides a cogent critique of the idea of Strict Liability:

> Many libertarians seem to assume the validity of some kind of "strict liability." They say this with respect to property, when they assume that the owner "is responsible" for harm that is done by or with his property.
>
> I believe this an unjustified assumption, and is based on lack of careful analysis of property rights. Property is the *right to use* or control a scarce resource. It is not immediately clear why the right to use would imply obligations. Thinking this way clouds other property-related issues like IP. People say, for example, that IP is not problematic just because it limits what you can do with your own property—after all, your rights in your property are not unlimited, since you can't use your property to commit aggression against others.
>
> This latter phrase is said repeatedly by libertarians. I can't count how many times I've heard it over the years. The problem is it improperly links the prohibition on aggression to ownership of one's own property, thus implying that property rights are limited. But a crime is simply an action, and actions employ *means*. But the actor *does not need to own the means*. If I steal

A's handgun to shoot B, I am the murderer, not A. I violated A's right to control the gun; but A's right to the gun does not make him the murderer. We can see that the idea of strict liability as it applies to 'responsibility for owned things' is deeply flawed.

In other words, just because you have no right to commit aggression (via *any* means, whether the means are your owned property or not, or even other humans, whether owned or not) does not mean that property rights are "limited." The non-aggression principle limits what *actions* you are permitted to engage in. And since inanimate property does not act by itself, then it never commits crimes. It is people who commit crimes. If the owner commits a crime, he is liable, whether he uses his own property or not. But if another person uses my property to commit a crime, why should I be liable? It was not my action. Therefore, we can see that the assumption that 'ownership implies responsibility' is relatively mindless, unthinking, and useless.[159]

Tort/Negligence

Torts are relevant in the context of pollution and other environmental concerns, especially in a society characterized by a libertarian legal system.[160] Kinsella provides insight on the task of detailing the

---

[159] Stephan Kinsella, "The Libertarian Approach to Negligence, Tort, and Strict Liability: Wergeld and Partial Wergeld" (published in a blog post on stephankinsella.com, September 1, 2009), <http://www.stephankinsella.com/2009/09/the-libertarian-approach-to-negligence-tort-and-strict-liability-wergeld-and-partial-wergeld/>

[160] Cornell University Law School defines torts as "civil wrongs recognized by law as grounds for a lawsuit. These wrongs result in an injury or harm constituting the basis for a claim by the injured party. While some torts are also crimes punishable with imprisonment, the primary aim of tort law is to provide relief for the damages incurred and deter others from committing the same harms. The injured person may

libertarian approach to negligent torts in general:

> A wrongdoer is someone who intentionally causes harm or does something that gives the victim or recipient of the action a right to forcefully respond. This is true in the case of aggression; threats (the action of attempting harm, or making someone fearful of receiving a battery gives rise to a right to use force in response); fraud (the defrauder intentionally and knowingly takes property of the victim without the victim's genuine consent)...

> So how should we view negligence? I believe it should be viewed as being on a spectrum between non-action or mere behavior, and fully intentional action (crime). It is "partially" intentional. As I noted in Causation and Aggression:

> > ... when we ask if someone was the cause of a certain aggression, we are asking whether the actor did choose and employ means to attain the prohibited result. For there to be 'cause' in this sense, obviously there has to be cause-in-fact— this is implied by the notion of the means employed "attaining" or resulting in the actor's end. Intentionality is also a factor, because action has to be intentional to be an action (the means is chosen and employed intentionally; the actor

---

sue for an injunction to prevent the continuation of the tortious conduct or for monetary damages."

intends to achieve a given end).

Notice that this analysis helps to explain why damages or punishment is greater for intentional crimes than for negligent torts that result in similar damage. For example, punishment is an action: it is intentional and aims at punishing the body of the aggressor or tortfeasor. In punishing a criminal, the punishment is justified because the criminal himself intentionally violated the borders of the victim; the punishment is therefore symmetrical …. However, in punishing a mere tortfeasor, the punishment is fully intentional, but the negligent action being punished is only 'partially' intentional. Therefore punishing a tortfeasor can be disproportionate; it would be symmetrical only if the punishment were also 'partially' intentional. But punishment cannot be partially intentional; therefore, the damages inflicted (or extracted) have to be reduced to make the punishment more proportionate.[161]

Kinsella's interpretation of torts creates a justification for punishment in the event of a "partially intentional" property rights violation. Moreover, it demonstrates why an "eye for an eye" punishment is inappropriate when applied to such cases where negligence is the cause of a property rights violation. For instance, if Peter were to, with full intention, run over and kill Bill, then executing Peter would be a justifiable punishment due to its symmetry with the crime. However, if Peter were to run over and kill Bill due to negligence, then executing Peter as punishment would be unjustified. This is because the act of executing Peter is not symmetrical with Peter's act of involuntary manslaughter.

Action is defined as the deliberate use of means aimed at achieving a certain end(s). An action aimed towards execution is not commensurate with an action aimed away from killing that yields this unfortunate result nonetheless. Though Peter's action was not explicitly aimed at killing Bill, his act is still considered "partially intentional" towards this end as it did involve the deliberate use of means to achieve an end which necessarily put Bill at risk (otherwise Bill could not have been killed as a result of the action). Thus, it would be more appropriate to reduce Peter's punishment, to a level commensurate with the degree of risk he placed on Bill's life. If Peter's act placed Bill's life at a 25% chance of being extinguished, then Peter's punishment should *at least* be reduced 75% with respect to the ultimate penalty of execution. How one's level of intentionality is to be determined, the percentage of risk his actions placed on others assessed, and what punishments correspond with negligence related reductions cannot be known for certain in advance, and, as such, would be determined by arbitration, available evidence, and case precedent.

Of course, there are other mitigating factors to consider where Peter could run over and kill Bill, but he might be held less liable, or not be held liable at all. For instance, if Bill jumped in front of Peter's car, then Peter would likely not be held legally liable as Bill would be assessed as the cause of his own death. Alternatively, if Charlie ran Peter off the road, causing Peter to run over and kill Bill, then Charlie would be held liable for Bill's death, not Peter despite the fact that he was the one who ran Bill down. Finally, should Peter have suffered from an unforeseeable seizure while driving that caused him to swerve and crush Bill, then he should not be held liable, as this would be the result of Peter's completely unintentional behavior as opposed to his "actions" (intentional behavior). Thus, one's criminal or tortious liability is contingent upon whether or not his *actions* are judged to be the cause of a property rights violation.

---

[161] Kinsella, "The Libertarian Approach to Negligence, Tort, and Strict Liability: Wergeld and Partial Wergeld."

ENVIRONMENTALISM

Externalities

Often times, environmental damages such as pollution and ozone depletion are referred to as externalities: external effects of one's private actions. Many argue negative environmental externalities warrant the intervention of the State, as their very existence supposedly reflects shortfalls of free markets (i.e. "market failures"). In short, the theory of externalities refers to those

> ... cases where some of the costs or
> benefits of activities 'spill over' onto third
> parties. When it is a cost that is imposed
> on third parties, it is called a negative
> externality. When third parties benefit
> from an activity in which they are not
> directly involved, the benefit is called a
> positive externality.[162]

Thus, the common rationale for State intervention is to use its legislative powers for the purpose of restricting negative externalities, such as pollution, and promoting positive externalities via subsidies, such as public education. However, what is often overlooked are the means required to take such measures, and the externalities *these means* produce. The true cost (or benefit) of any given action to another individual is impossible to objectively determine; this follows from the fact that one cannot compare value interpersonally. One may determine that the actors involved in a voluntary trade must see it as mutually beneficial, but one cannot ascertain the exact degree of benefit each party gained, much less the negative or positive effects the transaction had on uninvolved third parties. Therefore, to promote aggressive State solutions to remedy negative externalities is to impose a concretely destructive and unjustified activity for the pursuit of an outcome whose net beneficial or destructive effects cannot be known.[163]

Ironically, however, the common law legal mechanisms which were used to effectively defend against negative externalities were curtailed by the State centuries ago in pursuit of the "greater public good." The prior legal mechanisms were simple, consistent, justified, and effective as they were guided by the ultimate end of upholding private property rights. Walter Block describes the solution:

---

[162] Gene Callahan, "What Is an Externality?" *The Free Market* 8th ser. 19 (2001).
[163] For an advanced overview of the Austrian perspective on value and utility, see Jeffrey Herbener, "Further Explorations in Austrian Value and Utility Theory" (lecture presented at Mises University, Ludwig Von Mises Institute, Auburn, Alabama, August, 2005).

There *was* a way to force private polluters to bear the social cost of their operations': sue them, make them pay for their past transgressions, and get a court order prohibiting them from such invasions in the future.

Upholding property rights in this manner had several salutary effects. First of all, there was an incentive to use clean burning, but slightly more expensive anthracite coal rather than the cheaper but dirtier high sulfur content variety; less risk of lawsuits. Second, it paid to install scrubbers, and other techniques for reducing pollution output. Third there was an impetus to engage in research and development of new and better methods for the internalization of externalities: keeping one's pollutants to oneself. Fourth, there was a movement toward the use of better chimneys and other smoke prevention devices. Fifth, an incipient forensic pollution industry was in the process of being developed. Sixth, the locational decisions of manufacturing firms were intimately affected. The law implied that it would be more profitable to establish a plant in an area with very few people, or none at all; setting up shop in a residential area, for example, would subject the firm to debilitating lawsuits.[164]

Preserving the Earth's Natural Treasures

When one discusses the privatization of any currently socialized service, one of the most common objections levied is that doing so would diminish the capacity to preserve and maintain the resources involved for posterity. What is implicit in this objection is the unproven premise that the

---

[164] Walter Block, "Environmentalism and Economic Freedom: The Case for Private Property Rights," in *Journal of Business Ethics* 17 (1998): 1887-99.

State is indeed better suited at taking care of these resources than any private owners could be. As illustrated by the tragedy of the commons, the incentive structure for agents of the State to take care of public lands and properties is simply not as compelling as the incentive structure of private ownership where the owner stands to directly benefit from maintaining and building on the capital value of these goods. For example, say a wealthy businessman acquires Yellowstone National Park. In freed markets, the incentives he faces support a more productive use of those resources. Perhaps tourism to an ecological preservation is less rewarding to all parties than transforming the land into a space center, an amusement park, a sports stadium, selling parcels of it for residential purposes, etc. While the maintenance of Yellowstone as an ecological site is visible under State care, it is not clear that such a purpose is the most value-productive end to which it could be put – only the interactions between individuals in a marketplace can tend to arrive at the most productive use. Because money is able to purchase an entire spectrum of goods and services, transforming the land – or carefully preserving it as a preservation – will tend to follow from his desire to act in ways which he believes will yield him the greatest monetary profits. Thus, if the owner appraises that the most profitable use of the land is to preserve it for recreational use and appreciation, then he may spend resources to preserve its integrity and he may charge visitors admission.

It is also important to recall that, in most cases, for someone to acquire the wealth needed to purchase a landmass such as Yellowstone, he would first need to sell goods or services that people valued more than the price he asked for them. The desires of others in society would have already played a large factor in this person's decisions regarding how to allocate his resources. This is due to the effects of free trade; arranging his property in a way that benefits society is how he would have generated his great wealth in the first place. In the alternative case where someone merely inherits wealth or wins it in a lottery, if such people do not allocate their resources wisely, they will incur losses and progressively lose control over a wider range of resources unless and until they start taking into account the preferences of others in their allocation. This same analysis may be applied to lakes, rivers, and any other owned thing.

Walter Block illustrates this with his lake example. If the owner believes his lake is more profitable when used for dumping, he will likely convert the lake accordingly and charge customers to dump. Conversely, if he views the most profitable use of the lake to be recreation, he will use it towards this end, charging people admission for its enjoyment. When deciding between the two uses, the owner will also likely take into account that he can switch his lake from a recreational use to a dumping one but that it would be more difficult to do the reverse. On the surface, some may find this disturbing as it would undoubtedly result in some lakes being used for dumping. However, the supply and demand forces of the market will direct lake owners away from creating too many dumping lakes by means of the profit/loss system. As more lakes would be used for dumping, there would be relatively fewer lakes for recreation. Due to the shortage, recreational lake owners may be able to charge higher prices for admissions, generating more profits, causing future lake owners to act in kind, and even to convince dumping owners and other non-owners to join the recreational lake market, pushing the price down further.[165] This, of course, is also equally and simultaneously true with regards to lakes for fishing, for exploration, for scientific testing, and for any end to which lakes can be put.

The motive to maintain the capital value of one's property will also serve to prevent an over-harvesting of trees from a forest or fish from the sea. If a landmass is valuable due to its lumber, then one has a natural incentive to not harvest more than he is able to replenish, so that he may maintain his future cash flow. Likewise, if one's section of ocean or lake derives value from the number of its inhabitants, it will be in the owner's best financial interest to not consume more of them than he is able to replenish.

Pricing Mechanism

The subject of an untainted pricing mechanism warrants specific mention as it has great implications for the advocacy of private control. As prices reflect the relative scarcities, demands, and opportunity costs of using resources in particular ways, they represent a quantitative metric by which easy assessment of the value of one's actions is possible – by monetary profits and losses. An entrepreneur experiencing losses indicates he is employing his resources in a way that members of society value less than they did prior to the entrepreneur employing them in such a manner. The reverse is true for profits. An owner profiting from his employment of resources means that he is transforming existing resources in a manner that members of the market value more than they valued the state of their previous arrangement.

Naturally, then, the existence of money and money prices allows for rational economic calculation; entrepreneurs have something real by which they can measure their performance. The driving force of the entrepreneur is the desire to create value and give others a reason to part with their money. If he earns more than it cost him to start the project, it's a success – if not, it's a loss. With prices derived from private ownership, it's possible to examine the economic configuration of one's resources. One can examine not simply what to produce, but *how* to produce it. Thus, the

---

[165]   Walter Block, "Economics and the Environment: A Reconciliation," (interview, 1985). https://youtu.be/XMxgYY_q-AI

central error with State or public ownership remains that no such objective and accurate pricing mechanism exists to guide the actions of State actors to employ resources under their command in the most efficient manner possible, i.e., in a manner that generates the lowest opportunity costs for those resources. This is because the State's income is not voluntarily provided; it is provided via coercive and aggressive mandate. When people are compelled by force to hand over their money, it becomes impossible to determine their actual preferences as the amount of income received is not commensurate with the level of desirability of a given good or service.[166] Contrast this with entrepreneurs in a free market where contributions are entirely voluntary and, therefore, do reflect such desirability. When politicians regulate the uses of public resources, they are more compelled to employ them in the direction of special interests and political pursuits as opposed to employing them in such a way as to maximize their capital value. This, of course, results in over-consumption and misallocations as their command over such resources is temporary yet their positions do not allow them to reap direct benefits from their capital value. This leaves the politicians with only one personally advantageous course of action: to exploit and consume the resources under their command as much and as quickly as possible.

Water Privatization

Today, unfortunately, most aqueous resources are owned by the State:

> First, the rivers. The rivers, and the oceans too, are generally owned by the government; private property, certainly complete private property, has not been permitted in the water. In essence, then, government owns the rivers. But government ownership is not true ownership, because the government officials, while able to control the resource cannot themselves reap their capital value on the market. Government officials cannot sell the rivers or sell stock in them. Hence, they have no economic

---

[166] Murray N. Rothbard, "Toward a Reconstruction of Utility and Welfare Economics," in *On Freedom and Free Enterprise*, edit. Mary Sennholz. (Princeton: Van Nostrand, 1956), 23.

incentive to preserve the purity and value of the rivers. Rivers are, then, in the economic sense, 'unowned'; therefore government officials have permitted their corruption and pollution. Anyone has been able to dump polluting garbage and wastes in the waters.[167]

Because many aqueous resources are not privately owned, the tragedy of the commons plagues their use and integrity. Over-fishing, dumping, oil spills, and other forms of pollution abound as no one has a direct and exclusive means to privatize the benefits of taking measures to maintain the integrity of the water. This contrasts with the incentives private owners have to prevent others from unjustly dumping trash or otherwise polluting their water. The cleaner one's water resources, the greater market value they have. The private owners would have a more direct and vested interest in preserving the quality of the aqueous resource for whatever end they deem to be most profitable in the long run.

Furthermore, geographic coordinates can serve as barriers for adjacent, contiguous water resources. Despite the water moving in and out of one's territory, it is possible to homestead sea space and establish norms governing pollution of that space. If Sarah purchases a property with a river running through it that has pollutant level X, and her neighbor upstream begins to dump in the river such that the pollutant level exceeds X, she will have legal grounds to enjoin her neighbor's polluting activities. Of course, such legal means would only be necessary if Sarah and her neighbor had not or could not work out some voluntary arrangement, such as payment for the excess dumping.

As for the question of *how* one may create borders in such aqueous resources, this is merely a technical problem. Walter Block suggests the law should consider future scenarios openly:

> This scenario assumes, of course, that the necessary complementary technological breakthroughs occur, such as either genetic branding, or perhaps better yet, electrified fences, which can keep the denizens of the deep penned in where deep sea fish farmers want them. Yes, this seems unlikely at present, given that under present law there would be no economic benefit to such inventions. But

---

[167] Murray N. Rothbard, "Conservation, Ecology, and Growth," in *For a New Liberty: The Libertarian Manifesto* (New York: Macmillan, 1973), 317-18.

this is due, in turn, not to any primordial fact of nature or law. Rather, it is because the law has not yet been changed so as to recognize even the possible future scenario where ocean privatization would be economic. The public policy recommendation stemming from this analysis is merely that the law should now be changed so as to recognize fish ownership in a given cubic area of ocean when and if such an act becomes technically viable. Then, whether or not it actually occurs is only an empirical question. It will, if and only if the complementary technology is forthcoming to make it feasible. But under this ideal state of affairs, there would be no legal impediment, as there now is, in this direction. That is, suppose that the needed innovations never occur, or are always too expensive, compared to the gains to be made by herding fish instead of hunting them. Then, of course, there can be no private property rights used in this manner in the ocean, as a matter of fact. But as a matter of law, things would still be different under the present proposal. There would always be the contrary to fact conditional in operation that if technology were such, then it would be legal to fence in parts of the ocean for these purposes. Under this state of affairs, there would be no legal impediments to the development of the requisite technology.[168]

One other benefit of privatizing water resources is that doing so would create an incentive to implement and invent non-water polluting industrial activities and technology. Not only this, but the development of water polluting forensics would also take place to assist damaged parties in establishing proof regarding whom exactly is causing harm to whose property. These go hand in hand; as more effective forensic techniques are

---

[168] Walter Block, "Water Privatization," (unpublished manuscript) http://thelibertycaucus.com/wp-content/uploads/2014/01/waterprivate.pdf

developed, so too are the incentives for would-be polluters to not pollute so that they may avoid any potential legal liability.

In regards to oil spills, people who own certain portions of shipping lanes in the ocean may charge more for the passage of single hulled oil tankers than double hulled ones, as the former present a larger risk for spillage which will have a direct impact on the value of their owned section of the ocean. In this way, terrible environmental externalities like oil spills may be mitigated by market forces.

Air Pollution

Rothbard writes of Robert Poole, that he:

> cogently defines pollution 'as the transfer of harmful matter or energy to the person or property of another, without the latter's consent.' The libertarian — and the only complete — solution to the problem of air pollution is to use the courts and the legal structure to combat and prevent such invasion.[169]

Much of the same reasoning applied to water pollution also applies to air pollution. Polluting the air on another's property without invitation is considered either a trespass or harmful nuisance (provided an easement to pollute was not previously attained), and, as such, may be stopped or enjoined by court order. Just like water pollution, upholding private property rights will: deter dirty companies from establishing their facilities near residential communities, incentivize such companies to devise ways to mitigate their pollution, and create a greater demand for the development of forensic techniques to help identify polluting culprits. Rothbard summarizes the criteria to be met before someone may justifiably be held liable for air pollution:

> We have established that everyone may do as he wishes provided he does not initiate an overt act of aggression against the person or property of anyone else. Anyone who initiates such aggression must be strictly liable for damages against

---

[169] Rothbard, *For a New Liberty.*

the victim, even if the action is 'reasonable' or accidental. Finally, such aggression may take the form of pollution of someone else's air, including his owned effective airspace, injury against his person, or a nuisance interfering with his possession or use of his land.

This is the case, *provided that:*

1) the polluter has not previously established a homestead easement;
2) while visible pollutants or noxious odors are *per se* aggression, in the case of invisible and insensible pollutants, the plaintiff must prove actual harm;
3) the burden of proof of such aggression rests upon the plaintiff;
4) the plaintiff must prove strict causality from the actions of the defendant to the victimization of the plaintiff;
5) the plaintiff must prove such causality and aggression beyond a reasonable doubt; and there is no vicarious liability, but only liability for those who actually commit the deed.[170]

Many may object to this methodology by citing the current day technical limitations in determining which emitters are responsible for pollution and to what degree they are responsible. This is, of course, a genuine concern, but is, once again, merely a technical one, and technical limitations do not justify imposing aggressive measures to compensate for their shortfalls. Even from a utilitarian standpoint, such aggressive measures create a slew of effects which contribute to the deterioration of the overall standard of living for society and cannot, without arbitrary decree, be said to mend more issues than they create. To employ them also sets a dangerous precedent upon which more may be imposed for similar ends.[171] Rothbard warns about taking this seemingly easy way out:

---

[170] Rothbard, "Law, Property Rights, and Air Pollution."
[171] Today's positivistic State-supported legal system is a prime example of what may result from this line of thinking.

The prevalence of multiple sources of pollution emissions is a problem. How are we to blame emitter A if there are other emitters or if there are natural sources of emission? Whatever the answer, it must not come at the expense of throwing out proper standards of proof, and conferring unjust special privileges on plaintiffs and special burdens on defendants.[172]

Animal Extinction

Animals, like all other scarce goods, are subject to the destructive effects of the Tragedy of the Commons. If they are prohibited from being privately owned, then humans will invariably tend to consume them in an uneconomic manner. Walter Block uses the Cow and Buffalo analogy to express this concept:

It is a well-known fact, at least within the free market environmental community, that the cow prospered, due to private property rights which could avert the tragedy of the commons, while the bison almost perished as a species due to lack of the same. Nowadays, happily, this problem has been remedied with regard to the buffalo. But the whale, the porpoise, edible fish and other sea species are dealt with, at present, in precisely the same manner which almost accounted for the disappearance of the bison.[173]

Of course, certain species may go extinct if they are viewed as a nuisance to the great majority of humans e.g., locusts, mosquitoes, etc. This being a work on environmental economics and not biology, there will be no attempt to identify which species has the potential to benefit mankind on net and which ones do not. However, for those species appraised to have some market value, there will be a demand to maintain their populations. Perhaps universities may want to acquire certain species of reptiles or

---

[172] Rothbard, ibid.
[173] Block, ibid.

254

insects for medical research, or someone else may want to preserve populations of deer for sport, etc. There is also, of course, the opportunity for strict preservationists to pool their money or resources and purchase land for the mere sake of preventing other humans from using it in a way they feel is destructive of its natural integrity. This method may be used to preserve lands, waters, certain animal species, mineral resources, and more. Some people prefer to abstain from consuming certain animals or other resources, and, for this reason, may receive the greatest amount of psychic profit from establishing such preserves. Nothing about setting up such preserves would be in any way incompatible with private property rights or free enterprise.

Waste Disposal

The negative externalities associated with waste disposal may also be internalized if free people are permitted to perform these services and to own dump sites privately. Private, in this context, is not intended to reference the fascistic relationship of waste management firms being contracted out for public use paid with tax dollars. This setup creates moral hazard for the consumer when deciding what types of items to buy – and how to dispose of his unwanted goods – as the bill for disposing them has already been paid despite how much he or she dumps. Truly private dump site owners may be inclined to charge more for materials which are scientifically shown to be more toxic or harmful. Such higher charges may be used to compensate the owner for potential liability costs or for the mitigation of his property's value by their contamination. Likewise, consumers may be charged more to dispose of items containing Styrofoam or plastic, and they may become more inclined to purchase products packaged in less environmentally destructive materials to reduce disposal costs. This, of course, does not mean that people will stop using plastic and Styrofoam altogether, but rather that such materials would only be used when one subjectively determines that the unique benefits of their usage exceeds the high costs of their disposal, as he will now be bearing its full costs. In this way, the self-interest of the dump site owner to make as much money as possible coincides with the consumer's desire to save as much money as possible; they are harmonized with the actions requisite to maintain the environmental integrity of the Earth. This is not to say that such a paradigm will create an environmentally pure utopia, but merely that the incentive structures would be much more appropriately aligned toward promoting behavior which is more environmentally friendly than the incentive structure present in today's State managed paradigm. Andrea Santoriello explains in concrete terms:

In the case of solid-waste management, plastic companies and their customers escape from the cost of disposing of plastic after the consumer is finished with it. This is because most garbage collection is organized through the public sector. The cost of disposing of the plastic and the other waste is undertaken by the government, and a citizen is typically taxed without regard to the amount of trash he generates. Once the citizen pays his taxes, he has no incentive to choose environmentally sound goods because disposal costs are in effect free to him. If, instead, there were complete privatization of the garbage disposal industry, those who generate trash would directly pay for disposal costs. The owner of a private dump tends to charge tipping fees that vary with different kinds of trash. The price will be significantly higher for material that creates toxic waste because the dump owner will be liable for any harmful leaks from his site. The hauling firm, which collects the garbage from the homeowner and must pay the tipping fee, will pass the price onto consumers. Consumers, knowing that they will have to pay more for the disposal of more plastic, will tend to substitute toward less costly, and thus more environmentally sound, containers. In the jargon of economists, the negative externality will disappear; the cost of trash disposal will be internalized, brought to bear on the responsible parties.[174]

Freeing markets and protecting the environment are not mutually exclusive, in fact, they both operate under the same principles and are managed in the same organic and decentralized manner. There is no

---

[174] Andrea Santoriello, "Externalities and the Environment," in *The Freeman* (Foundation for Economic Education: Nov. 1996. <http://www.fee.org/the_freeman/detail/externalities-and-the-environment>.

bureaucrat, technocrat, or politician who effectively manages all of Nature's functions, nor is there any single component of Nature which handles this task alone. What do exist are voluntary groupings of animals with symbiotic relations whose members have the capacity to divorce themselves from such relationships as soon as they deem prudent. There is also predator and prey. Though these animals are not bound by concepts like the Non-Aggression Principle – as they have little to no capacity to recognize and understand its meaning – we can still bear witness to the beauty and complexity of the spontaneous order that results absent a central director with the sole legal power to violently impose its will upon all others. If the population of a predator species grows too large, its food supply will diminish, which will, in turn, diminish the population of said predator species. Even the plants which survive harmoniously with their surroundings will thrive and multiply while the ones that do not will die off and give way to more suitable vegetation. Thus, Nature is not the antithesis of a free market society; it is, instead, a reflection of its efficacy in the non-human realm. Nature has no opinion or volition. It must operate according to its own laws where the system that results is one which is bottom-up, not top-down, and which responds immediately and perpetually to the ever-changing variables of its inhabitants. No single individual or group of individuals could ever hope to artificially replicate such an efficient and adaptable system. Thus, proponents of a free market do not seek to arrogantly replace Nature with a superior man-made system, but rather to operate under a set of principles whose prototype is Nature itself. It should be telling that the only assumption those who advocate freed markets make regarding human beings is that they act in ways to secure satisfaction, utility, and profit. The concept of a freed market is not a theory for idealists, but a perspective that recognizes and orients itself according to what is known about human nature, contrariwise to the assumptions advocates of State management make, who must assume their authority figures have a greater economic awareness or more benevolent intentions than the citizens over which they preside. Rothbard beautifully illustrates the confusion:

> Thus, when we peel away the confusions and the unsound philosophy of the modern ecologists, we find an important bedrock case against the existing system; but the case turns out to be not against capitalism, private property, growth, or technology per se. It is a case against the failure of government to allow and to defend the rights of private property against invasion. If property rights were to be defended fully, against private and

governmental invasion alike, we would find here, as in other areas of our economy and society, that private enterprise and modern technology would come to mankind not as a curse but as its salvation.[175]

---

[175] Rothbard, *For a New Liberty*, 327.

Chapter Fourteen

THE CORPORATION

CORPORATIONS ARE ONE of the most stigmatized and misunderstood institutions in the economy. This prejudice is held not only by the left leaning or socialist types, but pervades many libertarian circles as well. Like many other prejudices, however, this malcontent is not completely unfounded as various corporations and their agents have pushed for the implementation of harmful and exploitative measures. However, a great majority of the harm brought on or encouraged by corporations is ultimately rooted in their relationship with the State. Such harmful measures involve the erection of aggressive barriers to entry into various industries which include, but are not limited to: occupational licensure, intellectual property laws, minimum wage laws, taxes, and other expensive regulations with the ostensible purpose of protecting the consumer. Of course, there is nothing wrong with the stated *intent* of such regulations. Rather, the issue is the means by which they are enforced, and the fact that a single institution has the exclusive legal privilege to create, interpret, and enforce these regulations: the State.

As we discussed in previous chapters, the free market has its own organic (and non-aggressive) regulatory powers, which act as a network of checks and balances on the behavior of actors in the market. Natural competition serves to align business interests with the interests of the general consumer. However, attempting to change the organic regulatory system of the market into an artificially controlled one presents a danger in that such powers then become subject to human intrigue and error as opposed to being impartially exercised according to the financial demands of the consumer. Thus, when the State is able to usurp regulatory powers over the marketplace a destructive zero-sum game manifests. Whereas, before the organic regulatory functions of the market were merely reflections of various actors pursuing their own ends, they now become to an ever increasing degree the result of central direction and control. In this context, inherent human self-interest will drive many businesses or firms in the economy to appeal to the State for both defensive and offensive ends. Businesses will realize that choosing to take the noble high road of not appealing to this institution would only result in giving their less scrupulous competitors an unfair advantage. Hence, the formation of the State regulatory agency causes the entrepreneur's ultimate pursuit of profit to be entangled with two opposing ends: satisfying the consumer and satisfying the State.

It now becomes economic to spend millions of dollars on political campaigns to influence a particular politician to support bills harmful to one's competitors and favorable to themselves. The opportunity costs are the R&D, advertising, or reinvestment into a more robust capital goods infrastructure that may have otherwise taken place. Invariably, the larger a given firm becomes the more involved it will tend to be with matters of the State as its success increasingly comes to rely on compliance with an entrenched regulatory apparatus. In addition to this, a larger firm will have more resources by which to direct the State's power in its own favor and to the expense of its competitors.

It is important to note, that in a free market, the efficacy of a given firm's pursuit of profit is *completely* contingent upon the degree to which the consumers' demands are satisfied. This creates a win-win paradigm: the firm wins when the consumer does and vice versa. However, once the State enters the equation, a win-lose paradigm emerges where one firm may suppress competition via legislative edict.

The power to legislate *is* the power to perpetrate aggression and is thereby antithetical to private property rights, the free market, and justice. Before the State may do *anything* it must first confiscate the wealth of its "citizens" so that it may fund its own operations. It then confers upon itself the exclusive right to produce legislation. In other words, any other institution which attempts to produce, interpret, and enforce law will be violently vanquished. Finally, once said legislation has been produced, the State enforces it via the application or threat of physical violence. This would be perfectly legitimate if agents of the State were making such dictates over the use of their own justly acquired property, i.e., over resources which they originally appropriated/homesteaded or received through voluntary exchange.[176] In reality, all the resources the State wields were at one point expropriated or stolen from others, and they are now being used to further erode the property rights of its subjects by dictating to them what they can and cannot do with their property (above and beyond not using it as an instrument to aggress against the persons or property of others).

With all this said, it becomes quite clear why the corporation has come to be a notorious source of exploitation: the largest firms tend to be corporations due to their ability to generate and manage large quantities of capital, i.e., money, factors of production, other assets, etc. Because corporations tend to be the largest firms, they tend also to be the ones most intimately involved with the State, as their existence/profitability relies heavily on legal and regulatory matters. The argument put forth in this

---

[176] After all, what one does with his own property is his prerogative, so long as in so doing he does not aggress against the persons or property of others.

chapter is simply this: absent the State, corporations will be profit seeking and wealth producing institutions just like all others in the free market. True exploitation is difficult to imagine if property is respected. That said, any socially maligned behavior that is perpetrated by firms in a free market will be immediately met with losses and damaged reputation, each of which disempowers the exploiter and serves to deter others from acting in kind. The free market accomplishes this, not with aggressive edict, but with the precise and organic mechanism spawned by the presence of consumer choice and competition, namely the price mechanism. Many auditing institutions and private certification agencies may also arise out of the consumer demand for easily recognizable markers for reputable and dubious institutions alike. In essence, the best way to prevent massive exploitation, poverty, and interpersonal conflict is to establish a social order centered around private property rights. Unlike the State, the corporation is a type of firm compatible with such rights. Thus, what is commonly perceived as corporate exploitation is in fact a *symptom* of the State.

The Firm

Before delving into the details of the corporate model, it would behoove us to review the more foundational concept of "the firm." In the words of Nicolai Foss the firm is simply "an organization planned with the express purpose of earning profit."[177] Peter Klein defines the firm as: "the capitalist entrepreneur plus the factors of production that he/she or they own."[178] In layman's terms, a firm is a business, i.e. an explicit attempt to earn revenues over losses. In the following sections, we will briefly review the four most prominent legal forms a firm may take: Sole Proprietorship, Partnership, Cooperative, and the Corporation.

Sole Proprietorship

A sole proprietorship (aka proprietorship) is a firm where no legal distinction is made between the firm as an enterprise and the owner. The owner is personally liable for all losses and debts. Every asset and all profits are owned and to be used exclusively at the proprietor's discretion. The

---

[177] Nicolai Juul Foss, "The Theory of the Firm: The Austrians as Precursors and Critics of Contemporary Theory," in *The Review of Austrian Economics* 7.1 (1994): 31-65. <https://mises.org/journals/rae/pdf/rae7_1_2.pdf>.

[178] Peter Klein, "Production and the Firm" (lecture presented at Mises University, Ludwig Von Mises Institute, Auburn, Alabama, July 23, 2013).

advantages of a sole proprietorship may include:

- Only small amounts of capital are needed to start and run one
- Easier to organize as there tends to be fewer moving parts
- The owner has full discretion over how the firm is run
- Because the owner is fully and personally liable for debts, creditors may be more willing to extend credit to a sole-proprietorship than a limited liability firm
- The owner keeps all the profits

In contrast some disadvantages may include:

- Potential investors or other creditors may be wary of involving themselves with a proprietorship, as the owner has relatively few checks on his behavior when compared with other types of firms
- Proprietorships die with the owner, unless he is able to transfer it to someone else. This may be difficult as the successor would have to be both intimately familiar with the firm's operations and willing to accept total liability for its debts. This will likely be a factor considered by prospective investors and creditors.
- These firms tend to have relatively less collateral than other firm types, hence creditors may be more reluctant to extend large amounts of credit.

Partnership

A partnership is legally similar to the proprietorship with the exception that there are two or more owners as opposed to just one. All partners, just like in a proprietorship, are personally liable for the firm's losses and debts. Conversely, the partners of a firm divvy out the profits and managerial discretion amongst themselves. This alleviates some of the drawbacks of a proprietorship as its continuity is not contingent on a single individual and its debts may be distributed amongst multiple parties. Thus partnerships tend to have more collateral and a greater ability to attract investors and creditors than proprietorships. However, some unique drawbacks will be the inefficiencies and difficulties involved with dissension amongst partners as to what direction to take the firm and how it is to be managed. However, such conflict may be mitigated by the partners agreeing to abide by the outcomes of a majority vote or through some other procedural method. Having multiple owners of a firm presents a series of checks on its direction, which can bring unique costs and benefits. Thus it will be up to the entrepreneur to decide ultimately which organizational framework will be most suitable to his enterprise.

Cooperative

Cooperatives are firms which are owned by their patrons. These owners may be the firm's customers, employees, suppliers or any combination. The common thread here being that the owners have a direct connection or dealing with the firm. Some patrons may have larger shares of ownership over the firm based on their seniority or how much they have invested into it. Moreover, cooperatives tend to be democratically managed. They may or may not have limited liability. All members of the cooperative (or "co-op") receive a share of the profits in accordance with their proportion of ownership shares. Some co-ops may not even have members with varying levels of ownership, but instead provide an equal amount of shares to all and disperse the profits accordingly.

Corporation

A corporation is a firm whose legal identity is separate and distinct from its owners. Corporations may have their own assets, enter into contracts, sue and be sued, lend or borrow money, and hire employees. Investopedia defines it:

> A corporation is created (incorporated) by a group of shareholders who have ownership of the corporation, represented by their holding of common stock. Shareholders elect a Board of Directors (generally receiving one vote per share) who appoint and oversee management of the corporation. Although a corporation does not necessarily have to be for profit, the vast majority of corporations are setup with the goal of providing a return for its shareholders. When you purchase stock you are becoming part owner in a corporation.[179]

One of the distinguishing characteristics of a corporation is that its ownership shares may be held by those whom have no direct tie to the firm, i.e., by people who neither manage, work for, buy from, or supply it. In

---

[179] "Corporation" on *Investopedia*.
http://www.investopedia.com/terms/c/corporation.asp

addition, the shareholders of a corporation are only held financially liable for the firm's debts up to the amount they invested. For instance, suppose Joe buys ten shares from company X at one dollar each and the following day company X goes bankrupt. Suppose also that the company is divided into one hundred shares of ownership, and the company is one thousand dollars in the hole. With this being the case, Joe would own ten percent of the company but not ten percent of its debt. That is to say, if Joe were a ten percent *partner* he would have to fork over one hundred dollars to the creditors (ten percent of the company's debt). However, because Joe is merely a ten percent shareholder of a *corporation,* his stock merely loses all its value rendering him just ten dollars poorer (the amount he invested into the firm) as opposed to one hundred dollars (ten percent of the firm's debt). This is due to what is known as the *limited liability* characteristic of the corporation. Unlike partnerships and proprietorships, owners or shareholders in a corporation are not vulnerable to having their personal assets seized as remuneration for the firm's debts. The same goes for torts committed by employees of the corporation. That is to say, shareholders are not held legally liable for torts committed by the corporation's employees just because they are in its employ or were using its assets as the instruments for said torts.

Free Market Society

Though the previous four legal types of firms are the most common, this is not to say that in a free market society various hybrids of these firms may not arise. So long as no aggression/fraud is being committed, there would be no limitations or prohibitions on what form a given firm may take. Robert Hessen sums this up:

> Any firm, regardless of size, can be structured as a corporation, a partnership, a limited partnership, or even one of the rarely used forms, a business trust or an unincorporated joint stock company. Despite textbook claims to the contrary, partnerships are not necessarily small scale or short-lived; they need not cease to exist when a general partner dies or withdraws. Features that are automatic or inherent in a corporation—continuity of existence, hierarchy of authority, freely transferable shares—are optional for a

partnership or any other organizational form. The only exceptions arise if government restricts or forbids freedom of contract (such as the rule that forbids limited liability for general partners).[180]

The Corporation

Stocks

A firm may sell its stock (shares of ownership) either privately or publicly on a stock exchange as a means to generate capital. One who purchases stock from a given corporation may be said to own equity in the firm. The Mises Wiki offers an explanation of equity:

> Equity is the legal claim of individuals to the assets of a business after deducting all obligations to others, namely, the liabilities. They are often represented as shares of a business which can be traded (for instances in the corporate form of legal business organizations). Organizations formed to assist the exchange of ownership interests in businesses are called stock exchanges.[181]

Shareholders of a given corporation are allotted certain voting rights in proportion to the number of shares they own. In most cases, shareholders will elect a Board of Directors to oversee the corporation's management and represent their interests, i.e., to act as a governing body ensuring no actions are taken by the firm which could unduly jeopardize the value of its stock. Each shareholder is entitled to a percentage of a firm's profit commensurate with the percentage of the firm's shares he/she owns. Thus, if John owns ten percent of a firm's shares and that firm generates one thousand dollars in profit, then he is entitled to one hundred dollars. One of the important functions of the Board of Directors, however, is to decide whether or not to disperse these profits to the shareholders directly in the form of dividends, use the profits to reinvest and expand the firm, or to

---

[180] Robert Hessen, "Corporations" in *The Concise Encyclopedia of Economics,* Econlib <http://www.econlib.org/library/Enc/Corporations.html>.

[181] "Equity" on Ludwig Von Mises Institute." <http://wiki.mises.org/wiki/Equity>.

repurchase stock. Each of these courses of action may help enhance the growth and value of the firm. However, the action or combination of actions taken will be case-dependent and require information that the average shareholder simply may not possess. This may be because the average shareholder does not have the time or incentive to keep up with the day-to-day management of the firm of which he is a partial owner; this will be especially true if he holds a small stake in it.

It is for this reason that the discretion over what to do with the company's profits are delegated to the Board of Directors and the management they oversee. They are generally more aware of where the firm is and what it will take to maintain its growth and profitability. A given corporation may also publish earnings reports at regular intervals to attract creditors and/or investors. Corporations who do not publish their earnings have the benefit of retaining financial privacy from their competitors, but at the same time, they may find it more difficult to attract investors due to a lack of transparency. There is no universally right or wrong path for a firm to take in this regard; it is simply something that would have to be dealt with on a case by case basis and at the discretion of those with the localized knowledge to make profitable decisions.

Finally, the price of a given corporation's stock is ultimately driven by investor expectations of its current and expected future profitability. Put differently, one's willingness to purchase stock at a given price will be contingent upon his projections of its future dividends and/or appreciation. Such projections may be derived from pure intuition, a detailed understanding of the related industry and the prospective company's role in it, or from the assessments of credible investors (or a combination of these).

Stock Market

A stock market or stock exchange is a place where securities may be bought and sold. Mises Wiki defines securities:

> In finance, a security is an instrument representing ownership (stocks), a debt agreement (bonds) or the rights to ownership (derivatives). A security is essentially a contract that can be assigned a value and traded.[182]

---

[182] "Security (finance)" Ludwig Von Mises Institute,
<http://wiki.mises.org/wiki/Security_%28finance%29>

For the purpose of this chapter, we will be focusing on the corporation and stocks. The stock market allows one the ability to extend capital to any publicly traded company. This creates an indispensable market for capital and acts as an additional mechanism by which any market participant may influence the flow and allocation of resources. Other things equal, market actors will tend to invest in those firms which they believe to have the greatest prospects for profits. Subjective factors, however, do play a role. Investors, like everyone, seek to maximize psychic income – of which earning dividends happens to be a large portion.[183] In a free market society, those firms which enjoy large profits will tend to be the ones who add the greatest degree of value to society. The stock market allows anyone to further empower and become, in an additional way, the beneficiaries of various productive enterprises. Contrary to popular belief, such a market acts as a bottom up and organic means by which to direct the flow of capital. Mises comments on the integral functions performed by the stock market:

> A stock market is crucial to the existence
> of capitalism and private property. For it
> means that there is a functioning market in
> the exchange of private titles to the means
> of production. There can be no genuine
> private ownership of capital without a
> stock market: there can be no true
> socialism if such a market is allowed to
> exist.[184]

Limited Liability

One of the most perpetrated myths regarding corporations is that they are or must be creatures of the State. This is categorically false, and is often times mistakenly thought to be the case due to the modern day marriage between various mega-corporations and the State. However, this is merely a symptom of a State regulated economy. There is absolutely no reason why a corporate form of organization cannot be established by voluntary contract. Robert Hessen offers an opinion:

> Moreover, to call incorporation a
> 'privilege' implies that individuals have no
> right to create a corporation. But why is

---

[183] Rothbard, "Fundamentals of Human Action" *Man, Economy, and State*, 71-72.
[184] Rothbard, "A Socialist Stock Market?" *Making Economic Sense*.

governmental permission needed? Who would be wronged if businesses adopted corporate features by contract? Whose rights would be violated if a firm declared itself to be a unit for the purposes of suing and being sued, holding and conveying title to property, or that it would continue in existence despite the death or withdrawal of its officers or investors, that its shares are freely transferable, or if it asserted limited liability for its debt obligations? If potential creditors find any of these features objectionable, they can negotiate to exclude or modify them.[185]

Limited liability for debts is not an overly complex issue to resolve in a freed society. Corporate firms would identify themselves as such to potential creditors, who would thereby understand that if the firm defaulted on a loan, they could not go after the personal assets of its shareholders. Knowing these limitations, the creditor would be well within its rights to deny an extension of credit, raise the interest rate to compensate for a perceived increase in risk, or negotiate that a portion of the personal assets of the corporation's managers or officers be included as collateral. There is no fraud or private property rights violation in this situation, therefore there is nothing truly un-libertarian about a corporate model. The stickier issue, however, is limited liability for torts. To reiterate, this simply shields shareholders from torts committed by other employees while on the job or using the company's assets. It should be made very clear that this in no way alleviates the legal liability of those who actually commit the torts, but rather insulates the owners of the firm not directly involved with said tort from legal recourse. However, if it is found to be the case that a CEO or other corporate officer committed a tort, then they, of course, would be held responsible. In a free market society, this would not be a unique feature of corporations, but would apply for any owner of a firm whose employee perpetrated a tort absent his involvement. For example, suppose John is a proprietor of a pizzeria and his employee Fred crashes a company vehicle into Sue in the course of a pizza delivery. Should John be held liable for Fred's negligence? Of course not. In a libertarian society, no person would ever be held liable for the actions of another (absent a contract stipulating otherwise). It is silly to think that just because someone else commits a tort with your property, that you would somehow be at least

---

[185] Hessen, ibid.

partially responsible for the tort. It is not who owns the instrument of aggression that is legally liable per se, but rather the person who actually caused the property violation.

Now this is not to say that various corporations could not voluntarily make themselves liable for the actions of their employees for the sake of establishing themselves as a "socially responsible establishment" in the community. A firm may find the development of such a reputation to be conducive to its profit margin. In this case, a firm may declare "we hereby transfer title up to X amount of dollars to any person found to be damaged by the actions of any employee acting within the boundaries of company protocol." This creates a voluntary binding contract for a given firm to provide restitution for such potential future damages. Above and beyond the binding nature of this contract, a company may also choose to compensate individuals damaged by an employee acting *outside* the narrow boundaries of company protocol. A company may do this to avoid negative public perception which may impact its profits. Kinsella provides additional commentary on the compatibility of corporate firm types with libertarian principles:

> My view is that corporations are essentially compatible with libertarianism. As for voluntary debts being limited to the corporation's assets; this is no problem since the creditor knows these limitations when he loans money. What about limited liability for torts or crimes? As mentioned, the person directly responsible for a tort or crime is always liable; sometimes the employer (which is often a corporation) is also liable for the employee's actions, via *respondeat superior*. Who else should be responsible? In my view, those who cause the damage are responsible. Shareholders don't cause it any more than a bank who loans money to a company causes its employees to commit torts. The shareholders give money; and elect directors. The directors appoint officers/executives. The officers hire employees and direct what goes on. Now to the extent a given manager orders or otherwise causes a given action that damages someone, a case can be made that the manager is causally responsible,

jointly liable with the employee who directly caused the damage. It's harder to argue the directors are so directly responsible, but depending on the facts, it could be argued in some cases. But it's very fact specific. Perhaps the rules on causation should be relaxed or modified, but this has nothing to do with there being a corporation or not—for the laws of causation should apply to any manager or person of sufficient influence in the organization hierarchy, regardless of legal form of the organization (that is, whether it's a corporation, partnership, sole proprietorship, or what have you).[186]

The Principal-Agent Problem

A common criticism of the corporation is that because the separation of ownership and control is so wide, the conduct of the firm's managers will tend to stray further from the interest of the shareholders than other types of firms whose managers comprise the entire set of owners. This critique is commonly referred to as the "Principal-Agent Problem." Such a problem exists when a "principal" delegates powers to an "agent" who has access to greater amounts of and/or more accurate information (a.k.a. *asymmetric information*) than the principal and whose interests are not perfectly aligned with said "principal." In the case of a corporation the "principals" are the shareholders and the "agents" are the managers and officers of the firm. Because information is typically asymmetric in favor of the agents, it is said that it is difficult for the principals to hold them accountable. Remember, the only reason the principals delegate power to agents in the first place is because they have neither the time nor the expertise to manage said powers to a satisfactory degree of competence. So too, and for the same reasons, would it be difficult for the principals to monitor and hold accountable the agents for any risky or detrimental behavior. Such behavior may include the doling out of oversized bonuses, perks, expensive company cars, private jets, excessive staff, etc. However, varying internal and external control mechanisms have developed to mitigate the negative impact of the aforementioned concerns

---

[186] Stephan Kinsella, "Corporations and Limited Liability for Torts," in *Mises Economics Blog* (Ludwig Von Mises Institute, September 10, 2008). <http://archive.mises.org/9084/corporations-and-limited-liability-for-torts/>.

whilst maintaining many of the corporation's organizational benefits.

Internal Checks on Corporate Management

What should first be mentioned is that small investors in a firm will likely understand that, being small, they have little say in the direction the firm takes. Thus, if they do not like how a given corporation operates, then they may refrain from investing in it. Likewise, if they are already invested and do not care for the direction the firm is heading, they may sell their shares and invest elsewhere (or nowhere at all). If shareholders are buying or selling shares at substantial levels, this will convey important signals to the managers in the form of rising or falling share prices. The price of a stock reflects an equilibrium, however fleeting, of the current state of market demand - that is, the aggregation of millions of individuals' differing levels of desires and willingness to pay for this stock – and the corresponding supply of such stock. If speculators suddenly come to market looking to heavily purchase stock, they will initially purchase shares at the prevailing market price. As they purchase more, however (technically, as they satisfy sell orders on the stock exchange), the number of people willing to sell the stock at that prevailing market rate declines, and the only ones holding more of that stock are individuals demanding more money in exchange for them. Now, in order to purchase more stock, these optimistic speculators must purchase them from individuals with greater reservation demand than prior. Thus, with the elimination of those with lower reservation demands, the "market price" the stock would fetch increases. The opposite is true too: Market actors looking to unload their stock on the market will satisfy all the buy orders, and the price they receive for their stock will continue to decline. Generally speaking, substantial "purchases" of shares will result in increasing share prices whereas substantial "selling" will tend to result in decreasing share prices.

Perhaps the most visible defense against corporate mismanagement is the Board of Directors. The Board of Directors are typically comprised of experienced managers and experts in fields related to the given corporation's industry, and serve as an internal auditing group charged with ensuring shareholder interests are not being compromised by poor managerial practices. The members of the board thus owe their tenure to the continued satisfaction of the shareholders they represent. The Board of Directors also establishes major company policies. These may include but are not limited to the hiring and firing of executives, setting dividends, and determining executive compensation.[187]

---

[187] As a side note, recall that shareholders voluntarily and explicitly provide their resources to these organizations for their management, whereas the State requires no

If a prospective business decision is large enough, a corporate firm may even hold a shareholder vote on it. Shareholders can, of course, mail in their votes, and they are counted per share owned – not per person – unlike the case in most cooperatives.

A corporation may be set up in such a way that its managers and officers receive bonuses for good performance. This serves to more closely align the interests of the managers with shareholder interests. Officers, managers, and other employees may also be given company stock or stock options. This solution is obvious, as the more stock a manager has, the less separation there is between ownership and control; that is, the more a shares a manager holds, the more aligned his interests will be with other shareholders. The interests, of course, being to safely and securely maximize the corporation's profits. This does not mean managers will not take any risks or even that they should not, but rather that such risks will be taken with great care and caution. In other words, one is less inclined to be as deliberate with the disposal of other people's money and property than he is with his own. Thus, when the manager becomes subject to personal losses for the falling of company profits, then he will tend to be more prudent in his decision making.

Large banking institutions or other venture capitalists may purchase substantial equity in various corporations, and thus wield considerable regulatory power over their strategic operations. Moreover, some shareholders may pool their resources and invest as a "block" yielding them considerable influence over the firm's management as well. Such blocks may form around shareholders who share common interests or ideas as to what direction the given firm should take. Thus corporate managers will have many checks and balances to contend with when running the firm. The combination and degree of these restrictions will tend to evolve and modify according to what configuration is most efficient. After all, managers do require some discretion to be efficacious lest an excess of constraints hinder their ability to perform the very functions placed in their charge.

Last, but not least, is the potential for a manager or officer to lose his job to a subordinate if he is seen as being reckless or incompetent. In other words, there is an internal market for managers. It is not sufficient to make it to the top; one must also maintain considerable performance levels

---

such explicit sanction. Instead, it seizes the resources of its citizens at the threat or application of violence regardless of consent and exercises jurisdiction over the property of others; property that it has neither legitimate claim nor authority over as States never acquire said property via original appropriation/homesteading or voluntary exchange. Corporate entities, on the other hand, would have to *persuade* investors to invest and could only rightfully exercise control over resources they acquired through peaceful means. Finally, shareholders may at any time withdraw their funds without legal consequence. In other words, the difference is between voluntary and involuntary association.

to retain a high position of authority. For example, if a given CEO becomes frivolous with company funds purchasing lavish company jets, cars, and frequenting five star restaurants, then the Board of Directors may decide to terminate him and offer his job to the CFO or whomever else they deem suitable.

External Checks to Corporate Management

External competition in the market is perhaps the most obvious and visible factor regulating corporate management. If a firm is unable to keep up with changing consumer demand or is unable to match falling competitor prices for its products/services, then it will lose market share. If this trend is not stopped, it will be reflected by a decrease in its share price. Share prices communicate important signals to market actors outside of the firm as well. For instance, falling stock prices may invite investors or competitors to purchase a majority of a given firm's shares and institute overhauling measures which involve a restructuring of management. This process is commonly referred to as a "hostile takeover." Once the firm has been restructured to the satisfaction of the new majority shareholders, they may then decide to sell their shares for a substantial profit. These investors, often referred to as "corporate raiders," essentially act as organizational handymen revitalizing the productive capacities of various waning firms.

A bank may also temper corporate policy by threatening not to renew a recurring loan in cases where it perceives managing practices to be excessively risky or out of sync with market trends. Mises provides a cogent response to the "separation of ownership and control" criticism of the corporation:

> It is asserted that the corporation is operated by the salaried managers, while the shareholders are merely passive spectators. All the powers are concentrated in the hands of hired employees. The shareholders are idle and useless; they harvest what the managers have sown. This doctrine disregards entirely the role that the capital and money market, the stock and bond exchange, which a pertinent idiom simply calls the 'market,' plays in the direction of corporate business. The dealings of this market are branded by popular anticapitalistic bias as a

hazardous game, as mere gambling. In fact, the changes in the prices of common and preferred stock and of corporate bonds are the means applied by the capitalists for the supreme control of the flow of capital. The price structure as determined by the speculations on the capital and money markets and on the big commodity exchanges not only decides how much capital is available for the conduct of each corporation's business; it creates a state of affairs to which the managers must adjust their operations in detail.

The general direction of a corporation's conduct of business is exercised by the stockholders and their elected mandataries, the directors. The directors appoint and discharge the managers. In smaller companies and sometimes even in bigger ones the offices of the directors and the managers are often combined in the same persons. A successful corporation is ultimately never controlled by hired managers. The emergence of an omnipotent managerial class is not a phenomenon of the unhampered market economy. It was, on the contrary, an outgrowth of the interventionist policies consciously aiming at an elimination of the influence of the shareholders and at their virtual expropriation. In Germany, Italy, and Austria it was a preliminary step on the way toward the substitution of government control of business for free enterprise, as has been the case in Great Britain with regard to the Bank of England and the railroads. Similar tendencies are prevalent in the American public utilities. The marvelous achievements of corporate business were not a result of the activities of a salaried managerial oligarchy; they were accomplished by people who were connected with the corporation by means

of the ownership of a considerable part or
of the greater part of its stock and whom
part of the public scorned as promoters
and profiteers.[188]

Limitations on the Size of a Firm

A common objection leveled against the corporation, and more
broadly against capitalism, is the possibility that one firm may acquire a
monopoly on an essential resource. Murray Rothbard demonstrates,
however, that firms face natural limits on their size due to the calculation
problem, which, up until that point, was exclusively applied as a critique of
socialism. The calculation problem, however, applies to any resource or
good that has no market price regardless of the overarching economic or
political structure directing its use. If a given type of good, say oil, is owned
by only one entity it can by definition have no market price. Market prices
are derived through a bidding process which occurs in trade. Thus, if a
good is being exclusively utilized by one entity, by definition it is not being
traded and therefore cannot develop such a market price. Without knowing
the market price of a good, it then becomes virtually impossible to
determine whether or not it is being employed efficiently[189] . In other
words, if one were to own the entire amount of a given good he would have
no objective base of reference to determine the opportunity costs of
employing it in any given manner. The resulting inefficiencies would
ultimately hamper his profit margin and may even lead to substantial losses.
Thus, a given firm's size would ultimately be limited by the economic
necessity for an external market to exist for all of the goods used in its
production processes. Peter Klein expounds upon this limitation to firm
size:

> Rothbard's account begins with the
> recognition that Mises's position on
> socialist economic calculation is not
> exclusively, or even primarily, about
> socialism, but about the role of prices for
> capital goods. Entrepreneurs allocate
> resources based on their expectations
> about future prices, and the information

---

[188] Mises, "The Market," *Human Action*, 306-07.
[189] Efficiency as measured in terms of profits or losses – that is, efficiency relates to
whether transforming a good in a certain way has made it more valuable in the eyes
of the consumer than it was prior.

contained in present prices. To make profits, they need information about all prices, not only the prices of consumer goods but the prices of factors of production. Without markets for capital goods, these goods can have no prices, and hence entrepreneurs cannot make judgments about the relative scarcities of these factors. In any environment, then – socialist or not – where a factor of production has no market price, a potential user of that factor will be unable to make rational decisions about its use. Stated this way, Mises's claim is simply that efficient resource allocation in a market economy requires well-functioning asset markets. To have such markets, factors of production must be privately owned.

Rothbard's contribution, was to generalize Mises' analysis of this problem under socialism to the context of vertical integration and the size of the organization. Rothbard writes in *Man, Economy, and State* that up to a point, the size of the firm is determined by costs, as in the textbook-model. However, 'the ultimate limits are set on the relative size of the firm by the necessity for markets to exist in every factor, in order to make it possible for the firm to calculate its profits and losses'[190]

.....The use of internally traded intermediate goods for which no external market reference is available thus introduces distortions that reduce organizational efficiency. This gives us the element missing from contemporary theories of economic organization, an upper bound: the firm is constrained by

---

[190] Rothbard, "Particular Factor Prices and Productive Income," *Man, Economy, and State*, 599.

the need for external markets for all internally traded goods. In other words, no firm can become so large that it is both the unique producer and user of an intermediate product; for then no market-based transfer prices will be available, and the firm will be unable to calculate divisional profit and loss and therefore unable to allocate resources correctly between divisions. Of course, internal organization does avoid the holdup problem, which the firm would face if there were a unique outside supplier; conceivably, this benefit could outweigh the increase in 'incalculability.'[191] Usually, however, the costs from the loss of calculation will likely exceed the costs of external governance.[192]

Absent the State, the corporation is no threat to the free market. With the advent of the corporation, the general consumer is given the added option to purchase equity in the firm regardless of his interest in the products or services it may offer. This serves as a decentralized mechanism to fluidly and efficiently allocate capital across the market. The resulting added avenue for consumer input in the market will then enable it to more accurately adapt itself to the changing tides of consumer demand. Finally, there is simply no inherent characteristic of a corporation that is anti-libertarian. Creditors that are not comfortable with an institution whose managers and shareholders cannot be held personally liable for debts will simply not extend credit, and anyone who perpetrates a tort will still be held liable for damages. Thus, any attempt to impede the formation of a corporation would be an attempt to limit the freedom of contract which is itself sacred in a free society. If the objection is that corporations are economically inefficient and may only be propped up by the State, then their existence in a free market would be an impotent one. Whatever the case may be, only the most efficient institutions will thrive.

---

[191] On the inability for firms to economically calculate their internal opportunity costs, see Rothbard, "Particular Factor Prices and Productive Incomes," <u>Vertical Integration and the Size of the Firm</u>, ibid, 614.

[192] Peter Klein, "Entrepreneurship and Corporate Governance," *The Capitalist and the Entrepreneur* (Auburn: Ludwig Von Mises Institute, 2010), 33.

Chapter Fifteen

GETTING THERE

THE BULK OF this work has been dedicated to demonstrating why free market anarchism is superior both ethically and economically to any possible social alternatives. Once the truth of this perspective is established, the question becomes one of means. How do we bring about the libertarian society we desire? Admittedly, there is no objectively best way to determine this, however, in the course of this chapter, methods will be delineated which are optimally suited to achieving liberation. Such methods will be separated into five major categories: agorism & counter economics, hacktivism, education & outreach, peaceful parenting, and the formation of free communities.

Many critics will write off the idea of free market anarchism as Utopian, unrealistic, or even dangerous. Ironically, such criticisms are logically and empirically better aimed against the State. Though the advocates of such a libertarian society generally promote it as a result of their universal stance against aggression, they are under no delusion that physical conflict would disappear. Rather, given the existence of scarce goods and the fact that humans are self-interested, they believe that a purely free society is best equipped to harmonize and coordinate human action for maximum gain. Conversely, free market anarchists recognize that it is the State, in all of its forms, which perverts and obstructs the economic guidance of the invisible hand, and that it is the advocates of the State who naively believe that its agents are benevolent, competent, and altruistic. Thanks to insights made by the likes of Mises, Rothbard, and Hoppe, one may rest assured that even if such benevolent and competent individuals occupied every State office, they would still have no rational economic basis to determine the optimal array of services, the degree to which they should be produced, the method of their production, and how they should be allocated. In the absence of a rational rebuttal to the merits of free market anarchism, some may object: "No such society has ever existed!" – to which the appropriate response is: "Progress is by its very nature unprecedented."

Agorism/Counter-Economics

In an environment where the most innocuous transactions are regulated and subject to licensure and permit requirements, agorism provides some much needed relief. Agorism and counter-economics are fairly interchangeable concepts which have to do with the study and practice of all peaceful human action which is forbidden by the State. More specifically, agorist activities tend to be associated with black or grey market activities, i.e., economic transactions which are non-compliant with State regulations or prohibitions. This could include anything from selling cannabis to running a lemonade stand without a permit. Such activities are used not only to highlight the merits of a truly free market, but also save the entrepreneur the expense of paying taxes, while having the additional benefit of depriving the State of extra revenue.

The beauty of agorism is that it takes free market ideas from the ideological realm and brings them to life. It provides those people too impatient to wait for the State's demise an avenue to live and associate freely *now*. It also serves as an effective and popular form of passive resistance. There are many individuals who engage in these practices as a regular part of their everyday lives without realizing their implications. Thus, by informing these people of the wide ranging benefits of their activities, one may be able to easily segue into a conversation regarding the merits of free markets. It is much easier to demonstrate the benefits of such a system to those who live it and likewise to those entrepreneurs who have first-hand experience with onerous State regulations and taxes.

In the pursuit of streamlining such agorist activities, the market has produced some astounding innovations of which we will cover the two most prominent: cryptocurrencies such as Bitcoin and anonymous online markets such as the Silk Road. Digital cryptocurrencies provide an individual with an array of benefits unlike anything the market actor has ever experienced. They provide a means by which one may transfer wealth securely, anonymously, and with virtually zero transaction costs. Naturally, this allows one to safely avoid taxes in the course of a transaction as there is no means by which said transaction may be traced backed to him. More importantly however, the use of such digital currencies normalizes the idea of using private currencies to the general public. The State's status as the sole producer of money is one of its greatest sources of legitimacy and power; thus, the proliferation and expanding use of private currencies constitute effective means by which State rule may be peacefully undermined.

Likewise, the advent of anonymous online markets allows one to transact in a global market, thereby enhancing the value of agorist activity and rendering international borders ever more superfluous. Above and beyond agorist ventures, however, even legal innovations may sometimes alleviate dependency on State services and should likewise be encouraged. For instance, the development of E-mail has displaced to a large degree the monopolized service the United States Postal Service has on the delivery of first class mail.[193]

Agorist activities, as well as legal market innovations, demonstrate tangible and readily-understood benefits of the marketplace. With their proliferation, ever more people will begin to wonder to what extent the market may be extended, and, conversely, question to what degree the State itself is necessary. In truth, the State is always in a precarious position, as it requires the presence of a market in order to perpetuate its parasitic existence. Conversely, the market is at the same time a threat to State legitimacy as it provides a productive contrast to the State's inner workings. In distinct contrast, the market has no such need for the State. It may exist, in fact, much more vibrantly with no State at all. Once this truth is uncovered, there will be no turning back. The State will be just another embarrassing blip in human history, similar to chattel slavery.

Hacktivism

Hacktivism is simply the use of computers and computer networks to promote political ends. Hacktivist groups, like Anonymous, have been used extensively to combat government measures to censor and restrict access to the Internet. Such groups also have provided private citizens with the means to obstruct government surveillance over their online activities. As the police state grows, these groups of individual hacktivists will be invaluable to maintaining communication networks amongst various liberty activists while, at the same time, denying government surveillance and tracking of their activities. Hacktivist groups, like Anonymous, have also shown wide support for journalistic organizations like Wikileaks, which dedicate themselves to making classified government information available to the public. The organization of these hacktivist groups tends to be decentralized and amorphous, making them very difficult to target for centralized command-and-control State enforcement agencies.

It would behoove the liberty community, then, to form alliances with such organizations as well as recruit members who possess the skills to engage in such activism. One of the most dangerous threats to State power is the Internet itself. Thus, protecting it as an open and accessible resource for all is of paramount importance. More than simply a tool to coordinate

---

[193] "Privatizing the US Postal Service," *Downsizing the Federal Government*, Cato Institute
      http://www.downsizinggovernment.org/usps

and synthesize liberty activism, unrestricted access to the Internet is integral to general human progress. If we wish to effectively protect our liberties, we must likewise protect the World Wide Web from State encroachment.

Education/Outreach

Education is another key component to abolishing the State and organizing a free society. It is not sufficient for one only to have an understanding of the social problems which plague society; he must have an intimate understanding of superior alternatives as well. Most people are aware of the complex, social problems that persist today ranging from poverty, famine, and disease, to war, inflation, and terrorism. Although they may believe the State is not treating such issues competently, they are tragically unaware of any viable alternatives. The masses have been inundated with propaganda their entire lives from the public schools in which they were stuffed as children to the State controlled, nationalistic mass media opinions they ingest as adults. The predominate notion of Political Reform is sold to the public as their only redress of grievances, while whispers of State abolition are immediately discarded as absurd and dangerous.

Despite attempts by defenders of the State to undermine and discredit anarchist ideas, libertarian anarchists retain the advantage of having reason on their side. Think-tanks like the Ludwig Von Mises Institute and The Property and Freedom Society have served the end of advancing radical freedom by proliferating and expanding upon libertarian ideas in the academic realm, while defending them from the most sophisticated critiques. More populist mediums such as Facebook and YouTube have also enabled many libertarians/anarchists to introduce the masses to the ideas of liberty, effecting an enormous swell in number. This trend is expected to continue as the reliance on State regulated mass media and propaganda is continually undermined by the common man's access to the virtually endless depths of knowledge present on the Internet. Beyond this, younger generations, who feel more at home online than watching television, will demonstrate the superiority of free access to the marketplace of ideas regarding news and opinion on the Internet. Moreover, the growing popularity of home-schooling promises to curtail State control over the minds of the youth.

Though the Internet does provide an excellent medium for providing copious amounts of information to billions of people, there are still advantages to reaching out to others in a face-to-face manner. Offering a meeting presence at various popular events or other public places may help others experience these ideas in a more tangible way. In the transition from any degree of Statism to libertarianism, there are bound to be questions and spiraling conversations that cannot be addressed in reading Murray Rothbard's articles in PDF; a living, breathing libertarian discussing and deconstructing social premises can catapult a person beyond where their own capacity for curiosity and intellectual courage would have taken them. Having personal interactions with others helps humanize the ideas of liberty, and may be cause for an intrepid mind to consider such ideas with greater deliberation. Working with other organizations and people on like-minded causes may also be an effective way to synergize efforts and resources. Additionally, the members of such organizations may themselves be more open to the ideas of anarchism and free markets as a consequence of camaraderie developed while working on like goals. For the spreading of anarchist ideas to be effective, one must sell them not only as rational and effective, but also humanitarian and inclusive. It must be made clear that the only things precluded are legal *privileges*. Such a system does not require people to work for hierarchical corporations or even to use money. If individuals prefer to voluntarily pool their resources and live in money-less communes, then there would be nothing stopping them. In fact, free market anarchy is precisely that system which permits the largest scope of opportunity for people to live their lives as they see fit.

Last, but not least, one must be willing to spread these ideas with patience and empathy if he wishes for them to be well received. At one point, most libertarians and anarchists were either active or passive supporters of the State. Thus, showing compassion, empathy, and love for others will do wonders in the way of instilling them with the desire to learn these ideas. Furthermore, living a happy and healthy life will encourage them to emulate your lifestyle and to discover the virtues which serve as its foundation. Hoppe deliberates upon the critical importance of spreading the ideas of liberty:

> ...more than force is needed to expand exploitation over a population many times its own size. For this to happen, a firm must also have public support. A majority of the population must accept the exploitative actions as legitimate. This acceptance can range from active enthusiasm to passive resignation. But it must be acceptance in the sense that a majority must have given up the idea of actively or passively resisting any attempt to enforce

nonproductive and
noncontractual property
acquisitions. The class
consciousness must be low,
undeveloped, and fuzzy. Only as
long as this state of affairs lasts is
there still room for an
exploitative firm to prosper even
if no actual demand for it exists.
Only if and insofar as the
exploited and expropriated
develop a clear idea of their own
situation and are united with
other members of their class
through an ideological movement
which gives expression to the
idea of a classless society where
all exploitation is abolished, can
the power of the ruling class be
broken. Only if, and insofar as, a
majority of the exploited public
becomes consciously integrated
into such a movement and
accordingly displays a common
outrage over all nonproductive or
noncontractual property
acquisitions, shows a contempt
for everyone who engages in
such acts, and deliberately
contributes nothing to help make
them successful (not to mention
actively trying to obstruct them),
can its power be brought to
crumble.[194]

Peaceful Parenting

Peaceful parenting may seem peculiar or impertinent in regards to
the subversion of Statism, but it is of grave importance. It entails a
complete and holistic parenting style, but this focus will be on its primary

---

[194] Hoppe, *Private Property*, 127-128.

precept of non-violence against children. This includes smacking, spanking, hitting or threats made thereof. Such violent parenting tactics teach a child that "might makes right" and primes them for State subjugation which operates under mirrored premises. There is no other time in life where one is more susceptible to influence than when he is a child. Thus, it is critically important that extra care be taken not to instill our children with ideas or furnish them with experiences that aligns the child's personality to that of a drone or soldier, able and willing to serve an arbitrary authority at the soonest provocation. Instead, rearing children as peers encourages them to inquire more deeply about the world around them and their place in it. This curiosity allows them to improve their understanding of the environment and to better grapple with their environment in such a way that it may be more transformed to their liking.

Encouraging inquiry, negotiation, and discussion may not be conducive to dominating or controlling children, but it will greatly enhance a child's critical thinking and reasoning abilities. When children grow up in peaceful and free environments, they will view the State with great skepticism and contempt. The State will be nothing more to them than an anachronism or a morbid joke. As the number of individuals who had been "peacefully reared" grows, the State's power and legitimacy will correspondingly fade. These individuals will likely be among the more avid and vociferous promoters of the libertarian philosophy for two reasons: (1) They will not be as conditioned as their counterparts to accept edicts given by arbitrary authority figures, and the fear emanating from the State's threats will accordingly be less effective against them; and, (2) they will already have experienced how free associations organize and form, and the benefits they entail.

Forming Free Communities

For those who have difficulty dealing in abstracts, experiencing a freed community may be conducive to understanding the merits of liberty. Forming such communities allows insiders a valuable opportunity to live more freely while they hasten the collapse of the State. The most renowned examples of such communities include the Free State Project in New Hampshire and the Blue Ridge Liberty Project in Asheville, North Carolina, however other, similar communities are springing into existence more frequently than ever.

The Blue Ridge Liberty Project is significant in that its goals and methods are entirely in line with those presented herein. The Blue Ridge Liberty Project (BRLP) was established with a twofold mission: to spread the ideas of free market anarchism and peaceful parenting, while establishing a community of people who live accordingly. The methods employed by members of the BRLP include education, outreach, and the promotion of agorism and peaceful parenting. The interest and membership of the BRLP and other similar liberty communities have continued to grow as they offer comfortable safe havens from the more insufferable aspects of the State. Additionally, these communities have proven to be highly conducive to synergizing the efforts of like-minded activists while, at the same time, adding credibility to their cause with the increase in visible participation.

The members of these communities have often left their extended families and established careers in order to take part in the high and noble cause of liberty. They are willing to trade temporary material comfort and security for the opportunity to achieve a life aimed at something greater than mere sustenance. These staunch and passionate individualists are the greatest philanthropists of our time. One is reminded of a quote attributed to Samuel Adams: "It does not require a majority to prevail, but rather an irate, tireless minority keen to set brush fires in people's minds."

Though the above methods may be the most effective means to achieving liberty, this in no way suggests they are the only ones. Encouragement should be given to anyone to promote liberty because its presence or lack thereof deeply impacts every aspect of our lives. We live in a world with incredibly diverse and beautiful individuals, whose value and variety are hampered by the use of systemic aggression. The fight against aggression – which is the fight for liberty – is the most important one of our time and will continue to be until liberty has prevailed. Ending the story of our enslavement should be top priority for those seeking to liberate man from all manners of oppression, subjugation, and exploitation.

The question of the proper or improper use of violence warrants the highest level of scrutiny as it presents the greatest potential danger to human progress. If one is still critical of free market anarchy, then they should be encouraged to evaluate the State with an equal level of skepticism. Make no mistake; the cause of liberty will get darker before the proverbial dawn. However, there is great cause for hope. Now more than ever, we are connected with one another socially and economically. We are discovering innovative ways to streamline communication and break down cultural barriers and languages, which prevent us from connecting with one another. We now have the distinct honor and privilege to usher in a new era of enlightenment, peace, and prosperity. All we must do now is choose whether or not we want to be passive observers or active participants in this revolutionary phase. Such participation can entail something as simple as choosing to live your own life freely as Albert Camus once opined: "The only way to deal with an unfree world is to become so absolutely free that your very existence is an act of rebellion."

Resources

Foreword

1. Doherty, Brian. *Radicals for Capitalism: A Freewheeling History of the Modern American Libertarian Movement*. New York: Public Affairs, 2007.
2. Boaz, David. *The Libertarian Reader: Classic and Contemporary Readings from Lao-tzu to Milton Friedman*. New York: Free Press, 1997.
3. McCaskey, John P. "New Libertarians: New Promoters of a Welfare State" (April 14, 2014), http://www.johnmccaskey.com/joomla/index.php/blog/71-new-libertarians,
4. McElroy, Wendy. "Murray N. Rothbard: Mr. Libertarian," (July 6, 2000) http://www.wendymcelroy.com/rockwell/mcelroy000706.html
5. Miron, Jeffrey A. *Libertarianism, from A to Z*. New York: Basic Books, 2010.
6. Barnett, Randy E. *The Structure of Liberty: Justice and the Rule of Law*. Oxford: Clarendon, 1998.
7. Barnett, Randy E. "Foreword: of Chickens and Eggs—The Compatibility of Moral Rights and Consequentialist Analysis," 3 *Harv. J. L. Publc. Pol'y* 611.
8. Hoppe, Hans-Hermann. Introduction to *The Ethics of Liberty*, by Murray N. Rothbard. New York: New York University Press, 2nd edition, 1998.

Introduction

9. Hoppe, Hans-Hermann. State or Private Law Society? Lecture. Mises Brasil. April 9, 2011.

Chapter Zero

10. Hoppe, Hans-Hermann. *Economic Science and the Austrian Method*. Auburn Ludwig Von Mises Institute, 1995.
11. Mises, Ludwig von. *Theory and History*. New Haven: Yale University Press, 1957.
12. Mises, Ludwig von. *The Ultimate Foundation of Economic Science*. New York: Van Nostrand LTD., 1962.

Chapter One

13. Hoppe, Hans-Hermann. *A Theory of Socialism and Capitalism: Economics, Politics, and Ethics.* Boston: Kluwer Academic, 1989.
14. Hoppe, Hans-Hermann. *The Economics and Ethics of Private Property: Studies in Political Economy and Philosophy* Boston: Kluwer Academic, 1993.
15. Mises, Ludwig von. *Human Action: A Treatise on Economics.* New Haven: Yale University Press, 1949.
16. Rothbard, Murray N. *Egalitarianism as a Revolt against Nature, and Other Essays.* Washington, D.C.: Libertarian Review, 1974.

Chapter Two

17. Kinsella, Stephan, and Jeffrey Tucker. Goods, Scarce and Nonscarce. Ludwig Von Mises Institute, August 25, 2010. mises.org/daily/4630.
18. Rothbard, Murray N. Justice and Property Rights. *Property in a Humane Economy*, Edit. Samuel L. Blumenfeld. Lasalle: Open Court, 1974.
19. Kinsella, Stephan. *Against Intellectual Property.* Auburn: Ludwig Von Mises Institute, 2008.

Chapter Three

20. Kinsella, Stephan. A Libertarian Theory of Contract. *Journal of Libertarian Studies 17.II* (2003).
21. Hoppe, Hans-Hermann. *Eigentum, Anarchie Und Staat: Studien Zur Theorie Des Kapitalismus.* Opladen: Westdt. Verl., 1987.

Chapter Four

22. Rothbard, Murray N. Austrian Theory of Money. *The Foundations of Modern Austrian Economics.* Edit. Edwin G. Dolan. Mission: Sheed & Ward, 1976.
23. Murphy, Robert P. *Lessons for the Young Economist.* Auburn: Ludwig Von Mises Institute, 2010.
24. Hülsmann, Jörg Guido, *The Ethics of Money Production.* Auburn: Ludwig Von Mises Institute, 2008.
25. Hoppe, Hans-Hermann. How Is Fiat Money Possible? Or, the Devolution of Money and Credit. *The Review of Austrian Economics 7.2* (1994).

26. Mises, Ludwig von. *The Theory of Money and Credit*. New Haven: Yale University Press, 1953.
27. Rothbard, Murray N. The End of Socialism and the Calculation Debate Revisited. *The Review of Austrian Economics* 5.2 (1991).
28. Hoppe, Hans-Hermann. 'The Yield From Money Held' Reconsidered. Franz Cuhel Memorial Lecture. Prague, April 24, 2009.
29. Hutt, William H. The Yield from Money Held. *Freedom and Free Enterprise: Essays in Honor of Ludwig von Mises*. Edited by M. Sennholz. Chicago: Van Nostrand, 1956.
30. Hülsmann, Jörg Guido. Has Fractional Reserve Banking Really Passed the Market Test? *Independent Review*. Winter VII.3 (2003).
31. Fisher, Irving. The Debt-Deflation Theory of Great Depressions. *Econometrica* 1.4 (1933).
32. Hülsmann, Jörg Guido. *Deflation and Liberty*. Auburn: Ludwig Von Mises Institute, 2008.
33. Keynes, John Maynard. *The Economic Consequences of the Peace*. New York: Harcourt, Brace and Howe, 1919.

Chapter Five

34. Rothbard, Murray N. *Man, Economy, and State: A Treatise on Economic Principles; with Power and Market: Government and the Economy*. Auburn: Ludwig Von Mises Institute, 2009.
35. Dilorenzo, Thomas J. The Myth of Natural Monopoly. *The Review of Austrian Economics* 9.2 (1996).

Chapter Six

36. Hoppe, Hans-Hermann, The Economics of Risk and Insurance. Lecture. Ludwig von Mises Institute. July, 2001.

Chapter Seven

37. Beito, David T. *From Mutual Aid to the Welfare State: Fraternal Societies and Social Services, 1890-1967*. Chapel Hill: University of North Carolina, 2000.
38. Boyapati, Vijay. What's Really Wrong with the Healthcare Industry. Editorial. Ludwig Von Mises Institute. March 26, 2010. https://mises.org/library/whats-really-wrong-healthcare-industry.

RESOURCES

Chapter Eight

39. Kinsella, Stephan. <u>Punishment and Proportionality: The Estoppel Approach</u>. *Journal of Libertarian Studies* 1st ser. 12 (1996).
40. Kinsella, Stephan. <u>Legislation and the Discovery of Law in a Free Society</u>. *Journal of Libertarian Studies* 11.2 (1995).
41. Caplan, Bryan D. *The Myth of the Rational Voter: Why Democracies Choose Bad Policies*. Princeton: Princeton University Press, 2007.
42. Murphy, Robert P. *Chaos Theory: Two Essays on Market Anarchy*. New York: RJ Communications LLC, 2002.

Chapter Nine

43. Hobbes, Thomas. *Leviathan: Or the Matter, Forme, and Power of a Common-Wealth Ecclesiasticall and Civill*. Edited by Ian Shapiro. New Haven: Yale University Press, 2010.
44. Molinari, Gustave de. *The Production of Security*. New York: Center for Libertarian Studies, 1977.
45. Hoppe, Hans-Hermann. *The Private Production of Defense*. Auburn: Ludwig Von Mises Institute, 2009.

Chapter Ten

46. American Society of Civil Engineers. <u>Infrastructure Report Card</u>. <u>http://www.infrastructurereportcard.org/fact-sheet/roads</u>
47. National Highway Safety Administration. <u>http://www-fars.nhtsa.dot.gov/Main/index.aspx</u>
48. Block, Walter. *The Privatization of Roads and Highways: Human and Economic Factors*. Lewiston: Edwin Mellen, 2006.
49. Rothbard, Murray N. <u>How and How Not to Desocialize</u>. *The Review of Austrian Economics* 6.1 (1992).

Chapter Eleven

50. Rothbard, Murray N. *Education, Free & Compulsory*. Auburn: Ludwig Von Mises Institute, 1999.
51. Smith, Aaron. <u>The Costs of Compulsory Education</u>. Editorial. Ludwig Von Mises Institute, June 22, 2011.
52. Mises, Ludwig Von. <u>Planning for Freedom</u>. Speech. American Academy of Political and Social Sciences, 1945.
53. Paterson, Isabel. *The God of the Machine*. New York: G.P. Putnam's Sons, 1943.
54. Donleavy, B. T. <u>The Education Bubble</u>. Editorial. Ludwig Von Mises Institute, May 12, 2010.

55. French, Douglas. The Higher-Education Bubble Has Popped. Editorial. Ludwig Von Mises Institute, August 10, 2011.
56. McCloskey, Deirdre N. *The Bourgeois Virtues: Ethics for an Age of Commerce.* Chicago: University of Chicago, 2006.
57. Eaton, Judith S. Accreditation and the Federal Future of Higher Education. Editorial. American Association of University Professors, September-October, 2010.

Chapter Twelve

58. Hoppe, Hans-Hermann. Interview on Taxation. Interview. Nicolas Cori of Philosophe Magazine, March 10, 2011. http://www.hanshoppe.com/2011/03/philosophie-magazine-interview-on-taxation/
59. Powell, Benjamin. Sweatshops: A Way Out of Poverty. Interview. Ludwig Von Mises Institute, March 2014. https://mises.org/daily/6696/Sweatshops-A-Way-Out-of-Poverty
60. DiLorenzo, Thomas J. Markets, Not Unions, Gave Us Leisure. Editorial. Ludwig Von Mises Institute, August 23, 2004. https://mises.org/daily/1590
61. Williams, Walter E. *The State Against Blacks.* New York: New Press, 1982.
62. Rothbard. Murray N. *Making Economic Sense.* Auburn: Ludwig Von Mises Institute, 1995.
63. Westley, Christopher. The End of Unions *The Free Market* 26: 9 (Sept. 2005).
64. Edwards, James Rolph. The Cost of Public Income Redistribution and Private Charity. *Journal of Libertarian Studies* Summer 21.2 (2007). https://mises.org/journals/jls/21_2/21_2_1.pdf
65. Fulton, Joshua. Welfare before the Welfare State. Editorial. Ludwig Von Mises Institute, June 21, 2011. https://mises.org/daily/5388

Chapter Thirteen

66. Prosser, William and Werdner Keeton, *Prosser and Keeton on the Law of Torts.* St. Paul: West Publishing Company, 1984.
67. Rothbard, Murray N. Law, Property Rights, and Air Pollution. *Cato Journal* 2, No. 1 Spring (1982).
68. Kinsella, Stephan. The Libertarian Approach to Negligence, Tort, and Strict Liability: Wergeld and Partial Wergeld. Blog post, September 1, 2009. http://www.stephankinsella.com/2009/09/the-libertarian-approach-to-negligence-tort-and-strict-liability-wergeld-and-partial-wergeld/
69. Callahan, Gene. What Is an Externality? *The Free Market* 8th ser. 19

(2001).

70. Herbener, Jeffrey. Further Explorations in Austrian Value and Utility Theory. Lecture. Ludwig Von Mises Institute, August, 2005.

71. Block, Walter. Environmentalism and Economic Freedom: The Case for Private Property Rights. *Journal of Business Ethics* 17 (1998).

72. Block, Walter. Economics and the Environment: A Reconciliation. Interview. 1985. https://youtu.be/XMxgYY_q-AI

73. Rothbard, Murray N. Toward a Reconstruction of Utility and Welfare Economics. *On Freedom and Free Enterprise*, Edited by M. Sennholz. Princeton: Van Nostrand, 1956.

74. Rothbard, Murray N. *For A New Liberty: The Libertarian Manifesto*. New York: Macmillan, 1973.

75. Block, Walter. Water Privatization. Unpublished manuscript. http://thelibertycaucus.com/wp-content/uploads/2014/01/waterprivate.pdf

76. Santoriello, Andrea. Externalities and the Environment. *The Freeman*. Foundation for Economic Education: November 1996. http://www.fee.org/the_freeman/detail/externalities-and-the-environment

Chapter Fourteen

77. Foss, Nicolai Juul. The Theory of the Firm: The Austrians as Precursors and Critics of Contemporary Theory. *The Review of Austrian Economics* 7.1 (1994). https://mises.org/journals/rae/pdf/rae7_1_2.pdf

78. Klein, Peter. *Production and the Firm*. Lecture. Ludwig Von Mises Institute, July 23, 2013.

79. "Corporation." on *Investopedia*. http://www.investopedia.com/terms/c/corporation.asp

80. Robert Hessen, "Corporations." *The Concise Encyclopedia of Economics*. Econlib http://www.econlib.org/library/Enc/Corporations.html

81. "Equity" Ludwig Von Mises Institute." http://wiki.mises.org/wiki/Equity.

82. "Security (finance)" Ludwig Von Mises Institute, http://wiki.mises.org/wiki/Security_%28finance%29

83. Kinsella, Stephan. Corporations and Limited Liability for Torts. *Mises Economics Blog*. Ludwig Von Mises Institute, September 10, 2008. http://archive.mises.org/9084/corporations-and-limited-liability-for-torts/

84. Klein, Peter. *The Capitalist and the Entrepreneur*. Auburn: Ludwig Von Mises Institute, 2010.

Chapter Fifteen

85. "Privatizing the US Postal Service" *Downsizing the Federal Government.* Cato Institute http://www.downsizinggovernment.org/usps

22421919R00165

Made in the USA
San Bernardino, CA
06 July 2015